Who Are the Shī'a?

Their True Origins and Beliefs

Produced by the Ahl al-Bayt World Assembly
Faculty of Scholarly Research and Publications
Mahdi Farmānīān, General Director and Editor
Sabāh al-Bayātī, Project Leader

Translated and Annotated by
Blake Archer Williams

LANTERN
PUBLICATIONS

Lantern Publications
info@lanternpublications.com
www.lanternpublications.com

Ordering Information:
Quantity sales. Special discounts are available on quantity purchases by corporations, associations, and others. For details, contact the distributor at the address below.

Shia Books Australia
www.shiabooks.com.au
info@shiabooks.com.au

ISBN- 978-1-922583-15-4

First Edition

NATIONAL LIBRARY OF AUSTRALIA
A catalogue record for this book is available from the National Library of Australia

In the Name of God,
the Most Compassionate, the Most Merciful

Prayers of God's Peace and Blessings

In keeping with the Islamic practice of showing respect for the name of God, and sending prayers of God's peace and blessings whenever the name of His blessed Prophet, Lady Fātima, and the Twelve Imams is mentioned, as well as for asking God to hasten the reappearance of the Lord of the Age on the Earthly plane, one or more of the following Arabic symbols have been employed throughout the text. They are repeated for their great rewards.

سبحانه وتعالى	Used exclusively after the name of God, meaning "the Sublimely Exalted", or, as a prayer, "[May His name be] Sublimely Exalted".
صلى الله عليه وآله وسلم	Used exclusively after the name of the Prophet, meaning "May the peace and blessings of God be unto him and unto [the purified and inerrant members of] his family"
عليه السلام	Used for any of the Twelve Imams or past prophets of God, meaning "May God's peace be unto him".
عليهم السلام	Used for two or more of the Twelve Imams or past prophets of God, meaning "May God's peace be unto them".
عليها السلام	Used for Lady Fātima, meaning "May God's peace be unto her".
صلوات الله عليهم أجمعين	Used for a plurality of the Fourteen Immaculates, meaning "May God's peace be unto them all collectively".
عجل الله تعالى فرجه الشريف	Used for the Lord of the Age (the Twelfth Imam), meaning "May God hasten the advent of his noble person".

Table of Contents

Introduction 7

1 Islam and Submission 13
The *Ijtihād* of some of the Companions 17
The Great Effrontery 26

2 Sources of Religious Authority 31
The Prerequisites for Religious Authority 34
The Limits of the Membership of the House of the Prophet 42
Prophetic Proofs concerning the Designation to Succession 50
Other Scriptural Proofs relating to the Succession of Ali 54

3 The Seeds of Sh'īa Islam 103
Use of the Expression "Sh'īa" by the Prophet 108
At the Pledge of Allegiance to Ali 123
Another Deviation 124

4 The Continuation of the Path of Sh'īa Islam 141
Sects within Islam and the Deviations of the *Ghulāt* 145
The Meaning of Sh'īa Islam 149
The Meaning of Sh'īa Islam in its General Sense 153
The Meaning of Sh'īa Islam in its Specific Sense 157
The Creed of Twelver Sh'īa Islam 158
"There will be Twelve Imāms after me." 158
The Sh'īa Creed in Brief 162

5 Disambiguation from Deviated and Extremist Sects 167
Deviated Sects 167
Extremism and the Extremists (*Ghulū wa Ghulāt*) 171
The Sh'īa Position with respect to the *Ghulāt* 179

6 False Memes about Sh'īa Islam and their Disabuse 207
The Abdullāh b. Sabā Meme 209
The Meme of the Persian Origin of Sh'īa Islam 211
Other Causes for the Perpetuation of the Meme 217

Bibliography 221

The Names and Dates of the Twelve Imams

			Dates of Birth-Death	
No	Kunya	Name	Islamic	Christian
1	Ab'al-Hasan	Ali b.AbuTalib	-23 to 40	600–661
2	Abu Md.	Hasan ibn Ali	3–50	624–670
3	Abu Abdillah	Husayn b. Ali	4–61	626–680
4	Abu Md.	Ali b. Husayn	38–95	658–712
5	Abu Ja'far	Md. ibn Ali	57–114	677–732
6	Abu Abdillah	Ja'far ibn Md.	83–148	702–765
7	Ab'al-Hasan	Mūsā b. Ja'far	128–183	744–799
8	Ab'al-Hasan	Ali ibn Mūsā	148–203	765–817
9	Abu Ja'far	Md. ibn Ali	195–220	810–835
10	Ab'al-Hasan	Ali ibn Md.	212–254	827–868
11	Abu Md.	Hasan ibn Ali	232–260	846–874
12	Ab'al-Qāsim	Md. B. Hasan	255–Present	868–Present

A Note on Transliteration

The transliteration system used in this book is basically that of the ICAS Press (2015) method (which is based on the Library of Congress Romanization Tables), with the following changes: The *shamsi* and *qamari* consonants appear in the definitive article 'al' (in place of the 'l'). This is so that those who are not familiar with the pronunciation of the Arabic words can become familiar with the words as they should be pronounced (as opposed to how they are written), enabling them to pronounce the words properly. Persian words of Arabic origin are transliterated as they are pronounced in the Arabic language, rather than their Persian pronunciations. However, Persian words, proper names, and personal names are transliterated to reflect their proper Persian pronunciation. Thus, 'Bukhāri' is Bokhāri, Kulayni is Kolayni, etc. In such cases, the sound for the *kasra* is romanized by 'e' rather than by 'i', the *ḍamma* by 'o' rather than by 'a' or 'u'. Similarly, the ض, ذ, and ظ letters are all romanized by the letter 'z' (for Persian words only). Thus, the *ezāfe* (*iḍāfa*) is Romanized *-e* after a consonant, and *-ah* or *-ye* after a vowel.

Introduction

The question as to the truth of what the actual teachings of Sh' īa Islam are and the question as to their historical origins and development is a subject that has held the interest of numerous historians both contemporary and among the historians of old, and many different views have been put forward concerning these questions. Most scholars are of the opinion that Sh'īa Islam is a sect among the various sects of Islam which was formed at the time when creedal differences began to crystalize. During that time, most of the lands in the realm of Islam were embroiled in conflict as a result of divisions along ideological lines rooted in political affiliations and loyalties. This was at a time when less than half a century had passed since the death of the Most Noble Prophet ﷺ. These differences and the occurrence of various insurrections caused the community of Muslims to split into factions and to take up entrenched positions against each other and to consider the shedding of Muslim blood as something that was acceptable. Each sect believed that they were in the right and their adversaries were in the wrong, and would interpret and rationalize the text of the Quran and of the prophetic hadīth scripture in such a way as to prove their position. The situation became acute when certain factions began to fabricate hadīth reports in order to further their case and point the finger of reproach and blame at their adversaries. In this way, false hadīth reports such as the following one were introduced, where the Most Noble Prophet ﷺ is claimed to have said, "Soon there will arise out of my community a sect known as the Rawāfeḍ. Kill them, for they are infidels!" This is obviously a fabricated hadīth report because historians of these sectarian disputes tell us that it was Zayd b. Ali b. al-Husayn that first used this label for those who abandoned him during his revolt against the Umayyads. Therefore, this label and others like it that were attached to factions that held positions that were contrary to that of the majoritarian position did not have currency at the time of the Most Noble Prophet ﷺ for his Eminence to make use of them.

Among such hadīth reports, there is one that has undeservedly gained near-*mutawātir*[1] status. All sects have reported the report that states that the Islamic community will be divided into seventy-three sects, all but one of which will be damned. Consequently, each sect has striven to prove that it is the sect that will be saved and that the rest of the sects within Islam are deserving of the fires of eternal damnation!

---

[1] *Mutawātir* - The highest possible classification of reliability of a hadīth report. A hadīth report is considered *mutawātir* (having reached the threshold of *tawātur*) when it has been transmitted with a frequency of transmission through different chains of narrators in exactly the same way to the extent that there can remain no doubt concerning the authenticity and reliability of the text in question. *Mutawātir* is a technical term which makes its appearance in the science of hadīth, referring to a report that has been transmitted by so many different transmitters (and in different chains of custody) with the exact same wording as not to leave room for a shadow of a doubt as to the integrity both as to the chain of custody and as to the reliability of the text itself. A *mutawātir* hadīth is a 'successively' narrated report conveyed by narrators so numerous that there can remain no doubt concerning the authenticity and reliability of the text in question, as it is not conceivable for them to have agreed upon an untruth; it is a hadīth report which is unquestionable in its veracity.

What fanned the flames of sectarianism even further was that the beliefs based on these false reports gradually penetrated further into the mindset of its adherents and were further disseminated to new circles. This state of affairs continued to the point where future generations believed with certainty that these words were uttered by the Most Noble Prophet ﷺ. In contrast, during the time of the Prophet ﷺ and for a time after his passing, no such beliefs were held. These beliefs did not find wide distribution and acceptation until the period of the intensification of *kalāmic* (dogmatic or creedal theology) debates. These debates occurred at the cusp of the encounter of the Muslim community with the alien cultures of Byzantium and Persia. This encounter and the resultant tensions increased on an almost daily basis with the introduction of newly translated philosophical texts. Thus, each intellectual disposition took up its own philosophical position, and these ideologies were accretions that had been lent to the Arabs by Byzantium, Persia, India and elsewhere.

With the dawning of the era of the compilation, inscription and redaction of hadīth reports, Muslim thinkers began to apply their efforts to different fields of intellectual endeavor, not the least among which was the issue of what the nature of the polity or form of government was supposed to be; the difference, in other words, between the two views of the imāmate and the caliphate. Most of the thinkers active in this field, such as Shahristānī, Baghdādī, and others, were of the majoritarian persuasion. The majority faction later came to apply the term *Ahl as-Sunna wa'l-Jamā'a* to themselves (which was later abbreviated simply to Ahl as- Sunna or simply to "Sunni"). All of the writings of the majoritarian persuasion centered on one objective, and that was the attempt to demonstrate the reality of the supposed "seventy-three" sects, after which their focus shifted to convincing their interlocutors that they are "the saved sect", and that all the other sects, including the Sh'īa, are destined for the fire. Moreover, in order to establish their position and to prove their claim, all sorts of different views and opinions were proffered concerning the origins and beliefs of Shī'a Islam. At times, the Sh'īa were considered to be followers of the imaginary figure Abdullāh b. Sabā whom it was alleged acquired his opinions from Judaism; and at other times, the Magian beliefs of the Persians were ascribed to the Sh'īa; and at other times still, they would say that Sh'īa Islam was formed as a reaction to the martyrdom of Imām Husayn ﷺ in Karbalā, or before that, to the martyrdom of Imām Ali ﷺ.

In this way, different accounts were given concerning the historical origins of Sh'īa Islam. Some considered it to have originated at the Saqīfa,[2] whilst others believed it to have started during the troubles in the reign of 'Uthmān; some others thought that Sh'īa Islam originated as a result of the Battle of the Camel or the Battle of Siffīn, and yet others ascribed its origins to the aftermath of the martyrdom of Imām Husayn ﷺ. Such opinions were at variance with historical realities, and the reason they were held is because the proponents of these views had not understood the truth of Sh'īa Islam, which was the expression of true Islam in all its multi-faceted aspects and beliefs. They did not realize that Sh'īa Islam was not a new-fangled belief or ideology imported from other religions and nations, and that it was a completely Islamic belief in every aspect of the word, whose initial seed was sown by the Most Noble Prophet ﷺ himself. This seed grew into a sapling which grew in strength daily, and it was nurtured by the People of the Household [of the Most Noble Prophet ﷺ] (*ahl al-bayt* ﷺ), who kept false beliefs and reprehensible innovations away from it, and

[2] The Saqīfa was a portico of the Banī Sā'ida where the Ansār (the clans of Yathrib/Medina who had entered into Islam and were its "Helpers") had gathered immediately upon the death of the Prophet ﷺ in order to determine who was to rule their city. It became the scene of the first manifestation of a carefully planned plot according to which six chieftains of Quraysh were to succeed, one after another, in taking the reins of leadership of the community after the Prophet's ﷺ passing.

exposed as frauds those false pretenders who attempted to associate themselves with the Household of the Most Noble Prophet ﷺ as a means of furthering their political and worldly objectives.

Unfortunately, many people did not understand the truth of Sh'īa Islam and would try to conflate the beliefs of false claimants with those of Sh'īa Islam in their books and rhetoric. They would accuse the Sh'īa of holding aberrant views, of having practices that were reprehensible innovations (*bid'a'*), and of having exited the fold of the religion of Islam. They even went so far as to accuse Sh'īa Islam of resorting to any deviant thought whatsoever in order to destroy Islam and the Arab identity!

These accusations were sketched out by the early antagonists and were fleshed out by those who followed them and by the contemporary adversaries among the majority, who paid heed to the claims of the enemies of Islam in furtherance of their anti-Sh'īa invective. All this, without troubling themselves to bother to do the bare minimum of the research required to learn of the beliefs of any given sect from the mouths and pens of those who actually self-identify as Sh'īa Muslims. The acuteness of the situation is all the more apparent in this day and age where there are plenty of facilities for acquiring such information and when any sincere seeker of truth can enter into a dialogue with knowledgeable people in other sects.

It goes without saying that sincerity in seeking the truth should be the most important motivational factor for any scholar and historian. For if this characteristic were absent, one could not hope to find the truth from among the pages of his writings. Fortunately, there still exist a number of historians whose sole objective is discovering the truth. Thanks to the efforts of these scholars, the veil has been lifted from the truth, just as some good work has been produced by certain orientalists as well. Moreover, Sh'īa scholars have made available authoritative sources so that the path is laid open to anyone who is genuinely interested in seeking the truth.

The work that is before you is an effort at one such opening, and we pray that Almighty God ﷻ makes it available and of benefit to all those who seek the truth.

1 - Islam and Submission (*Taslīm*)

Ibn Manzūr writes,

> "Islam and [self]-surrender [unto God ﷻ] mean submission, and [the meaning of] Islam in [the context of] the sacred law (*sharīa'*) is the attestation to humility [before God ﷻ] and [the acknowledgement of] one's obligation to [obey] the sacred law (*sharīa'*) and [all] that which the Most Noble Prophet ﷺ has delivered [from Heaven]. Upon [one's entering into] Islam, the [wonton shedding of] blood becomes prohibited and how beautifully has Tha'lab summed up this matter: 'Islam is a bearing of witness by the tongue and an attaining to faith by the heart'. However, concerning Islam it must be said that Abū-Bakr Muhammad b. Bashshār has said: 'When it is said that so and so is a Muslim, there are two possibilities concerning [the meaning of] this: (1) that such a person has submitted to God's ﷻ injunctions and ordinances, and (2) only that he is sincere in his worship of God ﷻ."[3]

[3] Ibn Manzūr, *Lisān al-Arab*, 12:393.

This definition clarifies a distinction that might not have been apparent at first glance, namely, that there is a difference between one who is sincere in his worship of God ﷻ and a person who has submitted to God's ﷻ injunctions and ordinances only outwardly. The first case speaks more to the reality of one's faith, and to the individual's relationship with his Lord; whereas the person who "has submitted to God's ﷻ injunctions and ordinances" encompasses absolute surrender to all that which God ﷻ has commanded without the individual having any will whatsoever against the will of his Lord. Pursuant to this utter submission, the individual shows humility and submits absolutely to all that the Most Noble Prophet ﷺ has brought from God ﷻ, and also believes that the Most Noble Prophet ﷺ does not speaks of his own will, but rather, expounds divine revelation without any additions to or subtractions therefrom. Thus, the Muslim considers as binding upon him all of the prescriptive and proscriptive imperatives (*awāmir wa nawāhī*) of the Most Noble Prophet ﷺ, whether they concern the injunctions of the law and directions concerning rituals and acts of worship, or imperatives concerning differences that might arise between people and the ways in which these conflicts are to be resolved. Furthermore, the Muslim considers the taking on of these commitments as acts of obeisance to God's ﷻ command, as mentioned in these noble revelations (*āyāt*):

وَمَا آتَاكُمُ الرَّسُولُ فَخُذُوهُ وَمَا نَهَاكُمْ عَنْهُ فَانتَهُوا ۚ وَاتَّقُوا اللَّهَ ۖ إِنَّ اللَّهَ
شَدِيدُ الْعِقَابِ...﴿٧﴾

> [59:7] Hence, accept [willingly] whatever the Apostle gives you, and refrain from [demanding] anything that he withholds from you.

فَإِن تَنَازَعْتُمْ فِي شَيْءٍ فَرُدُّوهُ إِلَى اللَّهِ وَالرَّسُولِ إِن كُنتُمْ تُؤْمِنُونَ بِاللَّهِ
وَالْيَوْمِ الْآخِرِ ﴿٥٩﴾

And: [4:59] And if you differ over any matter, refer it unto God ﷻ and the Apostle, if you [truly] believe in God ﷻ and the Last Day.

فَلَا وَرَبِّكَ لَا يُؤْمِنُونَ حَتَّىٰ يُحَكِّمُوكَ فِيمَا شَجَرَ بَيْنَهُمْ ثُمَّ لَا يَجِدُوا فِي
أَنفُسِهِمْ حَرَجًا مِّمَّا قَضَيْتَ وَيُسَلِّمُوا تَسْلِيمًا ﴿٦٥﴾

And lastly: [4:65] But nay, by thy Lord of Providence! They do not [really] believe unless they make thee [O Prophet] a judge of all on which they disagree among themselves, and then find in their hearts no bar to an acceptance of thy decision and give themselves up [to it] with utter conviction.

It is abundantly clear from the above *āyāt* (verses) that the self-surrender (*islām*) that God ﷻ demands of his servants entails an utter surrender to the decisions and commands of the Most Noble Prophet ﷺ. To the extent that even if such a posture might be at odds with what the individual might want or with that which he thinks more expedient to that which the Most Noble Prophet ﷺ has decided.

Almighty God ﷻ has ordained that self-surrender to God ﷻ and to His Apostle ﷺ has priority over the exigencies of expedience as seen from the individual's perspective and over that which they are bound to by way of tradition. When properly understood, Islam demands humility and absolute self-surrender to the will of the Most Noble Prophet ﷺ as he is the expounder *par excellence* of God's commands ﷻ, such that obedience to him is tantamount to obedience to God the Most Exalted.

As to the second meaning, which has to do with the purity of one's worship of God ﷻ: this entails the purity of ritual worship of one's Lord that includes aspects of worship that concern bodily movements, such as *salāt* (the obligatory daily ritual prayer and devotions), fasting, the Hajj pilgrimage, and so on.

The scope of this second definition is more limited than utter submission to all of the prescriptive and proscriptive imperatives of the Prophet ﷺ because many people strive in the path of their obedience to the injunctions of the sacred law and are co-equal in this regard, save for the fact that some among them do not bow in submission to rulings of the Law which they find to be inexpedient.

The Noble Quran points to both meanings and makes a distinction between the two, calling the first *īmān* and the second *islām*. Addressing the Arabs, the Noble Quran says:

قَالَتِ الْأَعْرَابُ آمَنَّا ۖ قُل لَّمْ تُؤْمِنُوا وَلَٰكِن قُولُوا أَسْلَمْنَا وَلَمَّا يَدْخُلِ الْإِيمَانُ
فِي قُلُوبِكُمْ ۖ وَإِن تُطِيعُوا اللَّهَ وَرَسُولَهُ لَا يَلِتْكُم مِّنْ أَعْمَالِكُمْ شَيْئًا ۚ إِنَّ
اللَّهَ غَفُورٌ رَّحِيمٌ ﴿١٤﴾

> [49:14] The Bedouin say, "We have attained to faith (*Īmān*)." Say [unto them, O Muhammad]: "You have not [yet] attained to faith; you should [rather] say, 'We have embraced Islam,' for faith has not yet entered into your hearts."

What this means is that the Bedouin did not come short when it came to carrying out the religious duties incumbent upon them as a result of their having entered into Islam. However, the Quran tells us that there is more to it than that, and that the carrying out of religiously incumbent obligations is not in itself an indication of a faith (*īmān*) that is a guarantee of an absolute submission to the will of God the Most Exalted and that of the Most Noble Prophet ﷺ, because the true nature of the stance of at least some of these Bedouins had been exposed for all to see at the Battle of Tabūk.[4]

For example, when the Bedouins disobeyed the order of the Most Noble Prophet ﷺ, *āyāt* were revealed which reprimanded them because they saw their welfare in their disobeying the order of the Most Noble Prophet ﷺ and thought that there was leeway and laxity in such matters through which they could justify their act of disobedience. However, the Noble Quran severely rebuked and reprimanded them and several Companions who had joined them in their disloyalty.

The *Ijtihād*[5] of some of the Companions

A study of the history of the time of the Prophet ﷺ reveals that the action of some of the Companions fell a degree shy of absolute submission to God ﷻ and His Prophet ﷺ.

Some of the Companions considered the prescriptive and proscriptive imperatives (*awāmir wa nawāhī*) of the Most Noble Prophet ﷺ to be commands which were to be obeyed at all costs, but these companions made up a very small minority. In contrast, there was a large number who allowed themselves to dispute with the Most Noble Prophet ﷺ concerning his commands when such commands conflicted

---

[4] The Battle of Tabūk is the final battle in which the Most Noble Prophet ﷺ participated personally and probably represents the opening conflict in the coming Arab–Byzantine wars. It took place during the months of Rajab and Sha'bān of the year 9/630 in the region of Tabūk. As the expedition was heading toward Tabūk to fight the Byzantine army, some among the ranks of the army refused to join the battle and tried to dissuade others from doing so, thereby weakening the morale of the army.

[5] Striving or effort expended for the derivation of sacred law.

with what they believed to be most expedient for themselves.[6] Additionally, they considered disagreeing with the actions of the Most Noble Prophet ﷺ to be a legitimate form of behavior where they considered this to be necessary, and would at times even act against the wishes of the Most Noble Prophet ﷺ. Some of these actions have been documented in the historical record:

1. Battle against Abū-Sufyān

When the Most Noble Prophet ﷺ had determined to pursue Abū-Sufyān's trade convoy, the convoy did not have the wherewithal to resist the small Muslim detachment. Thus, when Abū-Sufyān discovered the intention of the Muslims, he sent word at speed to the idolaters at Mecca concerning the imminent threat from the Muslim regiment. With the Quraysh army on the move and the inability of the Muslims to ambush the convoy, the situation had changed. The leaders of the Quraysh, with Abū-Jahl foremost among them, now insisted on war with the Muslims and considered the opportunity to destroy them a boon. If the Muslim expedition returned without engaging in battle, they would be considered to have fled from the scene of battle and would have emboldened the idolaters to pursue the Muslims and engage them in battle on their own lands, and this posed an even greater danger.

And so, given this, and given the fact that the Companions knew that the Most Noble Prophet ﷺ wanted to engage the idolaters in battle precisely in order to ward off the danger posed by the situation that they now faced, nonetheless, a number of them refused to accept the Prophet's ﷺ decision. Some of the Companions even went so far as to say, "Why did you not inform us to prepare for war? We came prepared [only] for a raid on their convoy!"

It is related in a hadīth report that this group of Companions said, "O Apostle ﷺ of God ﷻ! Let us pursue the trade convoy and leave

---

[6] Ibn Ishāq, *as-Sīrat an-Nabawīya*, 1:370-373.

the enemy be [in peace]." The Prophet's face colored after having heard these words. Abū-Ayyūb relates that a revelation was revealed concerning this matter:[7]

كَمَا أَخْرَجَكَ رَبُّكَ مِن بَيْتِكَ بِالْحَقِّ وَإِنَّ فَرِيقًا مِّنَ الْمُؤْمِنِينَ لَكَارِهُونَ ﴿٥﴾ يُجَادِلُونَكَ فِي الْحَقِّ بَعْدَ مَا تَبَيَّنَ كَأَنَّمَا يُسَاقُونَ إِلَى الْمَوْتِ وَهُمْ يَنظُرُونَ ﴿٦﴾

> [8:5] Even as thy Lord of Providence brought thee forth from thy home [to fight] in the cause of the truth, although some of the believers were averse to it, [8:6] [so, too,] they would argue with thee about the truth [itself] after it had become manifest – just as if they were being driven towards death and beheld it with their very eyes.

2. Fasting before the battle of Badr

When the Apostle ﷺ of God ﷻ was preparing to leave Medina for the Battle of Badr in the month of Ramaḍān, he fasted for one or two days. He then returned, ordering the town crier to announce on his behalf: "O ye disobedient crowd! I have broken my fast (*iftār*) and am not fasting; you, too, then, should break your fasts!" The reason for the need for such an announcement was that he had previously given the command for the Muslims to break their fasts and some among them had not complied.[8]

Rather, history tells us that "the position and opinion of certain [persons among the Muslim nation] was [intended] to weaken the spirit of the Apostle ﷺ of God ﷻ and the Muslim community! When his Eminence consulted with his Companions, 'Umar b. al-Khattāb (the

[7] Ibn Ishāq, *as-Sīrat an-Nabawīya*, 1:371.
[8] Al-Wāqidī, *al-Mughāzī*, 1:47-48.

second caliph) said, 'O Apostle ﷺ of God ﷻ! I swear [upon my oath] with God ﷻ, the Quraysh has come out [to battle] with the entirety of its forces. I swear [upon my oath] with God ﷻ, from the time that they have found favor [with God ﷻ], they have never been humbled! I swear [upon my oath] with God ﷻ, from the time that they became unbelievers, they have never attained to faith. I swear [upon my oath] with God ﷻ, they will never surrender their honor and respect to you and will fight you [to the end]! And the Apostle ﷺ of God ﷻ turned away from him."[9]

On the other hand, we see other Companions whose position is the opposite of this first group. For example, in this same scene, Miqdād b. Amr arose and proclaimed, "O Apostle ﷺ of God ﷻ! Execute that which the Lord has commanded and know that we are with you. I swear [upon my oath] with God ﷻ! We will not act as the Israelites who told [their prophet]: [5:24] *[But] they said: "O Moses! Behold, never shall we enter that [land] so long as those others are in it. Go forth, then, thou and thy Lord of Providence, and fight, the two of you [together]! [For] behold, we shall remain [right] here!"* Rather, what we say [Miqdād continued] is 'Go forth, then, thou and thy Lord of Providence, and fight, the two of you [together]! And we too shall be by your side. I swear upon my oath to He who commissioned you [in your ministry]! We will follow you even if you lead us into fire;' at which point the Apostle ﷺ of God ﷻ prayed for him."

After this, Sa'd b. Mu'ādh arose and said, "… We have attained to faith in you and affirmed you and testified that all that which you have brought is the truth, and entered into a [sacred] covenant with you to obey you in any and all circumstances. O Apostle ﷺ of God ﷻ! Act in whichever way you deem fit and I swear upon my oath to He who commissioned you [in your ministry] that if you head toward the sea and get swallowed up by it, we will follow you to the last person!

---

[9] Al-Wāqidī, *al-Mughāzī*, 1:47-48.

Establish relations with whomsoever you will, and sever relations with whomsoever you will, and take what you desire of our belongings, and know that, that which you take is better for us than that which you leave. I swear upon my oath with He in Whose hands my soul rests! I have never traversed this path and do not know of its [dangers]. [But] we have no fear in confronting the enemy tomorrow. We are [= you shall find us to be] solid in the field of battle and shall not turn our backs to the enemy. And it might come to pass that Almighty God ﷻ will use us as a means by which to brighten your eyes."[10]

This speech makes clear the position of the Companions concerning their submission to the will of the Apostle ﷺ of God ﷻ and the absence of such a submission. Furthermore, some of the Companions would take positions and give voice to opinions that ran counter to the position of the Apostle ﷺ of God ﷻ, and in a sense, theirs was an *ijtihād* that ran against the letter and spirit of scripture. This act in itself is an indication of their failure to abide by the commands of their Prophet.

The application of these types of "*ijtihād*" can be seen to have occurred on many different occasions. For example, it has been reported from Abū-Khidrī that "Abū-Bakr came to the Apostle ﷺ of God ﷻ and said, 'O Apostle ﷺ of God ﷻ! I passed such and such a valley in which I saw a humble and handsome man at prayer.' The Most Noble Prophet ﷺ commanded [Abū-Bakr]: 'Go and kill him!' Abū-Bakr went back to that valley, but when he saw the man in this posture, he could not bring himself to kill him and returned to the Apostle ﷺ of God ﷻ. The Apostle ﷺ of God ﷻ then commanded 'Umar to go and kill him. 'Umar [also] went and when he saw the man in this posture, he could not bring himself to kill him and returned to the Apostle ﷺ of God ﷻ and said, 'O Apostle ﷺ of God ﷻ! I saw this man praying in [all] humility, so I

[10] Al-Wāqidī, *al-Mughāzī*, 1:47-48.

did not want to kill him. The Apostle ﷺ of God ﷻ said, 'O Ali ؑ! Go and kill this man!' And Ali ؑ went to execute this command, but he did not find that man. He returned and informed the Apostle ﷺ of God ﷻ that the man had left and that he had not found him. The Most Noble Prophet ﷺ said, 'That man and his followers recite the Quran, but its [effect] does not rise above their throats. They shall exit the fold of religion just as an arrow flies out of a bow, and will not return to the fold of religion just as the [spent] arrow does not return to the bow. Kill them [whenever you see them] as they are the worst creatures on the face of the earth.'"[11]

Here is another example: it has been recorded in the annals of history that "the Most Noble Prophet ﷺ accepted [all] the demands of the idolaters in the negotiations leading up to the Treaty of Hudaybīya."[12] At this juncture, it is reported that some of the Companions said that His Eminence had accepted a humiliating treaty; whereas the Apostle ﷺ of God ﷻ had signed the treaty being better aware of the interests of the Muslim community. It is impossible to imagine that he would do something that was to the detriment of his community. Nonetheless, a number of the Companions had the temerity to object to the decisions of the Most Noble Prophet ﷺ to the point that 'Umar b. al-Khattāb himself is related to have reported by Bokhārī: "I said in admonition, 'Are you not a true prophet of God ﷻ?!' He said, 'Certainly.' I asked, 'Is it not the case that we are in the right and our enemies are in the wrong?' He answered in the affirmative. I [then] asked, 'Then in that case, why are we accepting the humiliation of this treaty?' He said, 'Verily I am the Apostle of God ﷻ and I do not

---

[11] Ahmad b. Hanbal, *Musnad*, 3:15.

[12] The Treaty of Hudaybīya was a pivotal treaty between the Most Noble Prophet ﷺ, representing the state of Medina, and the Quraysh tribe of Mecca, in March 628 (*Dhu'al-Qa'da*, 6 HQ). It helped to decrease tension between the two cities, affirmed a 10-year peace, and authorized the Muslims to return the following year in a pilgrimage to Mecca in peace.

disobey Him, and He shall provide me with the aid [that we need].' I asked, 'Had you not said that we would go to the Sacred Sanctuary (*bayt al-ḥarām*; i.e. the Ka'ba) and shall circumambulate it?' He said, 'Yes, but did I say that we will do so this very year?' I said, 'No.' He said, 'You shall come to the Ka'ba and will circumambulate it.' I then went to Abū-Bakr and asked him, 'O Abū-Bakr! Is he not a true prophet of God ﷻ?! He said, 'Certainly.' I asked, 'Is it not the case that we are in the right and our enemies are in the wrong?' He answered in the affirmative. I [then] asked, 'Then in that case, why are we accepting the humiliation of this treaty?' He said, 'O man! Verily he is the Apostle of God ﷻ and does not disobey his Lord of Providence (*rabb*), and He shall aid His prophet. So cling to his robe for upon my oath with God ﷻ, he is in the right!' I asked, 'Had he not said that we would visit the Sacred Sanctuary and shall circumambulate it?' He said, 'Yes, but did he say that we will do so this very year?' I said, 'No.' He said, 'You shall come to the Ka'ba in the future and will circumambulate it.' [And 'Umar said,] 'I have made some arrangements to prevent this treaty from taking effect.'"

[Bokhārī continues his report from 'Umar:] "After the treaty had been written [and signed], the Apostle ﷺ of God ﷻ ordered his Companions to arise and to slaughter the sacrificial camels. Upon my oath with God ﷻ, no one arose until his Eminence repeated his order three times. When no one stood up, the Most Noble Prophet ﷺ entered Umm Salama's [tent] and told her why he was upset with his Companions. "O Apostle ﷺ of God ﷻ! [Umm Salama said,] If you want them to obey your command, leave the tent and without speaking a word to anyone, slaughter your sacrificial camel and tell the barber to shave your head.[13] His Eminence acted on this suggestion, and when

[13] This was part of the hajj ritual which the Muslims had been deprived of partaking in on account of the treaty (but which pilgrimage they had been promised they could partake in during the following year without being molested.)

the people saw this, they arose and slaughtered their sacrificial camels and shaved each other's heads and well-nigh killed each other on account of their grief and sorrow."[14]

Again, this episode gives us an insight into the attitude of some of the Companions of the Apostle ﷺ of God ﷻ. In this episode, after the Most Noble Prophet ﷺ tells 'Umar b. al-Khattāb that he is an apostle of God ﷻ and that he does not disobey his Lord (which reason alone should suffice anyone of the veracity of the Apostle ﷺ of God's ﷻ position), 'Umar then presses the Apostle ﷺ of God ﷻ, who then tells him that he shall indeed come to the Ka'ba in the future and will circumambulate it. But it seems that even this answer was not convincing enough for 'Umar, who then proceeds to Abū-Bakr and poses the same questions to him! Furthermore, this is after his Eminence ﷺ had ordered them to get up and slaughter the sacrificial camels!

The disobedience of the Companions of the commands of the Most Noble Prophet ﷺ were repeated on numerous occasions after the Treaty of Hudaybīya, to the point that his Eminence felt the need openly to complain of the constant harassment and defiance of his associates. It is related by Muslim and Ahmad b. Hanbal, among others from 'Āisha: "While for or five days had passed of the month of Dhu'l-Hijja, the Apostle ﷺ of God ﷻ entered the house while he was [manifestly] angry and upset. I asked him, 'Who has made you upset, O Apostle ﷺ of God ﷻ? May God ﷻ curse him to hell!' He said, 'Have you not noticed that I ordered the people to do something and the people have waivered from performing it? If I begin to do something, I will not turn away from it. I have not brought these sacrificial [animals]

[14] Bokhārī, *Sahīh*, 2:81. Muslim, *Sahīh*, in the chapter on the Treaty of Hudaybīya.

other than for the purpose of sacrificing them!' His Eminence then disrobed from his pilgrimage attire and the others followed suit."[15]

'Āisha reports in a similar vein: "The Most Noble Prophet ﷺ did something lawful and permissible, and despite this, a number of the Companions refrained from following his example. When the news of this reached his Eminence, after praising God the Sublimely Exalted, he asked, 'What is preventing some from following my example in carrying out certain tasks?' I swear [upon my oath with God ﷻ] that I am more aware than anyone among them as to what is [right and what is wrong in the eyes of] God ﷻ, and have more humility and God-consciousness (*taqwā*) than any one of them."[16] It seems that a number of people considered themselves to be more pious and God ﷻ-conscious than the Most Noble Prophet ﷺ, for otherwise, what could possibly have been the motivation behind such skepticism and doubt concerning actions that were performed by the Most Noble Prophet ﷺ? Why else would they believe that the acts of his Eminence ran counter to the Divine will, preventing them from following suit?!

The situation even got to the point that some people countermanded his Eminence's commands on matters great and small. Apparently, these Companions believed that they had the right to interfere in the decision-making process and to determine positions

---

[15] Muslim, *Sahīh*, 4:34. Ibn Māja, *Sunan*, 2:993. Ahmad b. Hanbal, *Musnad*, 4:286 & 6:175. In a report from Berā' b. 'Āzib, it is reported that the Most Noble Prophet ﷺ stated, "Turn your Hajj [pilgrimages] to '*umra* [pilgrimages]." The people said, 'O Apostle ﷺ of God ﷻ! How can we turn them into '*umra* pilgrimages when it has [already] become unlawful for us [to perform] the Hajj [pilgrimage]?' The Apostle ﷺ of God ﷻ said, 'Pay heed to that which I command you, and do that which I command.' But they did not accept his words." Dhahabī writes, "This is a *sahīh* (sound) *hadīth* report related by al-'Awwālī which Ibn Māja has excised [from his compilation]." (*Seyr I'lām al-Anbiyā*, 8:498).

[16] Bokhārī, *Sahīh*, 8:145.

concerning sacred law that were at odds with the expressly stated position of the Most Noble Prophet ﷺ himself. It is reported from Jābir: "The Apostle ﷺ of God ﷻ forbade us from approaching our wives upon returning from a night journey, but later we did this [anyway]!"[17]

The Great Effrontery

The effrontery of some of the Companions relative to the directives of the Apostle ﷺ of God ﷻ proceeded to the point where they would interpret and rationalize his categorical directives in accordance with their own desires. Some among these considered themselves bound to obey only those directives that were revealed as part of the Quranic revelation itself and which concerned matters of ritual worship, considering themselves exempt from having to comply with social and political directives which bore on the formation of the new norms of society which the Prophet Muhammad ﷺ was commissioned to establish. They considered it their right to act on their own opinions and what they considered to be their interests on political matters and on issues having to do with governance and the way in which society was to be ordered after the Apostle ﷺ of God ﷻ had passed, even if their position was in direct opposition to the letter of what the Most Noble Prophet ﷺ had determined was best for them.

This attitude can be seen very clearly in the example provided by the case of the appointment of Usāma b. Zayd as the commander of the Muslim army, which was mustered to battle with the Byzantines. "Even though the Most Noble Prophet ﷺ had appointed Usāma b. Zayd to command the army and had fixed the standard for him with his own blessed hands, some of the Companions objected to this decision and ridiculed it. They claimed that Usāma is too young and that he does not merit the command over the elders of the *muhājirūn* (Emigrants)

[17] Abī-Shayba, *al-Masnaf*, 7:727; Hamīdī, *al-Masnaf*, 2:543; Ahmad b. Hanbal, *al-Musnad*, 3:373.

and *ansār* (Helpers) such as Abū-Bakr, 'Umar, Abū-Ubayda and others who were in the ranks of the army.

After the news of these objections and mockery reached the Most Noble Prophet ﷺ, he left his chambers irritated and in anger and despite the fact that he was seriously ill, and went up to the pulpit and said, 'O People! What [kind of] talk is this that [I have heard] you say concerning the command of Usāma? If today you mock and scoff at Usāma's command, you [equally] reviled the command of his father aforetime. But I swear [upon my oath] to God ﷻ! He merited the command [then], just as his son merits the command today!'"[18] And despite the adamant and emphatic command of the Most Noble Prophet ﷺ concerning the command of Usāma and the rapid dispatching of his army in the direction of the Syrian border, the troops stonewalled and stalled and would not allow the army to be dispatched. This stonewalling continued until the passing of the Most Noble Prophet ﷺ from the earthly plane; and still the army was encamped in Medina and its dispatch, which the Most Noble Prophet ﷺ had been most emphatic about, came very close to being cancelled, or at a minimum, was threatened with the change of its command.[19]

It must be said that the temerity of certain of the Companions in their disobedience to the Apostle ﷺ of God ﷻ had reached its nadir in the last days of his blessed life. A few historians, chroniclers of hadīth scripture and biographers of the Apostle ﷺ of God ﷻ have related from Ibn Abbās (here we cite the version by Bokhārī): "When the Most

---

[18] Ibn-Sa'd, *Tabaqāt al-Kubrā*, 2:190; Ya'qūbī, *at-Tārīkh*, 2:74; Ibn Athīr, *al-Kāmil fi't-Tārīkh*, 2:317; Ibn Abī'l-Hadīd, Abdul-Hamīd, *Sharh-e Nahj al-Balāgha*, 1:53; Abul-Faraj al-Halabī, *as-Sīra' al-Halabīa*, 3:207; Ibn Hishām, *as-Sīra' an-Nabawīya*, 2:339; Muttaqī al-Hindī, *Kanz al-U'mmāl*, 5:312; Balādhūrī, *Ansāb al-Ashrāf*, 1:474; Wāqidī, *al-Mughāzī*, 3:1119.

[19] Tabarī, *Tārīkh ar-Rusul wa'l-Mulūk*, 3:226; Ibn Athīr, *al-Kāmil fi't-Tārīkh*, 2:335; Abul-Faraj al-Halabī, *as-Sīra' al-Halabīa*, 3:209.

Noble Prophet ﷺ fell ill and was in his death throes, a number of the Companions were present in his chambers, including 'Umar b. al-Khattāb. The Most Noble Prophet ﷺ said, 'Bring [me] a scroll and inkpot so that I can write an inscription for you, after which you will never go astray.' 'Umar b. al-Khattāb said, 'This man is delirious! Among you is the Book of God ﷻ, and the Book of God ﷻ is sufficient unto us!'

"The Companions present in the Prophet's ﷺ chambers disagreed and divided into two groups. Some called for a scroll and inkpot to be brought so that the Apostle ﷺ of God ﷻ could write something 'after which they would never go astray,' and another group was with 'Umar! After much argumentation and bickering, his Eminence said, 'Get out from my presence!' And Ibn Abbās would always say, 'Verily, the greatest calamity [to have befallen our community] was that the Apostle ﷺ of God ﷻ was prevented from writing that which would have precluded the community from going astray.'"[20]

A slight variant of the text of the report of this same episode [also] appears in Bokhārī, who relates it from Ibn Abbās by way of Sa'īd b. Musayyib: "It was a Thursday. What a Thursday! He [Ibn-'Abbās] was overcome by tears and wept until the granules of sand [before him] became wet [with his tears]. He then said, "The Prophet's illness became acute on this day. He said, bring me a scroll so that I can write a letter for you by [adherence to] which you shall never go astray. Those present at [the deathbed of] his Eminence (*haḍra*^{t}) differed [as to what was to be done]: one group said, 'Carry out the order of the Prophet!' Another group said, 'No! Do not bring a scroll!' The crowd began to quarrel, whereas it is not appropriate to squabble in the presence of the Prophet, for the Quran tells us, [49:2] *O you who have attained to faith! Do not raise your voices above the voice of the Prophet.* They said, "The

[20] Bokhārī, *Sahīh*, 1:22 (The Book of Knowledge).

Prophet is delirious!" [They well understood what the Most Noble Prophet ﷺ wanted to write, but pretended not to understand and repeated what they said. And] the Prophet, [with the broken heart of a loving parent confronted with the disrespect and outright contumacy of a wayward son,] said, "Leave me to myself. [The severity of] the pain [that I am suffering due to my illness] is more palatable to me than the hurt of your [impudence]." He then said, "I commend you to three things: drive the idolaters out of the Arabian Peninsula, treat the delegations [of non-Muslims] as I have treated them [in the past], and ..." he was silent when it came to the third item, or he said "I have forgotten the third"![21]

What kind of "expedience" could possibly justify the prevention of the Most Noble Prophet ﷺ from writing his last will and testament; a testament the adherence to which would have prevented the entire community from ever going astray; and which prevention prompted Ibn Abbās to characterize it as "the greatest calamity [to have befallen our community]"? (According to some reports, when Ibn Abbās used to relate the story of this tragic episode, he wept to such an extent that the sand between his feet became wet with his tears. The only possible way to explain such "expedience" is to say that it was not expedient to the interests of certain of the Companions, as shall be made clear further in our discussion. It was for this reason (and not for the reason of the expedience of the community as a whole) that the Most Noble Prophet ﷺ was prevented from writing his will.

---

[21] Bokhārī, *Sahīh*, 5:137. The silence concerning the third item, as reported by Ibn Abbās, (or its having been forgotten, according to Sa'īd's report) speaks to the importance of the issue; we shall return to this point later. Also see: Bokhārī, *Sahīh*, 8:61; Muslim, *Sahīh*, 5:75; Ahmad b. Hanbal, *Musnad*, 4:356, H # 2992, where it appears with a provenance title deemed to be sound (*Sahīh*) by Ahmad b. Hanbal.

2 - Sources of Religious Authority (or: *Nass* and *Ijtihād*)

In the past, religious authority (*marjaʿīa*^{t}) usually rested in the hands of the clergy, and statesmen did not have religious mandates. The pharaohs of Egypt claimed that they were descended from the gods, but this claim was false. Kings were not the custodians of religious matters. It was generally the clergy who took charge of the enactment of religious rites and rituals. It was usually the case that the pharaohs of Egypt and other kings had charge of political matters, set social policy and saw to the administration of the state. The priestly class saw to the enactment of religious rites and rituals in the temples, which were the limits of their domain. History tells us that this is generally the way things were in the past. However, the advent of the revealed religions changed the function and status of the custodians of religion. In Judaism, religious functions became the responsibility of the rabbi, and in Christianity, it became the popes', so that policymaking and governance were the exclusive domain of kings who pretended to religiosity and obedience to the clergy in order to lend an aura of legitimacy and sanctity to themselves and to their reigns. But these kings would not interfere in religious rites and rituals and concerned themselves only with the maintenance and expansion of the boundaries of their realms.

After the dawning of Islam and the emigration of the Most Noble Prophet ﷺ from Mecca to Yathrib (which was consequently called Medina), the first adumbrations of the Islamic form of government were formed when the Apostle ﷺ of God ﷻ took on the responsibilities of both religious matters and policymaking in unison. He became the mentor and guide of the people in all matters pertaining to religion and the ordinances of the sacred law, and he would explain all of the details of the injunctions of the law and the rituals of the religion, and would ask his followers to follow his example in all such matters. For instance, with respect to *salāt* (mandatory ritual worship), he would say, "Perform your *salāt* as you see me perform [mine]." At the same time, he was the political leader of his community and was in charge of the administration of the state. This was demonstrated at the very beginning of his migration to Yathrib, where his Eminence wrote a treaty upon whose basis, he arranged the political relations of the *muhājirūn* (Emigrants), the *ansār* (Helpers), and the Jewish tribes resident at Yathrib. In a similar vein, he took personal charge of his army in the larger battles and personally assigned his governors and commanders. He was both the political and the religious leader of the community in unison, and executed both offices.

From the teachings of their prophet, the Muslims realized that the union of these two offices was to continue after his passing. They were to follow the example of the successor to the Prophet who, in addition to having leadership and policymaking responsibilities in the social and political economy of the polity (as well as in security matters), was to have the capabilities and spiritual standing in order to function as the religious leader of the community in interpreting and implementing the ordinances and injunctions of the sacred law as revealed by the Book of God ﷻ and in continuing to personify the paradigmatic example and exemplary model set by the Most Noble Prophet ﷺ. Thus, in Islam, matters of religion and state were not separate, and anyone who was to succeed the Apostle ﷺ of God ﷻ was to follow the same policy and method of the continued integrality of these two domains. Moreover, in so far as every member of the community cannot be equally qualified and have the competence to shoulder the responsibilities of the succession to the Most Noble Prophet ﷺ, it follows that the person that is to be able to shoulder and therefore merit such a responsibility must be imbued with certain attributes and characteristics to enable him to ensure the sacred law of Islam is properly interpreted and implemented, and to safeguard its polity and territories from the dangers that it faced.

Clearly, some of the functions of governance are subject to personal interpretations and to a determination of what is most beneficial by way of consultation and council. On the other hand, matters which pertain to religion and sacred law are not subject to such interpretations and expedients. In point of fact, it is entirely possible that such personal interpretations and the application of expedients in the ambit of religion and sacred law will, in time, undermine the very basis of religion itself, because the gradual accretion of distortions and superstitions into what is held to be sacred will cause that which is truly sacred and which has been replaced to be forgotten, inevitably bringing about deviations from the right path. Thus, religious authority has specific conditions which cannot be fulfilled by just anyone. It is in light of this understanding of the nature and function of religious leadership that the question is resolved as to whether the Most Noble Prophet ﷺ considered the issue of his succession to be important, mentioned the conditions that it entailed, and expressly appointed a person or persons to the tenure of this office; or whether he left the question of succession open for the decision of the community to decide who is the fittest for the religious and political leadership of the community based on the exigencies and expedience of the time.

The Prerequisites for Religious Authority

Having identified the importance of the political leadership of the community also being vested with religious authority if the sacred law of Islam is to be preserved and maintained, it is essential to proceed to state the necessary conditions for the occupant of this office. These conditions can be summed up in the merits, specific attributes, and assets that this office's custodian must be endowed with. Such traits necessitate that a specific designation on the part of the Most Noble Prophet ﷺ must exist concerning the person who is indeed endowed with these characteristics, such that any dispute or conflict in the community concerning this matter is precluded so that discord and chaos are avoided.

In examining the history of the formative period of Islam and the history of the ways of the Apostle ﷺ of God ﷻ, ample textual evidence can be found wherein the Most Noble Prophet ﷺ specifically indicates the individual who is imbued with these characteristics. It is related by historians of hadīth scripture that "When the Apostle ﷺ of God ﷻ was returning from his farewell pilgrimage, he encamped in a place in Jahfa which was called Ghadīr Khumm. He then ordered his Companions not to seek the shade of the yonder trees that spotted the desert so that the caravan would not disperse. He then had the tumbleweed and bramble cleared from under the nearby trees[22] and called his people to communal prayer.[23] The Prophet's companions made him an impromptu canopy by throwing cloth over the thorn trees,[24] and the Prophet prepared to make the Noon Prayers there in the

[22] Haythamī, *Majma' uz-Zawāid*, 9:105. A description close to this is also found in Ibn Kathīr, *Tārīkh*, 5:209.

[23] Ahmad b. Hanbal, *Musnad*, vol. 6, p. 281; Ibn Māja, *Sunan*, in the chapter on the Excellences of Ali (as); Ibn Kathīr, *Tārīkh*, 5:209-210.

[24] Ahmad b. Hanbal, *Musnad*, vol. 4, p. 372; Ibn Kathīr, *Tārīkh*, 5:212.

insufferable heat.[25] He mounted a pulpit that had been improvised from camel litters and gave a sermon wherein he started by praising and glorifying God ﷻ, and preached [of his wisdom] to the gathering, and then said, "The time is soon approaching when I will be recalled [by God ﷻ] and I must respond [= comply with this call; i.e. the reference is to the approach of the Prophet's time of death]; and [a day shall come when] you and I shall be [held] responsible before God ﷻ. How will you respond to God ﷻ ['s queries] on that Day?" The throng cried out, "We will bear witness that you carried out your ministry in the best possible way, and guided us, and [will pray that] God ﷻ reward you with His blessings [for what you have done]." The Prophet then asked, "Do you [then] not testify to God's ﷻ unicity and to [the veracity of my prophethood and of] my ministry? Do you [then] not testify that Heaven and Hell exist?" The people called out, "Yea, verily, we testify to all these things!" The Final Prophet prayed, "Almighty God ﷻ, [pray] bear witness!" He then asked, "Can [all of you] hear my voice?" And when they responded in the affirmative, our blessed Prophet said, "O ye people, I will precede you [to the next world] and you will enter into my presence at the Pond of Kawthar, a pond whose width is [equal to] the length of the distance from Basrī to San'ā[26], around which are arrayed silver goblets, countless as the starts of the night sky; and [at that time], I shall ask [each of] you concerning the Two Weighty Trusts [= the two things of high value,] which I left amongst you in trust. So pay attention to how you treat these two after I have departed!"

Here someone cried out, "O Prophet of God ﷻ! What are those two things of value?" And the Prophet responded, "The first is the Book of God ﷻ, one end of which is in God's ﷻ hands and the other in yours. Keep it well and obey its decrees and do not allow any change to enter

---

[25] Ahmad b. Hanbal, *Musnad*, vol. 4, p. 281; Ibn Māja, *Sunan*, in the chapter on the Excellences of Ali ؑ; Ibn Kathīr, *Tārīkh*, vol. 5, p. 212.

[26] Towns close to present day Baghdad and Damascus respectively.

into it, for you will [surely] go astray [if you do]. The other is my Family (*itratī*), the Members of my House (*ahl al-baytī*) ‎. Almighty God ‎ has informed me that these two shall never be parted until they enter into my presence at the Pond of Kawthar – this I have asked of my Lord. Therefore, do not surpass these two if you are to be saved from perdition, and do not fall behind from them, for you will be annihilated. Do not [attempt to] teach them anything, as they are more knowledgeable than you." Some hadīth reports state that Apostle ‎ of God ‎ said, "As long as you hold fast unto these two [Trusts], you will not go astray."[27]

After relating a number of hadīth reports concerning the Two Weighty Trusts, Ibn Hajar al-Haythamī al-Makkī writes: "Know that there are many chains of narration (*turuq*) for the hadīth of the Two Weighty Trusts and that it has been related by more than twenty Companions... We have mentioned earlier different versions of this hadīth report. Some of them relate to the utterances made by the Prophet ‎ at Arafa in the course of his Farewell Pilgrimage; others to pronouncements made while he was on his deathbed in Medīna, surrounded by the Companions; another to his address at Ghadīr Khumm; and yet another to statements made while returning from Ta'if." He then adds: "None of these versions [which are reported to have been said in different locations] contradicts any other, for there is no reason [to assume] why he should not have repeated the same truth on all these occasions, and on others as well, given the great significance

[27] Hākim al-Haskānī an-Neyshāpurī, *al-Mustadrak fī Sahīhayn*, 3:109 & 3:533 (Dhahabī has concurred with Hākim's ruling that this hadīth is *sahīh* in his *talkhīs* (summarization or digest) of the *Mustadrak.* Also see, Ahmad b. Hanbal, *Musnad*, 5:181-189; Tirmidhī, *Jāme'*, 2:308 & 5:328 H#3874; Nasāī, *Khasāis Amīr al-Mu'menīn*, p. 21; Muttaqī al-Hendī, *Kanz ul-U'mmāl*, 1:44 & 1:47-48; Muslim, *Sahīh*, In the chapter on the virtues of Ali ‎; Dāramī, *Sunan*, 2:431; Ibn-Sa'd, *Tabaqāt al-Kubrā*, 2:2; Munāwī's *Kunūz al-Haqāiq*, 3:14; *Hilīat al-Awlīā*, 1:355, H#64; Haythamī, *Majma' oz-Zawāid*, 9:163-164.

that [the inter-relatedness of] both the Quran and his Progeny possess."[28]

We can summarize the hadīth of the Two Weighty Trusts and Ibn Hajar's commentary concerning it as follows: The Apostle ﷺ of God ﷻ stated in no uncertain terms which persons are to take on the responsibility of religious leadership after his passing, expressly positing these to be the People of his own Household (the *Ahl al-Bayt*) ﷺ who are on a par with the Noble Quran, which is immune from all falsity. Therefore, the Quran is the first source of reference for the sacred law of Islam and is the Greater Weighty Trust, and the People of the Household [of the Most Noble Prophet ﷺ] are the Lesser Weighty Trust. The repetition of the hadīth of the Two Weighty Trusts and the reference to the succession of the People of the Household [of the Most Noble Prophet ﷺ] (the Ahl al-Bayt ﷺ) on numerous different occasions speak to the extraordinary significance of this issue and is in fact a learning opportunity for anyone who has not yet heard of the hadīth report, and a cautionary reminder to those who have.

However, the Most Noble Prophet ﷺ did not leave it at that. Rather, he expressed his intention in a much clearer fashion as well. Muhammad b. 'Abd-Allāh al-Hākim an-Neyshāpurī (d. 1012 CE), who was an 'Asharite and the leading Sunni *muhaddith* (*hadīth* scholar) of his age, quotes Abū-Dharr al-Ghaffārī (may God ﷻ be pleased with him), one of the great companions of the Prophet, as saying (while holding onto the door of the Ka'ba), "O ye people! Those of you who know me: I am he whom you know; and those who doubt me [i.e. the words I am about to recount], [know that] I am Abū-Dharr. I heard the Prophet of God ﷻ say, 'The example of my Family (*ahl al-bayti*) ﷺ is

[28] Ibn Hajar, *as-Sawā'iq*, p. 89.

like the example of Noah's Ark: he who boards it is saved and he who does not shall drown.'"[29]

In another *hadīth* report from Ibn Abbās it is related that "The Most Noble Prophet ﷺ said, 'The stars are the protectors of those who dwell on the earth, and the People of my House are the protectors of my community and deliver them from misguidance and errancy. If a tribe from among the Arabs opposes them, dissidence will arise [among them] and they will become the followers of Iblīs (Satan).'"[30]

In certain reports, the following speech of the Most Noble Prophet ﷺ appears concerning the Members of his Household:

> "The first is the Book of God ﷻ one end of which is in God's ﷻ hands and the other which is in yours. Keep it well and obey its decrees and do not allow any change to enter into it, for you will [surely] go astray [if you do]. The other is my Family (*etrati*), the Members of my House (*ahl al-baytī*) ؑ, and Almighty God ﷻ has informed me that these two shall never be parted until they enter into my presence at the Pond of Kawthar

---

[29] al-Hākim an-Neshapuri, *Mustadrak*, vol. 2, p. 343, who writes that this report is sound (*Sahīh*) in accordance with the criteria of Muslim b. al-Hajjar, the great hadīth compiler. See also: al-Muttaqi al-Hindi, *Kanz ul-U'mmāl*, Vol. I, p. 250; Ibn Hajar, *as-Sawā'iq*, p. 75; al-*Qunduzī*, *Yanābi' al-Mawaddah*, p. 257. Ibn as-Sabbāgh, *al-Fusul al-Muhimmah*, p. 10; as-Sabban, *Is'af al-Raghibīn*, p. 111; ash-Shiblanjī, *Nur al-Absar*, p. 114; and many others, including *Majma' al-Zawāid*, Hiliat al-Awliā, *Tarīkh al-Baghdād*, *Dhakhāir al-Uqbā* (Muhibb at-Tabarī), *Kunūz al-Haqāiq*, *Feyz al-Ghadīr* and *as-Sawāiq al-Mahraqa*. In some of these reports, the People of the Household [of the Most Noble Prophet ﷺ] are described as the Gate of Humility (*bāb al-hitta*), and that anyone who enters into [their wisdom] is a true believer (*mu'min*), and anyone who exits their gate is an unbeliever (*kāfir*).

[30] Ibn Hajar, *as-Sawā'iq*, p. 140; al-Hākim, *al-Mustadrak*, Vol. III, p. 149 & 458, where al-Hākim affirms the *sahīh* status of these two *ahadīth*; *Kanz al-'Ammāl*, 6:116; *as-Sawāiq ol-Mahraqa*; *Majma' oz-Zawāid* 9:174; *Fayḍ al-Ghadīr* and *Dhakhāir ol-Oqbā* (Muhebb at-Tabarī).

> – this I have asked of my Lord. Therefore, do not surpass these two, if you are to be saved from perdition, and do not fall behind from them, for you will be annihilated. Do not [attempt to] teach them anything, as they are more knowledgeable than you."[31]

The Commander of the Faithful, Ali b. Abī-Tālib ﷺ has stated in a portion of one of his sermons, "Protect the People of the Household of your Prophet ﷺ and honor them and follow their example. They shall not lead you astray from [the path of true] guidance, and shall not lead you back to [the days of] ignorance and ignominy. If they adopt a posture of quiescence, then you too should adopt such a stance; and if they rise up in rebellion [against tyranny and injustice], then you too should do the same. Do not surpass them, for you will surely be lost, and do not fall behind from them, for you will surely perish."[32]

It has been related from Imām Zayn al-Ābidīn, "… so which persons are reliable in the explication of the proof (*hujja*) of God ﷻ and the interpretation of God's ﷻ commands? [These cannot be any] other than those who are the Justice of the Quran, the progeny of the Imāms of Moderation, and the Lamps of Guidance which Almighty God ﷻ uses as the perfect evidence [of all truth] and [shall use] as the conclusive argument and final proof [against all falsehood] (*al-hujja*)[33] against his bondsmen [on the Day of Reckoning], whom He does not leave

---

[31] Ibn Hajar, *as-Sawā'iq ol-Mahraqa*, p. 230.

[32] Ali b. Abī-Tālib ﷺ, *Nahj al-Balāgha*, 2:190 (Dār ol-Andalūs).

[33] *Hujjat* or *hujjatullāh*: the Proof [of God ﷻ] [36:12] … *For of all things do We take account in a manifest Imām* (*imāmin mubīn*) [who shall be called to testify and provide evidence on all matters on the Day of Judgment]. This is the meaning of the word hujjatullāh or God ﷻ's proof for mankind, which is one of the names given to the Imāms by the Quran: The *hujjat* is the perfect embodiment and "clear evidence" of all truth on Earth and the conclusive argument and evidentiary proof against all falsehood on Judgement Day.

without such evidence and proofs for an instance. Do you not know them? Or [is it the case that] you can find anything other than by way of the light of the branches of the Blessed Tree or by way of the Remnants of the Select, whom God ﷻ has rendered utterly free of all pollution, and has made their amity a religiously obligatory (*wājib*) duty?!"[34]

There is no doubt concerning the fact that the Most Noble Prophet ﷺ has designated certain persons to whom the faithful of his community can refer after his passing. These are the People of the Household [of the Most Noble Prophet ﷺ] (the Ahl al-Bayt ؑ), adherence to whom he has made a religiously obligatory (*wājib*) duty in parallel with the Quran, and has proscribed the faithful from turning away from them and disobeying their orders and has warned them about such disobedience on pain of being led astray and of eternal perdition.

Now if it is asked why the Most Noble Prophet ﷺ has limited the source of religious authority to his own household, it must be said that accepting the fact that his Eminence does not speak out of his own desire and that that [which he conveys to you] is but [divine] inspiration with which he is being inspired [35]. It follows that all that which the Apostle ﷺ of God ﷻ has commanded is done under the direction and at the behest of Almighty God, Who has made the People of the Household [of the Most Noble Prophet ﷺ] (the Ahl al-Bayt ؑ) the subject of His special attention and bestowed upon them special attributes that enable them to merit and have the capability to accept the heavy burden of responsibility of this office.

---

[34] Ibn Hajar, *as-Sawā'iq al-Mahraqa*, p. 233. The reference is to this *āya*: [33:33] *for God ﷻ only wants to remove from you all that might be loathsome, O ye Members of the House [of the Prophet], and to render you utterly free of all pollution.*

[35] [53:2] *This fellow-man of yours has not gone astray, nor is he deluded*, [53:3] *and neither does he speak out of his own desire*: [53:4] *that [which he conveys to you] is but [divine] inspiration with which he is being inspired.*

The categorical *āyāt* of the Book of God ﷻ also speak to this issue, as is evidenced in the Āya of Purification:

وَقَرْنَ فِي بُيُوتِكُنَّ وَلَا تَبَرَّجْنَ تَبَرُّجَ الْجَاهِلِيَّةِ الْأُولَىٰ ۖ وَأَقِمْنَ الصَّلَاةَ وَآتِينَ
الزَّكَاةَ وَأَطِعْنَ اللَّهَ وَرَسُولَهُ ۚ إِنَّمَا يُرِيدُ اللَّهُ لِيُذْهِبَ عَنكُمُ الرِّجْسَ أَهْلَ
الْبَيْتِ وَيُطَهِّرَكُمْ تَطْهِيرًا ﴿٣٣﴾

> [33:33] for God ﷻ only wants to remove from you all that might be loathsome, O ye Members of the House [of the Prophet], and to render you utterly free of all pollution.

In this Noble āya, God the Sublimely Exalted establishes that He has removed from the People of the Household of the Most Noble Prophet ﷺ all taint of impurity and any sort of moral pollution and shortcoming which most other people are afflicted with. This purity necessarily entails immaculacy, i.e., a state of sinlessness and inerrancy, including, for example, calumnies concerning God ﷻ. On the other hand, the Most Noble Prophet ﷺ has accredited specific other attributes to the Members of his Household among which we can mention the fact that he stated that "They are the most knowledgeable persons with respect to the ordinances of the sacred law of Islam," and this necessitates their being the sources of reference in religious matters and the touchstones of the Muslim community.

Furthermore, it follows from the fact that the Apostle ﷺ of God ﷻ encouraged everyone to follow and defer to them, and 'not to surpass them or to fall behind from them' that they indeed merit this important office. It is not the case that this critical appointment was merely on account of a familial relationship or due to his love for them; recall that the Most Noble Prophet ﷺ did not show any affection for Abū-Lahab, who was his uncle, but rather considered him an enemy on account of his unworthy deeds.

The Limits of the Membership of the House of the Prophet ﷺ

[Because of the significance the Prophet ﷺ bestowed on this phrase,] some people have attempted to include as part of "the Members of the House of the Prophet" ﷺ persons who do not belong. However, the Most Noble Prophet ﷺ took many measures on numerous different occasions to preclude any possibility of doubt whatsoever concerning the membership of this select group.

Historians of hadīth scripture have reported hadīth from certain Companions that expressly state the bounds of what is meant by the expression 'Members of the Household [of the Prophet ﷺ]', including a report from the Mother of the Faithful (*umm al-mu'minīn*) Umm-Salama (may God ﷻ be pleased with her):

The events that constituted the occasion for the revelation of the *āya* were the following, as related by Umm Salama, a wife of the Prophet renowned for her piety and nobility of spirit, in whose chambers the events took place: "One day, Lady Fātema عليها السلام, the daughter of the Prophet, brought a dish of food to her father. He told her to summon her husband Ali عليه السلام and their children, Hasan عليه السلام and Husayn عليه السلام, which she did. When they were all gathered and engaged in eating, the Āya of Purification was revealed. Thereupon the Prophet took a piece of cloth that he had on his shoulders and cast it over their heads, saying three times, 'O Lord, these are the People of my House; remove filth and impurity from them and render them utterly pure.'"[36] 'Umar b. Abī-Salama, who was a witness to the incident, described it as follows: "The Āya of Purification was revealed in the house of Umm Salama. Then the Prophet told Ali, Lady Fātima, Hasan, and Husayn to approach him and threw over their heads a piece of cloth that was

[36] Qundūzī, *Yanabī, al-Mawadda*, p. 125.

covering his shoulders, and said, 'These are the People of my House; remove from them all filth, and render them utterly pure.' Umm Salama then asked, 'O Prophet, am I also one of them?' He replied, 'Be content with your own place, for you are one of the virtuous.'"[37] 'Āisha also relates: "One day the Prophet ﷺ left the house with a piece of cloth slung over his shoulders. Hasan, Husayn, [Lady] Fātima, and Ali came to see him, and he threw the cloth over their heads, reciting the Āya of Purification."[38]

And among the events concerning which there is no controversy whatever is that the Most Noble Prophet ﷺ challenged the Christians of Najrān to a *mubāhala*, which is a somber ritual where two disputing parties mutually imprecate each other with the understanding that their curse will fall on the party who is not in the right. To this they agreed and set a time and place for the following morning, upon which the Prophet ﷺ appeared with Imām Ali, his wife Lady Fātima عليها السلام, and their two sons, Hasan and Husayn, and looking heavenward, said, "O Lord, these are the members of my family [which I offer to You in this somber contest of mutual imprecation]."[39] When the Christians saw

---

[37] Ibn al-Athir, *Jami' al-Usūl*, Vol. I, p. 101; al-Muhibb al-Tabari, *Riyad al-Nadirah*, Vol. II, p. 269; al-Haythami, *Majma' az-Zawa'id*, Vol. IX, pp. 119, 207. See also Ahmad b. Hanbal, *Musnad*, 6: 296 & 323; Hākim, *al-Mustadrak*, 3: 108 & 147; *Kanz ul-U'mmāl*, 7: 102 & 217; and *Majma' az-Zawa'id*, 1:167.

[38] Qundūzī, *Yanabī' al-Mawadda*, p. 124. See also, Muslim, *Sahīh*, The Book of the Excellences of the Companions, the Chapter on the Excellences of the Members of the Household of the Prophet; and; Hākim, al-*Mustadrak*, 3: 147, in which Hākim states that this *hadīth* is *sahīh* in accordance with the criteria of the *shaykhayn* (Bokhārī & Muslim). See also Bayhaqī, *Sunan* 2:149; Tabarī, *Tafsīr* 5:22. Fakhr ar-Rāzī has also included this report in his *Tafsīr* under the āya of the Mubāhila (mutual imprecation), and says that the hadīth is accepted by almost all scholars of *hadīth* and *tafsīr* (Quranic commentary); Tirmedhī, Jāmi' 2: 209 & 319; Ahmad b. Hanbal, *Musnad*, 6:306; *Asad al-Ghāba*, 4:209.

[39] The above narrative, together with this last sentence (for which purpose the narrative was cited) appear in countless Sunnite sources, including: Muslim's

that the Prophet had brought his family (and only his family, and had not brought his generals and foot soldiers, leaving his family at home), they were overtaken by anxiety and refused to participate in the *mubāhila*. But they still did not enter into Islam, preferring instead to live under the protection of the realm of Islam and pay the jizya tax imposed on religious minorities instead.

Now the question might arise that if the Members of the Household of the Prophet ﷺ are these five persons, then what basis do the Twelver Sh'īa have for stating that the Imāms of the Household of the Prophet are twelve in number? The answer is that the hadīth scripture that has reached us from the Most Noble Prophet ﷺ sets their number at twelve.

The reports which appear in this class of hadīth are numerous to the point of being *mutawātir*.[40] They appear in all of the authoritative Sunni books (as well as in the books of Sh'īa hadīth, of course), including those of the *sahīhayn* (of Bokhārī and Muslim), the *Musnad* of Ahmad b. Hanbal, the *Sunan* of Dāramī, the *Sunan* of Beyhaqī, and the *Mustadrak fī Sahīhayn* of Hākim-e Neyshāpurī. The text varies slightly in each report, but the meaning is exactly the same. We will present the one which appears in the *Sahīh* of Muslim (related by Jābir b. Samara):

Sahīh, where it appears in the section on the virtues of Ali b. Abi Taleb; Tirmidhi's *Jāmi'* (2:166, 209 & 319); Hākim's *Mustadrak 'alā as-Sahīhayn* (3:150), where the sheikh affirms the hadīth to be *sahīh* in accordance with the criteria of the *shaykhayn*; Bayhaqī's *Sunan* (2:149 and 7:63), and Wāhidī's *Asbāb an-Nuzūl*, p. 75.

[40] *Mutawātir* - The highest possible classification of reliability of a hadīth report. A hadīth report is considered *mutawātir* (having reached the threshold of *tawātur*) when it has been transmitted with a frequency of transmission through different chains of narrators in exactly the same way to the extent that there can remain no doubt concerning the authenticity and reliability of the text in question.

> "This religion will last until the Day of Resurrection, or until such a time that twelve caliphs [other versions have 'Imāms'; the meaning is the same in this context: leader; ruler], all of whom shall be of [the clan of] Quraysh, shall [continue to] rule over you."

In the *Sahīh* of Bokhārī the report appears as follows, "There shall be twelve emīrs (rulers) [over you]". Other versions have it slightly differently: "My successors will be twelve in number, just like the chieftains of the Banī Isrā'īl, and all of them [shall be] from the Quraysh [and according to one version of this hadith, from the Banī-Hāshim]"[41]

All of these *ahādīth* state something to the effect that there will be twelve rulers over the community of the faithful, after which there will be the chaos leading up to the Day of Resurrection.[42] Now this mention of the twelve successors can refer only to the Immaculate Imāms from the Progeny of the Prophet ﷺ, for neither were the first caliphs twelve in number nor do the numbers of the Omayyad and Abbāsid rulers conform to this numerical prophecy. More importantly, the crimes those rulers committed, far from assuring the welfare and happiness of the *umma*ᵗ, actually brought about the destruction of the religion, so that it is impossible to consider them the successors of the Prophet ﷺ in any way. Moreover, if we refuse to interpret the hadīth as referring to the Imāms of the Shī'a, we are left with no clear or reliable meaning for it whatsoever.

---

[41] Muslim, *al-Sahih*, Vol. VI, p. 2; al-Bukhari, *al-Sahih*. Chapter XV of *Kitab al-Ahkām*. Ahmad b. Hanbal, *al-Musnad*, Vol. I, p. 397, Vol. V, p.86; Ibn Kathīr, *al-Bidāya*, Vol. VI, p.245; Qundūzī, *Yanabī al-Mawadda*, p. 373.

[42] This is actually a very important scriptural proof of the super-natural longevity of the life of the Mahdi عجل الله فرجه, the twelfth Imam, but discussing that would take us far afield.

In what was discussed above, we stated the reasons for the competence and merit of the Members of the Household of the Prophet ﷺ for occupying the office of religious authority after the passing of the Most Noble Prophet ﷺ, and we provided several scriptural proofs for our position. We also stated that in Islam, religious authority is integral to and cannot be separated from statesmanship and governance. The Most Noble Prophet ﷺ shouldered these twin burdens in unison, and this was especially the case after the emigration of the Muslim community to Medina and the formation of the Islamic state, after which the Muslims could witness first-hand how political and religious leadership were integrated in the person of the Apostle ﷺ of God ﷻ. Thus, if his Eminence appointed someone as a religious authority, it necessarily followed that he had appointed him to political leadership as well. The Most Noble Prophet ﷺ determined the first ruler to succeed him on this very basis, just as he determined the rulers who were to follow his first successor. It was for this reason that after this determination by the Apostle ﷺ of God ﷻ, matters would fall into their natural place, and each of the successors to the Most Noble Prophet ﷺ would appoint the ruler who was to succeed him in turn, just as the Most Noble Prophet ﷺ had foretold.

When we look at the mode of conduct (*sīra*) of the Most Noble Prophet ﷺ, we notice that the Apostle ﷺ of God ﷻ paid special attention to the issue of his succession from the very beginning and paid special attention to the person who was to shoulder the burden of this responsibility. God's ﷻ special attention to this matter had caused the groundwork to be laid for the special prophetic training even before his Eminence had been commissioned to his prophethood. Ibn Ishāq has stated the matter in this way (as has reached us by way of the Ibn Hishām redaction):[43]

Of the blessings of God 🌸 for Ali b. Abī-Tālib 🌸 is that the Quraysh had been stricken with a severe drought. During this time, Abū-Tālib was married and had more children than he could easily support, and the famine weighed heavily upon him. Muhammad noticed this and felt that something should be done. The wealthiest of his uncles was Abū-Lahab, but he was somewhat remote from the rest of the family, partly no doubt because he had never had any full brothers or sisters amongst them, being the only child of his mother. Muhammad preferred to ask for the help of Abbās, who could well afford it, being a successful merchant, and who was close to him because they had been brought up together. Equally close, or even closer, was Abbās's wife, Umm al-Faḍl, who loved him dearly and who always made him welcome at their house. So he went to them now... and suggested that each of their two households should take charge of one of Abū-Taleb's sons until his circumstances improved. They readily agreed, and the two men went to Abū-Taleb, who said when he heard their proposal: "Do what ye will, but leave me Aqīl and Tālib." Ja'far was now about fifteen, and he was no longer the youngest of the family. His mother Fātema had borne yet another son to Abū-Taleb, some ten years younger, and they had named him Ali. Abbās said he would take charge of Ja'far, whereupon Muhammad agreed to do the same for Ali. It was about this time that [Lady] Khadīja had borne her last child, a son named Abdullāh, but the babe had died at an even earlier age than Qāsim. In a sense, he was replaced by Ali.

---

[43] The passage that follows is taken from Martin Lings' recension, *Muhammad, His Life Based on the Earliest Sources*; Chapter 13, The Household; Lings' recension is based on the Ibn Hishām redaction of Ibn Ishāq's *Sīra*, which is no longer extant.

The Apostle ﷺ of God ﷻ took Ali for himself and held him close… And so, Ali was nurtured and raised in the care of the Apostle ﷺ of God ﷻ, after which God the Sublimely Exalted commissioned him to his prophethood. Ali followed him and attained to faith in him and affirmed him. Ja'far was similarly under the guardianship of Abbās until he entered into Islam and was no longer in need of his uncle's protection.[44]

There are many instances where the Most Noble Prophet ﷺ has referred to the priority of Ali ﵇ in entering into Islam and has foretold his important future role and prepared him for the acceptance of this critical task. It is related from Salmān and Abū-Dharr (may God ﷻ be pleased with them both) that the Most Noble Prophet ﷺ said, "This [here] Ali [﵇] is the first person to attain to faith in me and shall be the first person to shake my hand on the Day of Resurrection, and he is the Greatest Truth-teller (*as-siddīq al-akbar*) and the Touchstone of the Community (*fārūq hadhā ummat*) for distinguishing truth from falsehood, and he is the Prince of the Believers."[45]

His Eminence Imām Ali ﵇ has referred to his great nurturing at the hands of the Most Noble Prophet ﷺ in a sermon. Here, in the sermon known as the *al-Qāsi'a*, Imām Ali ﵇ describes his upbringing at the hands of the Prophet:

And [all of] you are well aware of the intimacy of my familial relationship with the Prophet of God ﷻ, and the special rank I enjoyed in his sight… When I was a child, he supervised my upbringing in his own house. He used to hug me and hold me close to his chest and place

---

[44] Ibn Hishām, *as-Sīrat an-Nabawīya*, 1:246; Hākim al-Haskānī an-Neyshāpurī, *al-Mustadrak 'alā's-Sahīhayn*, 3:576; Ibn Abī'l-Hadīd, Abdul-Hamīd, *Sharh-e Nahj al-Balāgha*, 13:198; Tabarī, *Tārīkh ar-Rusul wa'l-Mulūk*, 2:313.

[45] Tabarānī, *al-Ma'jam al-Kabīr*, 6:269, H#61846; Muttaqī al-Hindī, *Kanz ul-U'mmāl*, 11:616, H#3299; Ibn Asākir, *at-Tārīkh al-Madīnat ad-Damishq*, 12:130; Ibn Abī'l-Hadīd, Abdul-Hamīd, *Sharh-e Nahj al-Balāgha*, 13:228.

me beside him in his bed, bringing his body close to mine, and affording me [the unique opportunity] to take in the sweet fragrance [of his body] and to feel its warmth. [Sometimes] he would [even] feed me with food which he chewed [for me]. Never did he hear a lie from me, nor did he ever see guile and hypocrisy in me. From the time the Prophet was weaned [from his mother's milk], God ﷻ coupled the greatest of his angels to him as his [ever-present] companion [and guard], so that he would spend his every waking hour in [the presence of the angel who displayed] the highest [standards of] character and righteous behavior, and all the while I followed him as a young camel follows its mother and each [and every] day, an indication of [some aspect of] his [supreme moral] character would be exhibited to me by way of instruction, which I would then emulate [and make my own]. Every year he would go into seclusion [in a cave] in the mountain of Hirā, where none but me witnessed his presence. In those days, no household was ordered on [the basis of the teachings of] Islam except that of the Prophet of God's ﷺ and [his wife] Khadīja, and I, who was the third of this threesome. I would see the light of divine revelation and inhale the scent of [his] prophethood. [Once,] when a revelation descended on the Prophet, I heard a crestfallen moan and asked, "O Prophet of God ﷺ! What was that moan??" He replied, "That was Satan, who [just] lost [all] hope of being worshipped. You see all that I see and hear all that I hear, except that you are not a prophet; you are a vizier (*wazīr*) on [the path of] virtue."[46]

[46] The Sermon known as "*al-Khutba al-Qāsi'a*" (variously numbered 190, 191 and 192 – and others; in any event, it is the longest sermon in the *Nahj al-Balāgha* and the passage appears at its end.

Prophetic Proofs concerning the Designation to Succession

The question of the succession to the Prophet ﷺ is one that is highly controversial and about which many debates have taken place between the various sects in Islam, especially between the followers of the caliphs and the followers of the Imāms of the Household of the Prophet (*ahl al-bayt*). The followers of the caliphs maintain that the Most Noble Prophet ﷺ made no explicit designation concerning his succession by any specific individual and that his Eminence left the affairs of the community to the members of the community themselves so that they could elect anyone whom they pleased to the office of leadership; whereas the Sh'īa maintain that the Most Noble Prophet ﷺ explicitly designated Ali b. Abī-Tālib to the succession, who was designated in his capacity as leader and guide of the Islamic community after the Most Noble Prophet ﷺ.

When we study the mode of conduct (*sīra*) of the Most Noble Prophet ﷺ, we notice that the Apostle ﷺ of God placed a lot of importance to the question of leadership and succession, and would designate successors in the simplest of matters. For example, whenever he would dispatch two people somewhere, he would designate one of the two as the leader; and whenever he would leave Medina in order to engage in battle or when he traveled for some other reason, he would personally choose someone to succeed him and would not leave this decision up to the people.

Therefore, when we consider that the Most Noble Prophet ﷺ considered the question of his succession to be of such importance during his lifetime, it stands to reason that he would have considered the question of his succession after his passing to be doubly important. Thus, he had to designate a competent and worthy successor for the community he worked so hard to establish, for the eventuality of the day when he knew he would be called back to meet his Lord.

What is interesting to note is the fact that all of the other Muslim leaders paid attention to this matter. We see, for example, that Abū-Bakr orders 'Umar b. al-Khattāb to succeed him (and does not leave the Islamic community to its own devices to choose whomever they will); and we also see 'Umar b. al-Khattāb stating that if Sālem, the freedman of Abū-Huzayfa, or Abū-Ubayda al-Jarrāh were alive, he would without a doubt have appointed one or another of them as his successor. Furthermore, despite the absence of these two candidates, 'Umar does not leave the Islamic community to their own devices in an absolute sense. However, he restricts the succession to six people of his own choosing, ordering them to choose one candidate from among themselves for the succession. It is axiomatic that it is not possible for us to accept that the Companions of the Most Noble Prophet ﷺ had understood the importance of the issue of succession but that the Apostle ﷺ of God ﷻ had not appreciated its significance and importance – while we all hold as a principle of faith that the Prophet ﷺ was the most intelligent of God's ﷻ creatures and the person most concerned for the long-term interests of the community which he founded.

However, when we look at the mode of conduct (*sīra*) of the Most Noble Prophet ﷺ, we see that His Eminence was indeed not heedless of this important matter upon which the future course of the community depended. He had in fact made indications concerning the religious and political leadership of the community from the very beginning of his ministry.

When we look at Sunni hadīth sources[47], we see that after the revelation of this very early Meccan āya [26:214] *Warn thy family who are thy nearest of kin*, the Prophet called Ali ؑ to him, and said:

---

[47] The following passage is taken from Martin Lings's *Muhammad: His Life Based on the Earliest Sources*, a scholar of Sunni affiliation, whose sources probably included Tabarī's *Tārīkh* 2:319; See also Ibn Asīr's al-Kāmel 2:62,

"God ﷻ hath commanded me to warn my family, my nearest of kin, and the task is beyond my strength. But make ready food, with a leg of mutton, and fill a cup with milk, and assemble the Banī ʿAbd ul-Muttalib that I may tell them that which I have been commanded to say." Ali did exactly as he had been told, neither more nor less, and most of the clan of Hāshim came to the meal, about forty men. "When they were assembled," said Ali, "the Prophet told me to bring in the food which I had made ready. Then he took a piece of meat, bit upon it, and cast it again into the dish, saying: 'Take it in the Name of God ﷻ.' The men ate in relays, several at a time, until not one of them could eat any more. But," said Ali, "I could see no change in the food, except that it had been stirred by men's hands; and by my life, if they had been but one man, he could have eaten all that I had put before them. Then the Prophet said: 'Give them to drink', so I brought the cup, and each drank his fill, though one man alone could have emptied that cup. But when the Prophet was about to address them, Abu-Lahab forestalled him and

---

Bayhaqī's *Dalāel on-Nubuwwaʿ* 1:428, and *Majmaʿ oz-Zawāid,* 9:113. In their commentaries on *āya* [26:214] where the gentle reader will recall that the Prophet ﷺ laid his hand on the back of Ali's neck and said: "This is my brother, my executor (*wasīy* = legatee) and my successor (*khalīfati*) amongst you. Hearken unto him, and obey him;" both Tabarī and Ibn-Kathīr take the liberty to substitute the words *kadha wa kadha* (which mean "such and such") for *wasīy'ī wa khalīfati fikum* (my executor (*wasīy* = legatee) and my successor (*khalīfati*) amongst you). The censorship continues through to the modern period, where Muhammad Husayn Haykal (d. 1956), the renowned Egyptian writer and erstwhile Minister of Education relates the hadīth along the lines of Tabarī and Ibn-Kathīr (with the words *kadha wa kadha*) in the first edition of his book *The Life of Muhammad* ﷺ, but eliminates the end of the hadīth in the later editions of the book, pointing only to Ali's brotherhood with the Prophet ﷺ.

> said: 'Your host hath placed a spell upon you' whereat they dispersed before he could speak." The next day the Prophet told Ali to do exactly as he had done the previous day. So another similar meal was prepared, and everything went as before, except that this time the Prophet was on his guard and made sure of addressing them. "O sons of 'Abd al-Muttalib," he said, "I know of no Arab who hath come to his people with a nobler message than mine. I bring you the best of this world and the next. God ﷻ hath commanded me to call you unto Him. Which of you, then, will help me in this, and be my brother, mine executor and my successor amongst you?" There was silence throughout the clan. Ja'far and Zayd could both have spoken, but they knew that their Islam was not in question and that the purpose of the gathering was to bring in others than themselves. But when the silence remained unbroken, the thirteen-year-old Ali felt impelled to speak, and said: "O Prophet of God ﷻ, I will be thy helper in this." The Prophet laid his hand on the back of Ali's neck and said: "This is my brother, mine executor (*wasīy* = legatee) and my successor (*khalīfati*) amongst you. Hearken unto him, and obey him." The men rose to their feet, laughing and saying to Abu Tālib: "He hath ordered thee to hearken unto thy son and to obey him!"[48]

This *nass* (used here in the sense of a scriptural source containing an injunction or burden of duty whose meaning is clear and self-evident), which the Most Noble Prophet ﷺ issued at the very beginning of his call, contains unambiguous wording concerning the succession to the Apostle ﷺ of God ﷻ. The explicitness of its meaning is to such an extent that it has led certain biased historians to distort its meaning by

[48] *Muhammad, His Life Based on the Earliest Sources* by Martin Lings.

deleting its most important words – words that underscore the fact that the Most Noble Prophet ﷺ did indeed designate his successor and made the people duty-bound to obey him (to the point that they laughed at Abū-Tālib, saying, "He hath ordered thee to hearken unto thy son and to obey him!").

Other Scriptural Proofs relating to the Succession of Ali ؑ

The words and deeds of the Most Noble Prophet ﷺ concerning Ali b. Abī-Tālib ؑ conveyed to the people the high status and spiritual rank he had in the eyes of the Apostle ﷺ of God ﷻ. This was all in the way of laying the groundwork and preparing the minds of the faithful for the future leadership which the Apostle ﷺ of God ﷻ had in mind for the continuation of his ministry.

The Hadīth of the Bond of Brotherhood (*Ukhuwwa'*)

One of these preparatory elements occurred at the beginning of the migration to Medina or at the beginning of the Islamic Era and calendar. This was the announcement to the people that Ali ؑ was the brother of the Apostle ﷺ of God ﷻ – a distinction that the Prophet ﷺ did not bestow upon anyone else. Ibn Ishāq relates in his *Sīra*: "The Apostle ﷺ of God ﷻ created bonds of brotherhood between the *muhājirūn* (Emigrants) and *ansār* (Helpers), saying: "Pair up with each other in the way of God ﷻ, creating bonds of brotherhood between yourselves!" He then took the hand of Ali b. Abī-Tālib ؑ and said, "He is my brother." In this way, the Apostle ﷺ of God ﷻ, who is the Lord of the Apostles and the Leader of the Righteous and unique in his moral status and superiority among men, entered into a bond of brotherhood with Ali b. Abī-Tālib ؑ.[49]

[49] Ibn Hishām, *as-Sīra' an-Nabawīya*, 1:504; Tirmidhī, *Jame'*, 5:595, H#3720; Hākim al-Haskānī an-Neyshāpurī, *al-Mustadrak 'alā's-Sahīhayn*,3:16, H#4289; Ibn-Sa'd, *Tabaqāt al-Kobrā*, 2:60; Abul-Faraj al-Halabi, *as-Sīra' al-*

The Hadīth of the Rank of Aaron (*Manzila*ᵗ*-e Hārun*)

Another example occurred nine years later, in the ninth year of the Islamic era. In the *Sahīhayn* (of Bokhārī and Muslim both), as well as in the *masanīd* of Ahmad b. Hanbal and Tayālasī, in the *Sunan* of Abu-Dāwud and Tirmidhī and Ibn Māja, and many other sources, it has been related through various narrators (to the point of *tawātur*)[50] that the Prophet said to Ali b. Abī-Tālib ﷺ, "You are to me as Aaron's *manzela*ᵗ (rank, office, station) was to Moses, except that there will be no prophet after me." This statement makes its appearances in a different context in an episode that has been recorded by Ibn-Sa'd in his *Tabaqāt* (Vol. 3, p. 15.), which we paraphrase here.

One day the Prophet ﷺ learned that the armies of Byzantium were mobilizing for an attack on Madīna in the hope of gaining a swift victory. Upon hearing this, he ordered precautions to be taken, and with a single order, he was able to assemble a large force of Muslims to confront the enemy. At the same time, a report reached the Prophet ﷺ that the Hypocrites were also gathering their forces with the aim of causing disorder in the city during the anticipated absence of the Prophet ﷺ by killing and inciting people to violence. The Prophet ﷺ appointed Ali ﷺ to guard the city on his behalf, and he ordered that he should remain in Madīna until he returned, administering the affairs of the Muslims. When the Hypocrites realized that their treacherous plans had been divulged, they began spreading idle rumors in the hope of weakening Ali's ﷺ position. They hinted that the Prophet ﷺ was angry

---

Halabīa, 2:20; Tabarī, Muhebbiddīn, *ar-Riyāḍ an-Naḍra*, 3:111 & 3:164; Ahmad b. Hanbal, *al-Faḍāel*, p. 194, H#141; Ibn Asākir, *at-Tārīkh al-Madīna*ᵗ *ad-Damishq*, 12:136; Ibn Jawzī, *Tazkirat ol-Khawās*, p. 24, where he has considered this *hadīth* to be *Sahīh*; Muttaqī al-Hindī, *Kanz ul-U'mmāl*, 13:106, H#36,345; Abī-Ya'lā, *Musnad*, 1:455, H#347. See also, *Masābīh as-Sina*, 4:173, H#4799 and *Mishkāt al-Masābīh*, 3:356, H#2609.

[50] That is to say, to the point that there is no longer any room for doubt about its authenticity.

with Ali ؑ and that it was for this reason that he had not been permitted to accompany him on a major military expedition. Ali ؑ was greatly troubled and saddened by the circulation of these rumors. He hastened to the presence of the Prophet ﷺ, who had already left Madīna. When he told him what had happened, the Prophet smiled and said, "O Ali ؑ, are you not satisfied to be to me as Aaron ؑ was to Moses ؑ, except that you are not a prophet?" Ali ؑ said, "Verily, O Prophet of God ﷻ, [I am indeed satisfied with this office.]" And the Prophet ﷺ replied, "This [your staying behind] is on account of that [office]."

By making this statement, the Prophet ﷺ clarified the special position of Ali ؑ relative to the Prophet ﷺ himself, including his succession to the community, with a single historic sentence once and for all time.

A slightly different version of this event has also reached us, where the circumstances leading up to the pronouncement of the historic sentence are different, but the pronouncement is the same. The Apostle ﷺ of God ﷻ left Medina to fight the Battle of Tabūk and appointed Ali b. Abī-Tālib ؑ as the legatee of his household [and ministry], and appointed Sabā' b. Arfata of the Banī-Ghaffār as the governor of Medina. Surprised at Ali b. Abī-Tālib ؑ being left behind in Medina, the hypocrites thought they would capitalize on this supposed opportunity and said, "The Prophet ﷺ has not taken Ali ؑ with him [on his expedition] as he did not deem him worthy to accompany him." When Ali ؑ heard of this talk, he took up his arms and left Medina. He joined the Prophet ﷺ at a waystation called Jarf and told him, "O Apostle ﷺ of God ﷻ! The hypocrites believe that you do not deem me worthy of accompanying you, which is why you have left me behind in Medina with the women and children!" The Apostle ﷺ of God ﷻ said, "They lie. I left you behind in Medina because of the dangers that threaten it. Return and be the successor [and legatee] of my household and [the executor] of your house. O Ali ؑ, are you not satisfied to be to me as Aaron ؑ was to Moses ؑ, except that you are not a prophet?"[51]

The Conveying of the *Sūra^{t} al-Barā'a^{t}* (The Execration)

The Most Noble Prophet ﷺ was intent on distinguishing Ali ؑ from all of the other Companions in terms of his superiority in order to demonstrate his merit and unequalled competence as his successor. Another significant incident which is widely reported in the Sunni sources provides additional support for our thesis, and this has to do with the conveying of the *Sūra^{t} al-Barā'a^{t}* (The Execration), which is the 19th Sūra of the Quran, also known as the Sūra of Mary. In the ninth year of the Migration (*hijra*^{t}), the Prophet ﷺ sent Abu Bakr to recite this *sūra* to the idolaters of Mecca, but shortly afterwards he decided[52] to send Ali ؑ instead, instructing him to take the scroll from Abu Bakr and recite it to the Meccans himself. When Ali ؑ caught up with Abu Bakr and the latter returned to Madīna, he despondently asked the Prophet ﷺ whether there had been an *āya* (revelation) revealed with respect to him. The Prophet ﷺ said, "No, but I have been told to convey

[51] Tabarī, *Tārīkh ar-Rusul wa'l-Mulūk*, 3:103; Ibn Athīr, *al-Kāmil fi't-Tārīkh*, 2:278; Bokhārī, *Sahīh*, in the chapter on the *manāqib* of Ali b. Abī-Tālib ؑ; Muslim, *Sahīh*, in the chapter on the *Faḍāil as-Sahāba, Fadāil Ali b. Abī*-Tālib ؑ; Tirmidhī, *Jame'*, 2:300; Tayālasī, *Musnad*, 1:29; Esfahānī, Ahmad b. Abdullāh, Abū-Nu'aym, *Hilīat al-Awlīā*, 7:195; 7:195; Khatīb al-Baghdādī, *Tarīkh al-Baghdād*, 1:324, 4:204 & 9:394; Nasāī, *Khasāis Amīr al-Mu'minīn*, pgs. 14-15; Hākim al-Haskānī an-Neyshāpurī, *al-Mustadrak 'alā's-Sahīhayn*, 2:337; Ahmad b. Hanbal, *Musnad*, 1:170, 1:175, 1:177, 1:184, 1:330, 1:330 and 6:369; Ibn-Sa'd, *Tabaqāt al-Kubrā*, 1:14-15; Muttaqī al-Hindī, *Kanz ul-U'mmāl*, 3:154, 5:40, 6:154, 6:156, 6:395, 6:405, and 8:215; Haythamī, *Majma' az-Zawāid*, 1:109-111; Tabarī, Muhibbiddīn, *ar-Riyāḍ an-Naḍra*, 2:162, 2:164, 2:195; Tabarī, Muhibbiddīn, *Dhakhāer al-Uqbā*, p. 120.

[52] Our sources tell us that this decision was at the prompting of the angel Gabriel.

the message of this *sūra* to the idolaters of Mecca either myself [personally] or by one who is [a part] of me."[53]

"Ali ﷺ is [a part] of me."

In the Battle of Uhud, after victory was near but was thrown away by the Muslims by the abandoning of their posts against the instruction of the Prophet in order to go after the war booty, it is related in Ya'qubī and other sources that there was only Imām Ali ﷺ and two others who were at the Prophet's side defending him against the continual onslaught of the idol-worshippers of Mecca. Imām Ali ﷺ, who had slain the standard-bearers of the enemy one after the other, now threw himself at the ranks of the Meccan army, putting his own life at risk in order to safeguard the life of the Prophet. With each new onslaught, the Prophet would let out the cry, "Repulse them, O Ali!" And Ali ﷺ would singlehandedly attack them and break up their ranks and kill them and scatter them away from where the Prophet was stationed, and by endangering his own life, would keep the danger away from the sacred presence of the Prophet of God ﷺ. The angel Gabriel, who was present in the battle-field at the side of the Prophet, said, "O Apostle of God ﷺ! These [sacrifices of Ali's on your behalf] are due to his fellowship (*muwāsa*: spiritual intimacy, κοινωνία [koinonia]) with you." The Prophet replied, "[I am not surprised by these acts of sacrifice of his, because] He is of me and I am of him." To which Gabriel responded, "And I am of you both (*wa ana minkumā*)".[54]

---

[53] Nasāī, *Khasāes*, p. 20; Tirmidhī, *Sahīh*, 5:257:3091; Ahmad b. Hanbal, *Musnad*, 1: 3, 151 & 330 and 3:283; *Kanz ul-U'mmāl*, 1:246; Tabarī, *Tafsīr*, 10:46-47; al-Hākim, *Mustadrak*, 3:51. See also Tabarī and Ibn Kathīr's histories, as well as Suyūtī's *Durr al-Manthūr*, and countless others, where Imam Ali is preferred over Abu Bakr on a matter of religion and state by prophetic command.

[54] Tabari, *Tārīkh ar-Rusul w'al-Mulūk* (Dār al-Ma'ārif), vol. 2, p. 514; Ibn Asīr, *al-Kāmil fi't-Tārīkh* (Dār al-Kitāb), vol. 2, p. 107; See also, *at-Tārīkh ad-*

What does this mean? What does it mean to say that three persons are "of" each other? In what sense are they the same? Gabriel is an angel, not a human being. The only possible common element that unites the three is the matter of the propagation of the religion: Gabriel would receive revelation from God ﷻ and deliver it unto the Prophet, who would receive the revelations and would propagate and promote them to the Muslim community, usually by himself, but at times, as we will see below, also by way of Ali, his vizier and successor. So we can conclude that the exchange between the Prophet and the angel Gabriel (The Prophet replied, "He [Ali] is of me and I am of him." To which Gabriel responded, "And I am of you both (*wa ana minkumā*)") means that the three of them are similar and at one with each other concerning the function of the transmission and propagation of the revealed religion, and that this similarity is such that in the ministration of this divinely ordained function, it is as if they are three parts of the same substance. Moreover, because the proper fulfillment of that function requires immaculacy, that therefore, that substance (all three parts of it) must necessarily be immaculate i.e., inerrant as well as sinless.[55]

Damishq (Beirut), vol. 1, pgs. 148-150; as well as *Sharh an-Nahj* (Ibrāhīm, Egypt, 1386) vol. 10, p. 182; *Tadhkerat al-Khawās* (Najaf), p. 38; and *al-Aghānī* (Sāsī), vol. 14, p. 17.

[55] Recall, in the context of the need for immaculacy, what we said at the beginning of the chapter concerning the attributes that are necessary for a leader who must necessarily integrate religious leadership with statesmanship: "Thus, in Islam, matters of religion and state were not separate and anyone who was to succeed the Apostle ﷺ of God ﷻ was to follow the same policy and method of their continued integrality. And in so far as it is not possible for every member of the community to be equally qualified and have the competence to shoulder the responsibilities of the succession to the Most Noble Prophet ﷺ, it follows that the person that is to be able to shoulder and therefore merit such a responsibility must be imbued with certain attributes and characteristics so as to enable him to ensure the sacred law of Islam is

"Ali is your Master after me."

With the passing of the years, the Apostle ﷺ of God ﷻ spoke repeatedly about Ali b. Abī-Tālib in terms which leave no doubt whatever concerning his meaning and intention. Indeed, some of these scriptural proofs have the Prophet ﷺ expressly designating Ali b. Abī-Tālib as his legatee and successor after him, and stipulate his regency (*welāya'*) over the community.

It is reported from Barīda that "The Apostle ﷺ of God ﷻ appointed Ali b. Abī-Tālib to head an army headed for the Yemen and appointed Khāled b. Walīd to head an army headed to Jabal. He then said, 'If you meet up, Ali shall command both forces.' These two regiments did in fact meet up while having gained much booty. Ali b. Abī-Tālib took a handmaiden for himself out of his share of the *khums* (the one-fifth share). Khāled b. Walid called me [Barīda] and said, 'Take advantage of the opportunity that has presented itself and inform the Apostle ﷺ of God ﷻ of this matter.' I went at speed to Medina and entered the mosque. The Apostle ﷺ of God ﷻ was in his house and a number of Companions had gathered around its entrance. They asked, 'What news, O Barīda?' I said, 'All is well. Almighty God ﷻ has granted the Muslims a great victory.' [They then asked:] 'What caused you to return to Medina?' I said, 'Ali b. Abī-Tālib has taken a handmaiden for himself out of his share of the khums of the booty, and I have come to inform the Apostle ﷺ of God ﷻ of this deed of Ali's.' They said, 'You have done very well! Let the Prophet ﷺ know so that Ali falls from his favor!' The Prophet ﷺ had heard the conversation and so he came to the door with anger and annoyance and said, 'What has caused some of you to find fault with Ali? Anyone who finds fault with Ali has found fault with me; and anyone who separates from Ali has separated from me. Verily, Ali is [a part] of

properly interpreted and implemented, and to safeguard its polity and territories from the dangers that it faced."

me and I am [a part] of him. He has been made of my substance (*tinaʿ*; literally, clay) and I have been made from Abraham's substance (*tinaʿ*), and [verily,] I am of a higher [spiritual] rank than Abraham; and we are all from the same seed (*dhurrīya*). And God ﷻ is All-Hearing and All-Wise.' He then said, 'O Barīda! Do you not know that Ali's ؑ right from the khums [fifth of the booty] exceeds [the value of] the handmaiden he has taken? And he is your *walīy* (lord and master; regent; viceroy) after me.'[56] I said, 'O Apostle ﷺ of God ﷻ! I will not part your [company] until you offer me your hand so that I can renew my pledge of fealty in Islam with you.' And I did not part [company] with him until I renewed my pledge of fealty in Islam with him."[57]

---

[56] Ahmad b. Hanbal, *Musnad*, vol. 5, p. 356; Nesāī, *Khasāis*, p. 24 (with a slight variation); Hākim, *Mustadrak*, vol. 3, p. 110 (ditto); as well as Bayhaqī's *Majmaʿ az-Zawāid* and al-Muttaqī al-Hindī's *Kanz ul-Uʿmmāl*, Ibn Abī-Shaybi (from Dārāmī) and Munāwī's *Kunuz ol-Haqāiq*.

[57] Tabarī, *al-Maʾjam al-Awsat*, 6:232; Ibn Asākir, *Tārīkh ad-Damishq*, 42:191, in which Barīda is reported to have said, "The Apostle ﷺ of God ﷻ had become so angry that I had never seen him in such a state of anger except for the day of the confrontation with the Banī-Qarīza and Banī-Nadīr [two Jewish tribes who had treacherously betrayed their contractual oaths with the Prophet ﷺ]. The Apostle ﷺ of God ﷻ then turned to me and said, 'O Barīda! Verily Ali ؑ is your *walīy* (lord and master; regent; viceroy) after me; so befriend Ali ؑ for he acts in conformance with that which has been commanded [by God ﷻ].'"

And Abdullāh b. ʿAtāʾ relates: "I discussed this matter with Abū-Harb b. Suʿayd b. Ghafla, who said, 'Abdullāh b. Habīda has kept a portion of the *hadīth* report from you. The Apostle ﷺ of God ﷻ told him, 'Will you turn into a *munāfiq* (hypocrite) after my passing, O Ibn Barīda?'" Tayālasī, *Musnad*, p. 360, *hadīth* 2752; in which it is related from Ibn Abbās that the Prophet ﷺ said to Ali ؑ "You are the *walīy* of every true believer (*muʾmin*) after me." The great Mālikī scholar Ibn Abd al-Barr has entered this hadīth report in his *al-Istīʿāb* (3:1091) complete with its provenance title (*sanad*) and has stated that there is no problems with the provenance title of this report, as it is sound (*sahīh*) and [all of] its transmitters are reliable in their truthfulness (*thiqa*). Ibn Abī-Shayba (d. 235 HQ) relates in his *Masnaf* (12:80) from Imrān b. Hasayn

In the above hadīth report, the Most Noble Prophet ﷺ established the regency (*walāya'*) of Ali b. Abī-Tālib ؏ over all Muslims without any exceptions in terms that leave no room for any doubt. This was while Abū-Bakr and 'Umar were among those present, so that it should be noted that no exceptions were made in their favor.

The Coronation of Ali ؏ at the hands of the Apostle ﷺ of God ﷻ

The issue of the integrality of religious and state authority was one which the Apostle ﷺ of God ﷻ constantly emphasized, and he stove to make the faithful within the community which he had founded understand all of its aspects in their entirety. Thus, on various different occasions, he would point out that it was only the Members of the Household of the Prophet (the *ahl al-bayt* ؏) who had the competence and aptitude to take on the burden of these two important responsibilities – a burden which had to be carried immaculately if the sacred law of Islam was to be preserved and the newly inaugurated state which was founded by the Prophet ﷺ was to take root and become properly established. On the majority of such occasions, the Most Noble Prophet ﷺ would make a connection between adherence to the Members of the Household of the Prophet (the *ahl al-bayt* ؏)

---

that the Apostle ﷺ of God ﷻ said, "What do you want of Ali? What do you want of Ali? What do you want of Ali?? Ali is [a part] of me and I am [a part] of him. He shall be the *walīy* of every believer after me." Ahmad b. Hanbal relates this same report in his *Musnad*, 4:438 and 5:356, in which it appears thus, "Leave Ali ؏ alone! Leave Ali ؏ alone! Verily, Ali ؏ is [a part] of me and I am [a part] of him. See also, Tirmidhī, Jami', 5:632; Nasāī, *Khasāes Amīr al-Mo'minīn*, pgs. 109; Abī-Ya'lā, *Musnad*, 1:293, H#355, where he considers the *hadīth*'s provenance title to be sound; Muttaqī al-Hindī, *Kanz ul-U'mmāl*, 13:142; Muhibbiddīn, *ar-Riyāḍ an-Naḍra*, 3:129; Tabarānī, al-Ma'jam al-Kabīr, 18:128; Hākim al-Haskānī an-Neyshāpurī, al-*Mustadrak 'alā's-Sahīhayn*, 3:110; Khatīb al-Baghdādī, *Tarīkh al-Baghdād*, 4:339; Ibn Asāker, *at-Tārīkh al-Madīna' ad-Damishq*, 42:102; and Muttaqī al-Hindī, *Kanz ul-U'mmāl*, 11:608.)

and the regency (*walāyaᵗ*) of Ali b. Abī-Tālib ﷺ, to the effect that Ali ﷺ is the first link in the chain of the *ahl al-bayt* ﷺ.

The best expression of this matter occurred on the 18th day of *dhul hijja*[58] in the tenth year after the *hijraᵗ*[59], upon the Prophet's return from the *hajjaᵗ al-widā*[60] at an area by the name of Ghadīr Khumm.[61] In discussing the hadīth of the Two Weighty Trusts, we pointed to this connection and said that the Apostle ﷺ of God ﷻ stated:

"The time is soon approaching when I will be recalled [by God ﷻ] and [when] I must respond... I shall ask [each of] you concerning the Two Weighty Trusts [= the two things of high value,] which I left amongst you in trust. So pay attention to how you treat these two after I have departed! ... "The first is the Book of God ﷻ, one end of which is in God's ﷻ hands and the other in yours. Keep it well and obey its decrees and do not allow any change to enter into it, for you will [surely] go astray [if you do]. And the other is my Family (*itrati*), the Members of my House (*ahl al-baytī*) ﷺ. Almighty God ﷻ has informed me that these two shall never be parted until they enter into my presence at the Pond of Kawthar – this I have asked of my Lord. Therefore, do not surpass these two if you are to be saved from perdition, and do not fall behind from them, for you will be annihilated. Do not [attempt to] teach them anything, as they are more knowledgeable than you." Some hadīth reports state that Apostle ﷺ of God ﷻ said, "As long as you hold fast unto these two [Trusts], you will not go astray."[62]

---

[58] Hākim Haskāni, v. 1, pgs. 192-193.

[59] The migration of the Prophet and the nascent community of Muslims from Mecca to Yathrib (later to be called Medina), the event to which the Islamic calendar is pegged.

[60] The last pilgrimage of the Prophet from Medina to the Ka'ba in Mecca. *Majma' az-Zawa'id*, v. 9, pgs. 105 & 163-165.

[61] Named after the pond (*ghadīr*) of Khumm.

[62] Hākim al-Haskānī an-Neyshāpurī, al-*Mustadrak 'alā's-Sahīhayn*, 3:109 & 3:533 (Dhahabī has agreed with Hākim in his digest that this hadīth report is

The Prophet then said[63], "Do you not acknowledge that I have a greater claim [of dominion] on each of the believers than they have on themselves?" And [his] people cried out [in unison], "Yes, verily, O Prophet of God ﷻ!" The Prophet asked again, "Do you not acknowledge [or testify] that I am *awlā* [have priority of dominion] over each believer?[64]" And [his] people [again] cried out, "Yes, verily, O Prophet of God ﷻ! [To this we testify!]" And so, the Prophet took Ali's ﷺ hand and raised it, such that the whites of their underarms showed[65], and then said, "O People! Almighty God ﷻ is my lord and master [*mawlā*], and I am your lord and master. Of whomsoever I have [hitherto] been lord and master [*mawlā*], [so too] this [here] Ali shall [henceforth similarly] be his lord and master." The Prophet then raised his hands in supplication and prayed, "Almighty God ﷻ, Be Thou a friend to whoever is a friend of Ali, and an enemy of whoever is his enemy; Be Thou a supporter of whoever supports Ali, and oppose whoever opposes him; be a friend of anyone who is a friend of Ali and be wrathful to whoever subjects Ali to his wrath."[66]

---

sahīh; Ahmad b. Hanbal, *Musnad*, 5:181-189; Tirmidhī, *Jami'*, 2:308 & 5:328, H#3874; Nasāī, Khasāis Amīr al-Mu'minīn, p. 89; *Kanz ul-U'mmāl*, 1:44 & 1:47-48; Muslim, *Sahīh*, in the chapter on the Faḍāel as-Sahāba, Fadāel Ali b. Abī-Tālib ﷺ; Dāramī, *Sunan*, 2:431; Ibn-Sa'd, *Tabaqāt al-Kubrā*, 2:2; Munāwī, Fayḍ al-Ghadīr, 3:14; Esfahānī, Ahmad b. Abdullāh, Abū-Nu'aym, *Hiliat al-Awlīā*, 1:355, H#64; Haythamī, *Majma' az-Zawāid*, 9:163-164.

[63] *Majma' az-Zawāid* (9:113 & 162-3 and 165); in addition, some of the wording of this report also appears in Hākim al-Haskānī al-Neyshāpurī, *Shawāhid at-Tanzīl*, 3:109-110 and Ibn Kathīr's *Tārīkh*, 5:209.

[64] [33:6] *The Prophet has a higher claim on the believers than [they have on] their own selves.*

[65] Hākim al-Haskānī al-Neyshāpurī, *Shawāhid at-Tanzīl*, 1:190 and 1:193.

[66] Quoting Dhahabī in his *al-Badāya wa'l-Nahāya*, the Hāfiz al-Qurān Ibn Kathīr states (5:214) that the uppermost part of this report is *mutawātir* and I am certain that the Apostle ﷺ of God ﷻ has stated these words; but the part where (اللهمّ والِ من والاهُ) is mentioned is an addition whose provenance title is strong [but does not reach the threshold of *tawātur*].

After the sermon, 'Umar b. al-Khattāb (the second caliph, after Abu Bakr) came up to Ali ؑ and congratulated him, "O son of Abu Tālib, may this great favor upon you be blessed, as you have brought the morning to the evening [i.e. passed this day] while becoming the lord and master [*mawlā*] of all the believers.[67] Happy your fortune, O son of Abu Tālib [*bakhin bakhin laka, yā ibn abī* Tālib]."[68]

The Prophet of God ﷺ had a black turban called a *sahāb* which he wore on special occasions such as the day of the conquest of Mecca[69]. This turban he placed on Ali's ؑ head after the sermon. It has been reported by Abd al-'Alā b. 'Adī al-Bahrānī who said that the Prophet called Ali ؑ unto himself and tied this turban with his own hands onto Ali's ؑ head, letting its tail end hang freely behind Ali's ؑ head.[70]

Furthermore, we have a report from the Commander of the Faithful himself that on the Day of Ghadīr Khumm, the Prophet of God ﷺ tied a black turban around his head and placed its tail end upon his shoulder. The report from the Commander of the Faithful about this event appears in Tiyālasī's *Musnad* and Bayhaqī's *Sunan* as follows: "On the Day of Ghadīr Khumm, the Prophet of God ﷺ wrapped a black turban around my head and let its tail-end loose behind my head, and then said, 'God ﷻ the Sublime and Exalted aided me in the battles of Badr and Hunayn with angels who wore turbans such as these.' And he went on to say, 'The turban is what distinguishes a Muslim from an idolater.'"[71] In another report, he said, "O Ali ؑ! The turban is the crown of the Arabs."

---

[67] Ahmad b. Hanbal, *Musnad*, 2:281.

[68] Hākim al-Haskānī al-Neyshāpurī, *Shawāhid at-Tanzīl*, 1:157-158. See also Ahmad b. Hanbal, *Musnad*, 2:281, Ibn Māja's *Sunan* (*bāb faḍāil Ali*), *ar-Rīyāḍ an-Naḍra* 2:169; and Ibn Kathīr, *Tārīkh*, 5:210.

[69] Muslim, *Sahīh*, (*Ketāb al-Hajj*, report #'s 451 & 452); Abu Dāwud, *Sunan*, 4:54

[70] *ar-Rīyāḍ an-Naḍra*, 2:289.

[71] *Kanz ul-U'mmāl* 20:45; Tayālasī, *Musnad* 1:23; Beyhaqī, *Sunan* 10:14.

The Competencies and Merits of Imām Ali ؑ for Leadership of the Community

There can be no doubt that the Apostle ﷺ of God ﷻ did not appoint his cousin and son in law Ali b. Abī-Tālib ؑ to the religious and political leadership of his community solely out of the love and affection which he felt for him. This was because his Eminence did not have the right to speak out of his own desire;[72] but obeyed the commands of God ﷻ in every instance, and affection for his next of kin was not more important to his Eminence than the interests and honor of the Islamic nation for which he underwent untold hardships and toiled for a quarter-century to establish. The first seeds of the Islamic form of governance had just begun to sprout after the onerous hardships that the Most Noble Prophet ﷺ had to endure in order to guide mankind to the path that would ensure their felicity in this world and in the world of the hereafter. Therefore, given that the Apostle ﷺ of God ﷻ protectively guarded this main objective which was the whole purpose of his ministry, is it even worthy to think that a man of his stature would leave the future of his community without a guide to its own devices and without having pointed his devout followers in the right direction such that they would be vulnerable at any given moment to misguidance and deviations from the straight path? This is something that is inconceivable of a prophet which the Quran has described in the following terms:

لَقَدْ جَاءَكُمْ رَسُولٌ مِّنْ أَنفُسِكُمْ عَزِيزٌ عَلَيْهِ مَا عَنِتُّمْ حَرِيصٌ عَلَيْكُم
بِالْمُؤْمِنِينَ رَءُوفٌ رَّحِيمٌ ﴿١٢٨﴾

> [9:128] Indeed, there has come unto you, [O mankind,] an Apostle from among yourselves: heavily weighs upon

---

[72] Reference to [53:3] *and neither does he speak out of his own desire.*

> him [the thought] that you might suffer [in the life to come]; full of concern for you [is he, and] full of compassion and mercy towards the believers.

Therefore, the choice of Ali b. Abī-Tālib ﷷ by the Prophet ﷺ was at the behest of the divine will, just as Almighty God ﷻ appointed Tālūt (Saul) to the leadership of his community on account of his primacy and merit in leadership. Thus, appointment to this office is by God ﷻ, and God ﷻ is more aware of the interests of his bondsmen and is better aware whom to appoint as their leader. It is from this vantage that we state that Imām Ali ﷷ had all of the attributes and qualifications which prepared him for the leadership of the Islamic nation after the Most Noble Prophet ﷺ. This included knowledge, the soundness of character, bravery, etc. all of which were well established by facts and events that took place in the early years of Islam and to which our august prophet made repeated reference.

Ali ﷷ as the Most Learned Person of the Community

Assuredly, the office which integrates religious leadership with statesmanship presupposes a great amount of knowledge and learning. There is much evidence that proves that Ali b. Abī-Tālib ﷷ was the most knowledgeable leader and the wisest of judges in the community after the Most Noble Prophet ﷺ, who testified to this, as did the honorable Companions as well as the events of history.

It is related from Ibn Abbās that the Most Noble Prophet ﷺ stated, "I am the City of Knowledge and Ali is its Gate. Anyone who desires to enter this City must enter it through its Gate."[73]

---

[73] Hākim, *Mustadrak*, 3:126, who considers it *sahīh*; also al-Khatīb al-Baghdādī, *Tarīkh al-Baghdād* 4:348, 7:127 & 11:48-49. See also, al-Khārazmī, *al-Manāqib*, p. 40; Ibn Hajar, *al-Sawā'iq*, p. 73; Ibn Athīr, *Usul al-Ghāba*, Vol. IV, p.22.

The Most Noble Prophet ﷺ has also stated: "I am the Abode of Wisdom and Ali is its Gate."[74]

These were a couple of examples of hadīth reports in which the Prophet ﷺ informed his followers of Imām Ali's ﷺ superiority in knowledge and wisdom – a precedence which merits priority to the succession after the passing of the Prophet ﷺ. In a hadīth report related by Salmān, the Most Noble Prophet ﷺ expressly linked the competence for the general leadership of the community to the superiority of knowledge: "I told the Prophet ﷺ, 'Every prophet has a *wasī* (legatee, executor and successor), so then who is your *wasī*?' His Eminence remained quiet and did not reply to me. Afterwards, when he saw me [again], he called to me and said, 'O Salmān! Come!' I went to him with speed and said, 'I am at your service.' He said, 'Do you know who Moses's *wasī* (legatee, executor and successor) was?' I said, 'Yes, it was Joshua (*Yūsha' b. Nūn*)' He said, 'On what basis?' I said, 'Because he was the most learned [of his tribe].' He said, 'Verily, my *wasī* and the person who is privy to [all of] my secret [knowledge], and the best person whom I leave behind [among my nation], and the person who will act on my commitments and fulfill [the obligations of] my religion is Ali b. Abī-Tālib ﷺ.[75]

Some of the Companions who had obtained these statements from the Most Noble Prophet ﷺ and had witnessed their truth relayed them to the rest of the people. For example, it was asked of Ibn Abbās what kind of person Ali ﷺ was. He replied, "His breast is full of wisdom

---

[74] Tirmidhī, *Jamī'*, 2:299; *Hilīat al-Awlīā* 1:64; *Kanz ul-U'mmāl*, 6:401.

[75] Heythamī, *Majma' az-Zawāid*, 9:113, wherein Haythamī states that Tabarānī has related this hadīth report, and that it should be noted that the purpose for the Prophet's ﷺ question to Salmān concerning the reason for the *wasīa*ᵗ (legateeship, successorship) to Moses of Joshua was to make manifest Ali b. Abī-Tālib's ﷺ superiority and priority in learning (*a'lamīa*ᵗ). See also Ibn Ishāq's *as-Sīra*ᵗ *an-Nabawīya*, p. 825, with a slightly different wording.

and knowledge and bravery and awe[-inspiring qualities]; furthermore, he was a close kin of the Apostle ﷺ of God ﷻ."

It is related from Amr b. Sa'īd b. Ās: "I asked Abdullāh b. Ayyāsh b. Rubayya, 'Why were people so predisposed to Ali b. Abī-Tālib ؑ?' He replied, 'O son of my brother! Ali ؑ was endowed with a copious amount of certain knowledge, came from a towering lineage, had priority in [adopting] Islam, and was the son-in-law of the Apostle ﷺ of God ﷻ; he had a deep understanding of the paradigmatic example (*sunna'*) set by the Prophet, had courage and gallantry in battle, and was generous and kind to the disadvantaged."[76]

It has also been related by Abdul-Mālik b. Sulaymān: "I asked 'Atā, 'Did there exist among the Companions of the Apostle ﷺ of God ﷻ anyone more learned than Ali ؑ?' He said, 'No, by God ﷻ! I know of no such person!'"[77]

The Commander of the Faithful, Ali ؑ said: "There is not a single āya in the Quran, the time and place of the revelation of which are not known to me. Abundant knowledge is stored in my breast, so ask me whatever you will before you lose me. Whenever an āya was revealed to the Prophet ﷺ and I happened not to be in his presence, he would wait until I arrived and then say to me: 'Ali, some *āyāt* were revealed while you were away,' and explain and interpret their meaning to me."[78]

And Ibn Abbās has reported: "'Umar said, 'Ali ؑ is the best judge among us.'"[79]

---

[76] Ibn Hajar, *Tahdhīb at-Tahdhīb*, 7:388.

[77] Ibn Athīr, *Usd al-Ghāba*, 6:22; Ibn Abdul-Barr, *al-Istī'āb*, 2:462; Munāwī, *Fayḍ al-Ghadīr*, Tabarī, Muhibbiddīn, *ar-Riyāḍ an-Naḍra*, 2:194.

[78] *Qunduzī*, *Yanabī al-Mawadda*, p.83. See also: Ibn-Sa'd, *Tabaqāt al-Kubrā*, 2:101, and Ibn Hajar, *Tahdhīb at-Tahdhīb*, 7:337.

[79] Bokhārī, *Sahīh*; Hākim al-Haskānī an-Neyshāpurī, al-*Mustadrak 'alā's-Sahīhayn*, 3:305; Ahmad b. Hanbal, *Musnad*, 5:113; *Hilīat al-Awlīā*, 1:65.

Ibn Mas'ūd has also reported: "We were discussing this matter together that the best Judge in Medina is Ali b. Abī-Tālib ﷺ."[80]

None of these transmitters reported anything without their having had corroborative evidence from the Prophet ﷺ himself, as in the case where his Eminence said, "Ali ﷺ is the best judge among my community."[81]

These reports prove that the prerequisite of having superiority and preeminence in learning (*a'lamīa'*) resided in Ali b. Abī-Tālib ﷺ, just as this prerequisite obtained for Seth, and this was the case to the point where even Imām Ali's ﷺ enemies admitted [the superiority of] his knowledge and learning; as witnessed by Mu'āwiya who upon learning of his Eminence's martyrdom stated, "Knowlege and understanding were buried with the son of Abū-Tālib."[82]

Ali ﷺ as the Most Courageous Person of the Community

Ali's ﷺ courage and the awe which he inspired instilled fear in the hearts of the enemies of Islam, and no one had any doubts about his courage and power. His enemies were the first to admit to this quality of his, and hastened to do so before his friends were able to. This quality of the Commander of the Faithful ﷺ was so well known that people would relate its legendary stories to each other and pass them down from one generation to the next throughout the centuries. The Commander of

---

[80] Hākim al-Haskānī an-Neyshāpurī, al-*Mustadrak 'alā's-Sahīhayn*, 5:135, where Hākim states that this hadīth report is *sahīh*. See also, Ibn-Sa'd, *Tabaqāt al-Kubrā*, 2:101.

[81] Tabarī, uii*ar-Riyāḍ an-Naḍra*, 2:198; Ibn Abdul-Barr, *al-Istī'āb*, 1:8, who relates another report from the companions and states that it has been related through different chains of transmission from 'Umar that he said Ali ﷺ is the best judge in the community.

[82] *al-Istī'āb*, 2:463.

the Faithful ﵇ was the standard bearer of the Apostle ﷺ of God ﷻ for all the difficult battles that were fought for the sake of Islam.[83]

Ali ﵇ in the Battle of Badr

Ali's ﵇ power, courage and self-sacrifice in the Battle of Badr was legendary. The books of history have recorded that "Ali ﵇ destroyed the major share of the idolaters singlehandedly."[84]

Ali ﵇ in the Battle of Uhud

In the Battle of Uhud, the Muslims had killed the standard bearer of the idolaters… and the person who had accomplished this feat was Ali ﵇ … Imām Ali ﵇, who had slain the standard bearers of the enemy one after the other, now threw himself at the ranks of the Meccan army, putting his own life at risk in order to safeguard the life of the Prophet. With each new onslaught, the Prophet would let out the cry, "Repulse them, O Ali!" And Ali ﵇ would singlehandedly attack them and break up their ranks and kill them and scatter them away from where the Prophet was stationed, and by endangering his own life, would keep the danger away from the sacred presence of the Prophet ﷺ of God ﷻ. The angel Gabriel, who was present in the battlefield at the side of the Prophet, said, "O Apostle of God ﷻ! These [sacrifices of Ali's ﵇ on your behalf] are due to his fellowship (*muwāsa*: spiritual intimacy, koinonia) with you." The Prophet replied, "[I am not surprised by these acts of sacrifice of his, because] He is of me and I am of him." To which Gabriel responded, "And I am of you both (*wa ana minkumā*)".[85]

---

[83] Wāqidī, *al-Mughāzī*, 1:147; Ibn Hishām, *as-Sīrat an-Nabawīya*, 1:708.

[84] Ibid.

[85] Tabarī, *Tārīkh ar-Rusūl wa'l-Mulūk*, 2:514; Ibn Athīr, *al-Kāmil fi't-Tārīkh*, 2:107; Ibn Asākir, *at-Tārīkh al-Madīnat ad-Damishq*, 1:148-150; Ibn Abī'l-Hadīd, Abdul-Hamīd, *Sharh-e Nahj al-Balāgha*, 10:182 and 14:251, where he states that the hadīth is *mashhūr; tadhkirat al-khawās* (Najaf), p. 38; and al-

At this time, a herald could be heard crying, "There is no hero like unto Ali [in bravery], and no sword [in its deadliness] like unto [Ali's] *dhu'l-fiqār* (the name of Ali's sword)."

Ali in the Battle of the Trench

In the Battle of the Trench or the Battle of the Confederates (*Ahzāb*), a trench had been excavated around Medina at the suggestion of Salmān the Persian as a protective measure against the attack of the idolaters of Mecca. However, there were parts of this trench that did not have the necessary depth or width, allowing the enemy to pass. The Apostle ﷺ of God ﷻ and the Muslims had prepared for battle and the idolaters had them surrounded. Nevertheless, no clashes took place until a few cavalrymen of the Quraysh, including Amr b. 'Abdwūd of the Abī-Qays put on battle armor and mounted their horses. When they passed alongside the dwellings of the Banī-Kanāna, they said, "O Banī-Kanāna! Prepare for battle, for these riders shall soon be upon you!" They proceeded to Medina, and when they reached the trench, they stopped and said, "By God ﷻ! This is a ploy of which the Arabs were unaware!" They went back and forth along the length of the trench until they settled on a narrow and proceeded along that point. They paraded about for a while until Ali b. Abī-Tālib and some others came forth and closed off their pass. The Quraysh cavalry approached them, and Amr b. 'Abdwūd was one of those who had sustained injuries in the Battle of Badr, which is why he had not participated in the Battle of Uhud and was now present on the front line of the Battle of the Trench in order to display his bravery. He went forward and challenged: "Are there any warriors [ready who are worthy of a fight]?"

Aghānī (Sāsī), vol. 14, p. 17; Ibn Hishām, *as-Sīra' an-Nabawīya*, 2:100; *ar-Riyāḍ an-Naḍra* 3:137; Tabarānī, *al-Ma'jam al-Kabīr*, 1:297, H#9214. See also: Ganjī, *Kifāyat at-*Tālib, 69:227; Khārazmī, *Manāqib*, 167:H200; and *Waq'a' as-Siffīn*, p. 478.

Ali ﵇ stepped up and said, “O Amr! You have covenanted with God ﷻ that if a man of Quraysh asks two things of you, that you will grant him one of those requests.”

Amr said, “Yes, this is true.”

Ali ﵇ said, “I call you to God ﷻ, and to His Apostle, and to Islam.”

Amr said, “No. I have no need for such things.”

Ali ﵇ said, “Then I call you to battle!”

Amr said, “Why, O son of my brother? Upon my oath to God ﷻ, it does not please me to have to kill you.”

Ali ﵇ said, “But by God ﷻ, it pleases me to bring an end to you!”

These words of Ali’s ﵇ made Amr angry. He jumped off his horse and went after him. They fought each other for a time, after which Ali ﵇ killed Amr, putting to flight the rest of his troop who had been witnessing the fight.[86]

وَرَدَّ اللَّهُ الَّذِينَ كَفَرُوا بِغَيْظِهِمْ لَمْ يَنَالُوا خَيْرًا ۚ وَكَفَى اللَّهُ الْمُؤْمِنِينَ الْقِتَالَ ۚ
وَكَانَ اللَّهُ قَوِيًّا عَزِيزًا ﴿٢٥﴾

> [33:25] Thus, for all their fury, God ﷻ repulsed those who were bent on denying the truth; no advantage did they gain, since God ﷻ was enough to [protect] the believers in battle - seeing that God ﷻ is most powerful, almighty.

[86] Ibn Hishām, *as-Sīra' an-Nabawīya*, 2:244; Tabarī, *Tārīkh ar-Rusul wa'l-Mulūk*, 2:573; Ibn Athīr, *al-Kāmil fi't-Tārīkh*, 2:181; Hākim al-Haskānī an-Neyshāpurī, al-*Mustadrak 'alā's-Sahīhayn*, 3:32.

In his *ad-Durr al-Manthūr*, in the commentary on the above āya, Soyūtī states: Ibn Abī-Hātam, Ibn Mardūda and Ibn Asākir have reported that Ibn Mas'ūd used to recite the āya thus: ... no advantage did they gain, since God ﷻ was enough to [protect] the believers in battle with Ali b. Abī-Tālib. Dhahabī has reported that Ibn Mas'ūd used to recite it as follows: ... since God ﷻ was enough to [protect] the believers in battle with Ali.[87]

The Muslims were afraid to fight Amr b. 'Abdwūd because they were aware of his reputation as a great warrior, and even the Prophet ﷺ was concerned when Ali ؑ engaged him in battle.

According to what Ibn Abī'l-Hadīd, the great Mu'tazilite scholar of the Shāfi'ī rite, has reported, Abū-Ja'far al-Iskāfī has related this tale and the emotional condition of the Prophet ﷺ in detail. He reports that the Apostle ﷺ of God ﷻ gave what council he deemed to be necessary to Ali ؑ and prayed to God ﷻ for his safety and victory, such that it is reported that on the day of the Battle of the Trench, after Ali ؑ went to fight Amr, his Eminence ﷺ raised his hands heavenward and prayed, "O Lord! On the Day of Uhud, you took Hamza away from me, and on the Day of Badr, you took Ubayd; so save Ali for me this day and do not leave me alone, for you are the best of [all] benefactors."

The Most Noble Prophet ﷺ would prevent Ali ؑ from going out to fight 'Amr, and when 'Amr cried out the challenge: "Are there any warriors [worthy of a fight]?" no one responded to his challenge, and Ali ؑ announced his willingness to fight him, but the Prophet ﷺ would not give him permission to enter the field of battle, until finally, the Prophet ﷺ told Ali ؑ:

"But he is Amr!"

And Ali ؑ said, "And I am Ali!"

The Prophet ﷺ brought Ali ؑ close to himself and kissed him and put his turban on his head and accompanied him for a portion of

---

[87] *Mizān al-I'tidāl*, 2:17.

the way to the field of battle as a gesture of farewell. It seems he was very concerned and anxious as to what might become of Ali ﷺ He then went to a corner and raised his hands and face to Heaven and constantly prayed for Ali's ﷺ safety, and waited to see what fate would befall him; and the Muslims stood close by without a sound or any movement, as if a bird had sat on their heads and they didn't want to scare it away, until the dust settled and the sound of Ali's ﷺ voice pronouncing the *takbīr* (*allāhū-akbār*; the proclamation of the sublimity of God ﷻ) was heard, and everyone knew that Ali ﷺ had vanquished Amr; and the Apostle ﷺ of God ﷻ pronounced the *takbīr* and the Muslims repeated it after him so loudly that the horde of the idolaters who were situated behind the trench heard their voices. And that is why Khuzayfa said, "If the virtues and excellences of Ali ﷺ in the Battle of the Trench in which he sent Amr to his doom were to be divided among every Muslim, it would be sufficient for them."

Ibn Abbās has commented with respect to the *āya* [33:25] *no advantage did they gain, since God ﷻ was enough to [protect] the believers in battle*, that what is meant by sufficiency here is the instrumentality of Ali b. Abī-Tālib ﷺ.

Ali ﷺ in the Battle of Khaybar

In the seventh year of the Hegīra,[88] the Apostle ﷺ of God ﷻ determined to conquer the highly fortified strongholds of Khaybar, and set out towards the fortifications with a large garrison. He began with sending some of his Companions to the forts, but they did not make any headway. Barīda reports, "Sometimes the Apostle ﷺ of God ﷻ would be afflicted with headaches which would cause him to remain in his chambers for one or two days. And when we got to Khaybar, the

[88] The migration from Mecca to Medina which is the event that the start of the Islamic calendar and era are pegged to.

Apostle of God was afflicted with a headache and remained in his tent. During this time, Abū-Bakr took the standard of the Apostle of God and left for the fortifications, and returned unsuccessfully after an intense battle. 'Umar followed suit after him and engaged in an even more intense battle, and [he too] retreated. The Apostle of God was informed [of the proceedings], and he said, 'I swear [upon my oath] to God! Tomorrow I shall give the standard to one who loves God and His Prophet and who is beloved of God and His Prophet, and he shall conquer the fortress by force.' Ali was not present during this speech. Consequently, each of the Companions wanted this prophecy of the Apostle of God to apply to them. On the morning of the next day, Ali, who was installed on a camel, seated the camel down next to the tent of the Apostle of God and dismounted. He had been suffering from an ailment of the eyes and had bound his eyes with cloth. The Apostle of God ask, 'What ails you?' Ali said, 'I have been stricken with an ailment of the eyes.' He said, 'Come close.' Ali went to the Apostle of God and his Eminence rubbed some of his blessed saliva onto Ali's eyes. After this, Ali never again suffered from this malady. He then gave the standard to Ali, who arose and went toward the fortresses with a red tunic draped on his shoulders.

The guard of a fort came from another direction, covered in armor and [carrying] arms, wearing a helmet of stone and [mockingly] singing a paean:

Verily, [all Khaybar] knows that I am the sentry, chock full of arms, battle-hardened and the champion [of battle].

In response, Ali chanted this paean:

I am that person whom my mother has called Heydar (lion)! And I shall pick you off like [so many] seeds; for verily, I am the lion of the fields of thickets and of the fields of battle.

The two engaged in battle and exchanged blows until Ali entered a blow on the sentry's head. Ali's blow broke the stone helmet and tore through the chain mail and rent the sentry's head in two down to his chin. Thus did he fulfill the prophecy and 'conquer the fortress by force.'"

It is reported from Abū-Rāfi', the freedman of the Apostle ﷺ of God ﷻ: "When the Apostle ﷺ of God ﷻ entrusted the standard to Ali ؑ, we moved alongside him toward the fortifications. When we reached their vicinity, their inhabitants came out to defend them. Ali ؑ engaged in battle with them. A Jew landed a blow and knocked his Eminence's shield to the ground. He took one of the doors of the fort that was to the side of the fort and used it as his shield. This door remained in his hand until God ﷻ granted him victory over Khaybar. After the battle was over, he put the door aside. At this point, seven people and myself, who made up the eighth, tried to move this door but could not do so."[89]

The chroniclers have also recorded this incident. Hākim related from Ali ؑ who asked Abū-Laylī: "O Abū-Laylī! Were you not with us at Khaybar?" He answered, "Certainly." Ali ؑ said, "Do you recall that the Apostle ﷺ of God ﷻ sent Abū-Bakr to Khaybar, who went with his troop but was not able to accomplish anything and had to retreat?" And it is also related from his Eminence that "The [Most Noble] Prophet ﷺ marched on Khaybar, and when he got there, he sent 'Umar together with a contingent to their fortifications. The Jews engaged them in battle and it was not long before 'Umar and his troops returned [in defeat]. After that, 'Umar and his men accused each other of cowardice."[90]

---

[89] Ibn Hishām, *as-Sīra' an-Nabawīya*, 2:334; Tabarī, *Tārīkh ar-Rusul wa'l-Mulūk*, 3:11; Ibn Athīr, *al-Kāmil fi't-Tārīkh*, 2:219;

[90] Hākim al-Haskānī an-Neyshāpurī, al-*Mustadrak 'alā's-Sahīhayn*, 3:37. In his summarization, Dhahabī has pronounced this report to be sound (*sahīh*) and has agreed with its conclusion.

Ali عليه السلام in the Battle of Hunayn

In the Battle of Hunayn. The Muslims had become proud of their large numbers because the Most Noble Prophet ﷺ had left Medina for this expedition with ten thousand troops who had participated in the conquest of Mecca, together with an additional twelve thousand who had joined them after the conquest. Nonetheless, the Hawāzin Tribe and their allies surprised them with a forceful attack.

Despite their numbers, the Muslims were defeated and fled, and only the Most Noble Prophet ﷺ and nine of his close friends remained steadfast. All of the Muslims had fled, and only these nine remained to form a protective ring around the Prophet ﷺ. Abbās had the reins of the Prophet's horse in his hands and Ali عليه السلام protected his Eminence ﷺ from the front, and the others acted to protect the Prophet ﷺ to either side of him, while the *muhājerūn* (Emigrants) and *ansār* (Helpers) had all fled.[91]

It is related from Anas: "In the Battle of Hunayn, the people had left the side of the Apostle ﷺ of God ﷻ and had fled, except for Abbās b. Abdul-Muttalib and Abū-Sufyān b. Hāreth, the Prophet's cousin. The Apostle ﷺ of God ﷻ ordered that it be announced: "O People of the Sūra of The Heifer (*Baqara*); O gathering of Ansār (Helpers)! O ...! Finally, this call was repeated by Banī-Harth b. Khazraj. When they heard this call, they returned [to the battle]. When this occurred, the fighting became [even] more intense, and the Apostle ﷺ of God ﷻ said, 'Verily, the kiln of battle has heated up!' He then picked up a fistful of white pebbles and, throwing them at the enemy, said, 'By the God ﷻ of the Ka'ba, you have been defeated!' On that day, Ali b. Abī-Tālib عليه السلام was the bravest warrior on the side of the Apostle ﷺ of God ﷻ."[92]

---

[91] Ibn Abī'l-Hadīd, Abdul-Hamīd, *Sharh-e Nahj al-Balāgha*.13:278

[92] Haythamī, *Majma' az-Zawāid*, 6:180. Tabarānī has considered this *hadīth* to be *sahīh*.

All of these reports testify to the fact that Ali b. Abī-Tālib ؑ was the vanguard of the army of Islam in battle and the bravest warrior of that army in the heat of battle. He never took command of any battle without returning victorious from it, just as Saul (*Tālūt*) led his nation to victory and drove Goliath (*Jālūt*) and his hoard out of Palestine, putting an end to the nomadic wandering of the children of Israel.

Reasons for the Conflict

It is by no means our intention in this essay to enumerate the virtues and excellences of Imām Ali ؑ exhaustively, for they are beyond measure, and many books have already been written on the subject. Rather, our purpose is to express the reasons which motivated the Most Noble Prophet ﷺ to introduce and appoint Ali ؑto succeed him, and to recount the vital role his Eminence played in the life of the Islamic community, be it at times of war or peace. It is hoped that in this way, it will become clear that the choice of Ali ؑ was not one that was based on the supposed only reason of his kinship with the Prophet ﷺ.

It can be seen clearly with a mere glance at the situation that it was only Ali b. Abī-Tālib ؑ who summed up in his person all of the necessary attributes and qualifications for the office of religious and political leadership of the community – and that is where the trouble begins.

Some among the nascent community had self-surrendered absolutely to the will of the Prophet ﷺ and considered all that he said to be tantamount to divine revelation – a posture that is affirmed by the Quran:

﴿وَمَا يَنطِقُ عَنِ الْهَوَىٰ ﴿٣﴾ إِنْ هُوَ إِلَّا وَحْيٌ يُوحَىٰ ﴿٤﴾﴾

> [53:3] and neither does he speak out of his own desire:
> [53:4] that [which he conveys to you] is but [divine] inspiration with which he is being inspired.

Yet some others do not own to this and say that perhaps the Apostle ﷺ of God ﷻ appointed Ali ؑ to succeed him on the basis of familial relations and his love and affection for his cousin and son-in-law; and this contingent reserve for themselves the right to question and object and even dissent against the express words and deeds of the Prophet ﷺ. Perhaps these objections were rooted in envy and other such baser emotions to which very few people are immune. These statements are not mere empty claims that are bereft of any historical documentary evidence; to the contrary: there are a multitude of hadīth reports to be found in such scriptural sources for proving this truth.

In the hadīth report where Barīda had been sent by Khālid b. Walīd on a mission, we stated that Khālid had sent him to the Prophet ﷺ and had told him that an opportunity had arisen which must not be squandered. We saw that even Companions that were standing outside the door of the house of the Prophet ﷺ encouraged Barīda to complain about Ali ؑ and hoped that Ali ؑ would thereby fall out of favor with the Most Noble Prophet ﷺ. It was this very fact that made the Prophet ﷺ angry and exit his chambers and explain to them that anyone who annoys Ali ؑ has annoyed the Prophet ﷺ himself.

It is related from Jābir that "in the Battle of Tā'if the Apostle ﷺ of God ﷻ spent a long time whispering confidences in Ali's ؑ ear, to the point that certain people were showing their discomfort and disapproval openly. They complained, 'Your whispering confidences with Ali ؑ today has taken on extended proportions.' To which the Apostle ﷺ of God ﷻ replied, 'It is not I who has chosen him as my confidante but rather this was something that was done at God's ﷻ behest.'"[93]

It is reported from Zayd b. Arqam that "the door of a certain number of the Prophet's Companions opened up into the mosque. The

[93] Tabarānī, *al-Ma'jam al-Kabīr*, 2:186; Ibn Asāker, *at-Tārīkh al-Madīna' ad-Damishq*, 2:312.

Apostle ﷺ of God ﷻ ordered that all of these doors be sealed, other than that of Ali's ﷷ. Some of the Companions spoke to the Apostle ﷺ of God ﷻ about this, who, having heard what they had to say, went up to the pulpit and said, 'I have been commanded to seal up these doors other than the door of Ali's ﷷ house. Some people have objected to this. I swear upon my oath to God ﷻ! I have not closed a door or opened a door on my own account, but have acted according to that which I have been commanded [by God ﷻ].'"[94]

It is reported from Sa'd b. Abī-Waqqās: "I was sitting along with two other people in the mosque talking ill of Ali ﷷ when the Apostle ﷺ of God ﷻ came forth in such a way that one could see the anger in his eyes, and I took refuge with God ﷻ from his anger. He said, 'What do you want with me? Anyone who annoys Ali ﷷ has [in fact] annoyed me!'"[95]

It is also reported from Ali ﷷ: One day the Apostle ﷺ of God ﷻ had taken my hand [in his] and we were walking the streets of Medina when we stopped in front of a garden. I said, 'What a beautiful garden, O Apostle ﷺ of God ﷻ!' He said, 'There will be better gardens for you in Heaven.' We went a little further and after we had reached a secluded alley, he took me in his arms and wept bitterly. I asked, 'What are you weeping for, O Apostle ﷺ of God ﷻ?' He said, 'There is rancor and hatred in the hearts of some people who will manifest these [feelings against you] after my passing.' I asked, 'O Apostle ﷺ of God ﷻ, will [my abiding by] my religion be secure under these circumstances?' He said, 'Your religion is secure.'"[96]

Hayyān al-Asadī relates from Imām Ali ﷷ, who stated that the Prophet of God ﷻ told him, "Verily, after my passing, the people of my community will plot against you and betray you, whereas you shall

---

[94] Hākim al-Haskānī an-Neyshāpurī, *al-Mustadrak 'alā's-sahīhayn*, 3:15.

[95] Heythamī, *Majma' az-Zawāid*, 9:29.

[96] Heythamī, *Majma' az-Zawāid*, 9:118.

remain [steadfast] upon my religion and will fight for [the establishment and preservation of] my *sunna*ᵗ (code of conduct) and values. At that time [and under those trying circumstances,] anyone who befriends you has [in fact] befriended me, and anyone who takes a stance of enmity towards you has [in fact] become my enemy. Verily, this will become [colored with] the pigment [of blood] of this, and he pointed to my visage and then to [the hennaed beard on] my head."[97]

Social and psychological circumstances caused the office of the succession to be taken from the Members of the Household of the Prophet ﷺ, the *ahl al-bayt* ؏. Envy was one of the factors which prevented prophethood and the office of succession to prophethood to be conjoined in the House of Hāshim (i.e. the House of the Prophet ﷺ), even though the envious knew full well that the Members of the Household of the Prophet ﷺ, the *ahl al-bayt* ؏, were the most deserving of the succession or caliphate; but they could not accept this fact.

These emotional complexes and inwardly-maintained enmities were revealed in a conversation between Ibn Abbās and 'Umar. It is reported by Abdullāh b. 'Umar, the son of the Second Caliph 'Umar b. al-Khattāb:

"One day, I was seated along with some other people at the side of my father. The conversation turned to poetry and the question as to who is the best poet among the Arabs. Everyone named a poet [of their choice] until Abdullāh b. Abbās came and sat among us. 'Umar said, 'The person who must answer this question has joined us!' He then asked, "O Abdullāh, who is the best poet among the Arabs?' He replied, 'Zahrayan Abī-Salmā.' ['Umar] responded, 'So recite a poem of his that you are more familiar with.' [Abdullāh b. Abbās] said, 'O Commander of the Faithful! He has composed this poem in praise of his tribe of

[97] The reference is to Imam Ali ؑ being martyred by being struck by the poisoned sword of Ibn Maljam, may God ﷻ curse him to hell.

Ghatfān, which goes under the name of [the clan of] the Banī-Sanān, and it goes like this. [Whereupon he proceeded to recite four couplets.]

'Umar said, 'I swear [upon my oath] by God ﷻ! He has composed the best poem, and I do not think that this song of praise is worthy of any clan other than the Banī-Hāshim due to their kinship with the Apostle ﷺ of God ﷻ.'

Ibn Abbās said, 'May God ﷻ grant you success, O Commander of the Faithful! And may you be successful always.'

'Umar said, 'O son of Abbās! Do you know what it was that caused the people to turn away from you?'

He replied, 'No, O Commander of the Faithful.'

'But I know the reason,' said 'Umar.

Ibn Abbās asked, 'What was the cause, O Commander of the Faithful.'

'Because the Quraysh did not like to allow both prophethood and the caliphate to be combined in your House, for with this you would feel arrogant and rejoice. Thus, Quraysh considered this and chose others for [the office of] the succession.'

Ibn Abbās said, 'Am I reprieved from the ire of the Commander of the Faithful so that I can speak [freely] and so that he can listen?'

'Umar said, 'Say whatever you want.'

Ibn Abbās said, 'As for your statement that the Quraysh did not like to allow both prophethood and the caliphate to be with us, it is not surprising, for God ﷻ has described many people who disliked what God ﷻ has sent down to them and thus render their deeds fruitless. [Reference to 47:9][98] And as to your saying that we would feel arrogant and rejoice, if we were wont to do this, we would have done so based on our kinship with the Apostle ﷺ of God ﷻ, but we are a clan whose

[98] [47:9] *this, because they hate [the very thought of] what God has bestowed from on high and thus He causes all their deeds to come to naught!*

mode of conduct is derived from that of the Apostle ﷺ of God's ﷻ about whom the Sublimely Exalted Lord has stated, [68:4] *for, behold, thou keepest indeed to a sublime code of moral conduct*; and Who commanded him, [26:215] *and spread the wings of thy tenderness over all of the believers who may follow thee.*

'But as to that which you said that Quraysh chose someone [else] for the caliphate, I must say that God ﷻ the Exalted has stated,

وَرَبُّكَ يَخْلُقُ مَا يَشَاءُ وَيَخْتَارُ ۗ مَا كَانَ لَهُمُ الْخِيَرَةُ ۚ سُبْحَانَ اللَّهِ وَتَعَالَىٰ عَمَّا يُشْرِكُونَ ﴿٦٨﴾

> [28:68] And [thus it is:] thy Lord of Providence creates whatever He wills; and He chooses [for mankind] whatever is best for them [without their having a choice in the matter]. Limitless is God ﷻ in His glory, and sublimely exalted above anything to which they may ascribe a share in His divinity!

O Commander of the Faithful, I know of a certainty that the Lord appointed for His bondsmen he whom He chose. Had the Quraysh looked at the matter from that same window, it would have attained to success, done good and been rewarded for it.'

'Umar said, 'O son of Abbās! You of the Banī-Hāshim constantly want to cheat in the affairs of the Quraysh and show enmity towards them.'

'Be gentle, O Prince of the Faithful,' said Ibn-Abbās, 'and do not describe [in such terms] the hearts of the people from whom God ﷻ has removed all kinds of uncleanliness and Who has purified them with a complete purification. [Reference to 33:33].[99] Moreover, the Prophet ﷺ himself belonged to the Banī Hāshim.

'And as to what you said, that the Banī-Hāshim still holds rancor and enmity towards the Quraysh, how can one not hold rancor and a sense of enmity toward one who has taken away his right, and who sees it in the hands of others [who are not worthy of it]?'

At this point, 'Umar became angry and said: 'I have heard many things about you, but I ignored them because of my regard for you. I am told that you think that we have taken away the caliphate from you through oppression and because of envy.'

Ibn-Abbās said, 'As concerns [the matter of] envy, so [also] it is obvious: Satan envied Adam and drove him from Heaven and we are the children of Adam and have [also] been subjected to envy. As for oppression, it is evident, and the Commander of the Faithful knows [full well] who is in the right.'

Ibn-Abbās then said, 'O Commander of the Faithful! Has not the Arab made a case against the non-Arab on the basis of the truth which was brought by the Apostle ﷺ of God ﷻ? And has not the Quraysh made a case against the other Arabs on the basis of the truth which was brought by the Apostle ﷺ of God ﷻ? And are we not more deserving of [spiritual kinship to] the Apostle ﷺ of God ﷻ compared to the rest of Quraysh?'

'Umar said, 'Now get up and go back to your home.' He got up and left. When he was leaving, 'Umar called to him and said, 'O Son of Abbās! I have respected [and shall continue to respect] your right to the extent of your [rightful] station [in life].'

Ibn Abbās turned around and said, 'O Commander of the Faithful! I have a right relative to you and to all the other Muslims on

[99] [33:33] *for God only wants to remove from you all that might be loathsome, O ye Members of the House [of the Prophet], and to render you utterly free of all pollution.*

account of my nearness [in spirit] to the Apostle ﷺ of God ﷻ. Anyone who respects and abides by this right has respected his own right, and anyone who disrespects it, has in truth disrespected his own self.'"¹⁰⁰

Over and above the factor of envy of the institution of prophethood and the office of succession to prophethood being conjoined in the House of Hāshim, there was an additional factor which certain people used as a pretext for circumventing Ali's ؑ right to the caliphate, and that was Ali's ؑ killing of many of the leaders of the idolaters in the various battles of the war that they had declared on Islam. This demonstrates that although they had entered into Islam (i.e. that they had accepted its outer trappings), their hearts were still full of the hatred and rancor towards the true core of Islam which they held during the Era of Ignorance (*jāhilīya*').

According to a hadīth report narrated by Ibn Abbās, 'Uthmān b. 'Affān (the third caliph) affirmed the realities of these feelings of hatred and ill will. Ibn Abbās reports: "A verbal quarrel broke out between 'Uthmān and Ali ؑ. 'Uthmān said, 'What can I do about [the fact that] the Quraysh do not like you? In the Battle of Badr you killed seventy of their ranks whose faces were like droplets of gold, and you brought their noses to the ground before their lips.'"¹⁰¹

Measures taken by Ali's ؑ Opponents (Usāma's Army)

The measures taken by those who owned to *ijtihād* (juridical striving for the derivation of law) and who were arrayed against the forces of those

---

¹⁰⁰ Ibn Abī'l-Hadīd, Abdul-Hamīd, *Sharh-e Nahj al-Balāgha*, 12:52 See also, Tabarī, *Tārīkh*, 1:2769. And Tabarī, 1:2770 ff.
¹⁰¹ Ibn Abī'l-Hadīd, Abdul-Hamīd, *Sharh-e Nahj al-Balāgha*, 9:22.

who believed in *nass*,[102] were very powerful and effective. They strove diligently to prevent the Members of the Household of the Prophet from attaining to the succession of the Apostle ﷺ of God ﷻ, and indeed, they succeeded in their task. They had started their plans prior to the death of the Most Noble Prophet ﷺ. After the Sermon of Ghadīr, it was perfectly clear that the Apostle ﷺ of God ﷻ had laid the groundwork for Ali's ؑ succession, and that he was intent on entrusting the religio-political leadership of the community to him.

As the Most Noble Prophet ﷺ knew that a number of people were not pleased with this decision, and that they would resist it, he decided to dispatch them to battle the Byzantines with Usāma's army so that they would not be present in Medina when death finally overcame him. But the main personalities to the "Ijtihād" party

---

[102] The literal meaning of the word *nass* is applied to a term or expression whose meaning is clear. In the technical vocabulary of the Islamic sciences, it is used for (1) any word or term whose implications of meaning are clear and self-evident, such that no other possibilities of meaning are assumed for it. (2) The Usūlīs also use the word *nass* as a descriptor of or as a reference to the words of scripture (i.e. of the Quran and the *Sunna*[t] of the Apostle ﷺ of God, which is derived from collections of hadīth reports (*sihāh*, *masānīd*, etc.), books of *sīra* (prophetic biography and mode of conduct), *tafāsīr* (commentary and exegesis), etc.); this usage (i.e. that which is synonymous with scripture) is used in contradistinction to *ijmā'* (scholarly i.e. juridical or creedal consensus) and *qiyās* (analogical reasoning) and their resultant juridical derivatives or products by way of *ijtihad* (juridical striving for the derivation of law). An example would be when it is said that "No *nass* exists for this particular issue;" which is another way of saying that "Scripture is silent on this particular issue;" meaning that there is no Quranic text and nothing in the hadīth report corpus that bears on this subject. Alternatively, one can say, "We have *nass* concerning this matter;" meaning a scriptural text (Quran or hadīth) that bears on this subject; and this second usage is utilized irrespective of whether or not the *nass* or text (sense #2) in question is related to the matter only literally (on its surface) and not in "*nass*" form, i.e. unequivocally (sense #1).

disobeyed the orders of the Apostle ﷺ of God ﷻ and began to proffer excuses as to why they should not join Usāma's army.

On one hand, the Apostle ﷺ of God ﷻ was on his deathbed and was preparing to meet his Lord; and on the other, Usāma's army was preparing to be dispatched to a far-away place, the outcome of which was indeterminate and the fate of all of those who had enlisted in the army would not be known until its return. Meanwhile, Ali ﵇ and his main supporters were not included in the muster list. Naturally, the leaders of the Ijtihād party had discerned the Apostle ﷺ of God's ﷻ purpose in the mustering of Usāma's army, and knew that ousting Ali's ﵇ opponents from Medina would prepare for a smooth and trouble-free transition to Ali's ﵇ succession. The hope was that the space afforded by this extended absence would allow for the process of the pledging of allegiance to Imām Ali ﵇ to successfully run its course, ensuring that everything goes his way and thereby precluding any possibility of opposition and resistance; the Ijtihād party would be presented with a fait accompli and would have no choice but to accept the reality that the rest of the people have accepted and pledged allegiance to Imam Ali ﵇.

Ali's ﵇ opponents understood this all too well, which is why those companions failed to comply with the Prophet's ﷺ order and instead withdrew from Usāma's army, staying at the periphery of Madīna and waiting in the wings for news about the deteriorating health of their Prophet ﷺ (and continuing their sabotage of the Prophet's ﷺ will) despite the Prophet's ﷺ insistence on the dispatching of Usāma's army and the numerous repetitions of this order by the Prophet ﷺ to "Dispatch Usāma's army immediately!"

The Most Noble Prophet ﷺ saw that his plan had not paid off and that his time had come prior to his being able to dispatch those who opposed the divine will. He thought of another plan at the last minute, so that perhaps he would thereby arrive at his objective and inscribe his will to have Ali ﷺ succeed him and have his will available in written form so that it would not be possible to circumvent it. For this purpose, he requested that a scroll and inkpot be brought to him so that he could write "a letter for you by [adherence to] which you shall never go astray." [Here is the story in its entirety.]

At the Prophet's Deathbed (The Hadīth of the Scroll and Inkpot)[103]

The Noble Prophet ﷺ was on his deathbed. These were the last moments for humanity to avail themselves of their connection with Heaven and to benefit from its (embodied) revelation. A few of the Companions had gathered around the Prophet. The wives of the Prophet were also present, veiled by a curtain, which company undoubtedly included Lady Fātima ﷺ. The narrator of the story is 'Umar b. al-Khattāb (the second caliph), who is relating the story to Ibn-Abbās:

> "We were in the company of the Prophet ﷺ. There was a curtain [drawn] between us and the wives of the Prophet. The Noble Prophet began to speak and said, 'Wash me down[104] with seven small skins of water. Then bring a scroll and an inkpot, and I will write a letter for you by [adherence to] which you shall never[105] go astray.' The wives of the Prophet called from behind the curtain [for us] to comply with the request of the Prophet. I ['Umar] said, 'Be quiet! You are like the womenfolk

---

[103] I have added this section. The text is taken from Blake Archer Williams, *Creedal Foundations of Walīyic Islam* (Forthcoming from Lantern Publications).

[104] Washing down with water was practiced in early times as a measure against fever. The practice works by bringing down body temperature through evaporation.

[105] The phrase here is *lan taḍillu*, which means you will never go astray because *lan* is used exclusively for negations which are absolute.

> who thronged around [the Prophet] Joseph and lusted after him. If the Prophet falls ill, you squeeze your eyes and shed tears, and if he is in good health you clutch at his collar and demand disbursement.' The Prophet said, 'They are better than you!'"[106]

Jābir relates the episode thus: "At the time of his death and the last hours of his life, the Prophet asked for a scroll in order to write a letter to his community [compliance with] which [would ensure that] neither would they go astray, nor would they lead others astray. Those who had gathered around his deathbed [i.e. of the] blessed [Prophet,] raised such a clamor and uttered such [shameless] nonsense that the Prophet desisted from his request."[107]

Finally, Ibn-Abbās's own version: "The Prophet was near death. He said, 'Bring [me] a scroll and inkpot so that I can write an inscription for you after which you will never go astray. 'Umar b. al-Khattāb started to speak, became cantankerous and said, 'No! [There still remains] all these towns [which] have not been subdued and must be conquered! So who is going to conquer them?' Zaynab bt. Jahsh, a wife of the Prophet said, 'Carry out the order of the Prophet! Do you not hear that he wants to write his will??' A tumult arose again, at which point the Prophet said, 'Get up and leave [me alone]!' No sooner had they left, that the Prophet passed away."[108]

Based on the above *ahādīth* and others which we will bring to bear shortly, all of which indicate that there are varying descriptions of exactly what took place, it seems reasonable to conclude that the Prophet repeated his demand several times and that those who opposed him said something different each time in order to obstruct his will: the

---

[106] Ibn Sa'd, *at-Tabaqāt al-Kubrā* (Beirut edition), vol. 2, pgs. 243-244.
[107] Ibid, p. 243.
[108] Ibid, p. 244-245.

Prophet would repeat his demand time and again because of his devotion to providing guidance to his community, and the forces who opposed his will would obstruct it and prevent him from writing down his will by raising a hullabaloo each time. Allama Askarī states that he believes that at first the Prophet asked for a scroll and inkpot so that he could write his will and that his Companions knew what he intended to write [based on numerous past indications, the most important and most recent being his sermon at Ghadīr Khumm, which had been delivered less than three months prior and was fresh in everyone's mind], and so they said, "No! We do not need your will! We have the Quran, and that is sufficient unto us." When the Prophet ﷺ repeated his demand a second time, they said, "The fever has gotten the better of the Prophet! The Quran is sufficient unto us and we do not need anything else!" And on the third repetition, they said, "This man is delirious! The Quran is sufficient unto us!"

In the *Sahīh* of Bokhārī there is a hadīth from Sa'īd b. Jubayr about this episode, who relates it from Ibn-'Abbās, who was an eye witness:

> [It was] a Thursday. What a Thursday! He [Ibn-'Abbās] was overcome by tears and wept until the granules of sand [before him] became wet [with his tears]. He then said, "The Prophet's illness became acute on this day. He said, bring me a scroll so that I can write a letter for you by [adherence to] which you shall never go astray. Those present at [the deathbed of] his Eminence (*haḍrat*) differed [as to what was to be done]: one group said, 'Carry out the order of the Prophet ﷺ!' And another group said, 'No! Do not bring a scroll!'

In such circumstances, if one is intent on preventing something from taking place, one can act in such a way and say certain inflammatory things that will change the whole atmosphere and divert the focus from the main matter at hand such that it is no longer possible for it to be realized, and that is exactly what happened here. Back to the *Sahīh* of Bokhārī and Ibn-'Abbās's narrative:

> The crowd began to quarrel, whereas it is not appropriate to squabble in the presence of the Prophet, for the Quran tells us, [49:2] *O you who have attained to faith! Do not raise your voices above the voice of the Prophet.* They said, "The Prophet ﷺ is delirious!" The Prophet ﷺ, with the broken heart of a loving parent confronted with the disrespect and outright contumacy of a wayward son, said, "Leave me to myself. [The severity of] the pain [that I am suffering due to my illness] is more palatable to me than the hurt of your [impudence]."[109]

And the hadīth makes its appearance in the *sahīh* of Muslim by the same narrator (Sa'īd b. Jubayr) thus:

> [It was] a Thursday. What a bad Thursday! On that occasion, tears streamed from Ibn-'Abbās's eyes and I saw his tears as a string of pearls upon his cheeks. [After he regained his composure,] he then said, "... bring lambskin and an inkpot [or an alternative which also appears in the same source]: bring a tablet and an inkpot so that I can write a letter for you by [adherence to] which you shall never go astray." [To which] they responded, "The Prophet is speaking irrelevance [= is delirious]."[110]

---

[109] Bokhari, *sahīh, bāb al-marad an-nabī wa wafātihī* (The Chapter on the Illness of the Prophet and his Death), vol. 3, p. 62; *al-Maghāzī* (Bulāq edition), vol. 6, p. 11.

[110] Muslim, *Sahīh*, vol. 3, p. 1259, hadīth 21.

In the *Sahīh* of Bokhārī there is another hadīth from Ibn-'Abbās, who relates,

> "... there were people in the room [gathered around] the Prophet, among whom was 'Umar b. al-Khattāb. [When the Prophet] ordered [them] to 'Bring something so that I can write a letter for you by [adherence to] which you shall never go astray', 'Umar said, 'The illness has gotten the better of the Prophet, and what he says is not based on sufficient [mental] health and intelligence [God ﷻ forbid!![111]]. Among you is the Book of God ﷻ, and the Book of God ﷻ is sufficient unto us!" Those present in the room disagreed and divided into two groups: one group was with 'Umar, and the other group opposed him. The Prophet ﷺ said, "Get out from my presence! [All] this noise and argument and bickering is not appropriate in my presence.[112]

Is it not plain to see what was said and done against the will of the Prophet ﷺ? At such a crucial moment, when he wanted to write his last testament and message to humanity, when he wanted to leave his legacy and to write his most important message of guidance after which "you shall never go astray"! How did such outrageous behavior affect the emotional state of our beloved Prophet ﷺ? What tremendous pain and suffering it must have inflicted on his daughter Lady Fātima عليها السلام, and on

---

[111] With this mentality, the veracity and integrity of any one of the *ahādīth* of the Prophet and even any āya of the Quran can be denied, which, in effect, would mean the unraveling of the soundness of the dual bases of our religion! And of course, this is why the issue of immaculacy (*Isma'*: Sinlessness and inerrancy) is of vital importance, and why *isma'* as defined by the Sh'īa means sinlessness and inerrancy.

[112] Bokhari, *Sahīh*, vol. 7, p. 156 and vol. 9, p. 137 of the Bulāq edition.

her husband, Imām Ali ﷺ, the would-be beneficiary of the Prophet's ﷺ will, and on their sons, Imāms Hasan ﷺ and Husayn ﷺ? If a great scholar or scientist, or even an ordinary person, is prevented from saying his peace in the most sensitive moment of his life – the time of one's death – it is undoubtedly a great tragedy. How, then, are we to gauge the magnitude of the tragedy when the perpetuity of guidance for a community is at stake? The guidance of millions of people; rather, the sacred guidance of the entirety of humanity until the end of time and the Day of Judgment!

In some of the redactions which appear in Bokhārī[113] and elsewhere[114], Ibn-'Abbās adds this important sentence: "*Musība*ᵗ (calamity, disaster, tragedy)! The tragedy (*musība*ᵗ) [of the] entire [affair] was that the Prophet ﷺ of God ﷻ was prevented from writing his will and testament (*wasīa*ᵗ)".[115] It is perfectly clear that the calamity and the pain and suffering of the Prophet ﷺ and his legatees and successors (*wasīy*; plural, *awsīā*) which Ibn-'Abbās refers to is not the Prophet's ﷺ death (as some apologists have tried to rationalize in their commentary on this hadīth, the letter of the hadīth and the sentence itself apparently notwithstanding), but that it has to do with the fact that in his dying moments, the Prophet ﷺ of God ﷻ wanted to provide his community with a message which was laden with salvific significance and was a sturdy handle against any possible division which

---

[113] Ibid, vol. 6, pgs. 11-12, and vol. 1, p.39, and vol. 7, p.156, and vol. 9, p.137. See also Muslim, *Sahīh*, vol. 3, p. 1259, hadīth 1639 and Ibn Sa'd, *al-Tabaqāt al-Kubrā* (Beirut edition), vol. 2, p. 244.

[114] See Muslim, *Sahīh*, vol. 3, p. 1259, hadīth 1639, and Ibn Sa'd, *al-Tabaqāt al-Kubrā* (Beirut edition), vol. 2, p. 244.

[115] *Wasīa*ᵗ is the abstract noun form from the tri-letteral root *wa-se-a* from which the word *wasī* (legatee, executor, and successor) is also derived. This investiture of Ali ﷺ using this precise word appears in many *ahadīth*. See for example Section 7.17 of Blake Archer Williams, *Creedal Foundations of Walīyic Islam* (Forthcoming from Lantern Publications).

would tear the community apart, and he was prevented from doing so by the "staunchest of his friends and comrades".

Besides, if 'Umar truly thought the Book of God ﷻ was sufficient for the solution of all problems, why did he muster Abu Bakr and hasten to the Saqīfa immediately after getting the news of the death of the Prophet ﷺ, so that they could ensure that the question of the caliphate should be resolved in accordance with their interests? Why did they not at that point refer exclusively to the Book of God ﷻ but rather chose to make no mention of the Quran? Clearly, this was a verbal ruse used to accomplish his express purpose of preventing the Prophet ﷺ from writing down his will.

Now we can fathom the depths of the pain and suffering of our beloved Prophet ﷺ, and it is in light of these *ahādīth* which we find in the *sahīhayn* (of Bokhārī and Muslim, as well as copious other sources) that the prophecy of the greatest of the prophets can be fully appreciated, where he is reliably reported to have said, "No prophet has been tormented like they tormented me."

As to the question of why the Prophet ﷺ did not continue to persist in having his will written down: there is the fact of his illness, and the fact that society in those days was almost pre-literate, meaning that only a very small percentage of the population were able to read and write, and that consequently, oral transmission was much more important as compared to today. Beside that, the Prophet ﷺ had made his will abundantly clear less than three months earlier at the fateful sermon at Ghadīr Khumm (as well as on many earlier occasions). Furthermore, we can state that a man who is capable of looking into the eyes of the Prophet and telling him to his face that he is delirious when the latter wants to write his will, and does so while laying claim to being a faithful follower of said prophet – such a man would also be capable, at a later date, of claiming that the Prophet ﷺ wrote this will while he was not fully in charge of his senses and that therefore, it was invalid.

This would be particularly the case if the man in question was able to find partisans of his (such as Abu-Ubayda al-Jarrāh and Mughīra[t] b. Sha'ba and 'Amr b. 'Ās (all of whom were his bosom buddies) to testify that yes, the Prophet ﷺ was not in full command of his senses and that the will was written under these circumstances. Of course, as mentioned earlier, this potential threat was a greater evil than the evil of not writing the will down, as it would cast doubt in the minds of some, about the purity of the entirety of the prophetic hadīth corpus and in time would become an indelible spot on the integrity of Islam itself. The Prophet ﷺ knew, bless his noble heart, that these men would stop at nothing to get their way in the matter of the succession. It was something they had coveted for themselves and held dear in their hearts for years, because he had been told what would happen in a revelation by the angel Gabriel which is alluded to in the first several *āyāt* of the *Sūra[t] at-Tahrīm.*[116] However, we are anticipating our story a little, which we will get to presently, God ﷻ willing; but not before putting one final finishing touch on this section.

Now that we have demonstrated the magnitude of the torment of the Prophet ﷺ and of his legitimate heirs, we will proceed to demonstrate the unmitigated extent of the duplicity that was involved. We read in the History of Tabarī and other standard sources:

> "When Abu-Bakr was passing the last hours of his life, he called for 'Uthmān. [When] the two were alone, Abu-Bakr said, "Write, In the Name of God ﷻ, the Compassionate, the Merciful, this is that which Abu-Bakr wills to the Muslims…" After these words, Abu-Bakr lost consciousness, and 'Uthmān proceeded to continue writing: "To proceed, I appoint as my successor after me 'Umar b. al-Khattāb, and in doing so, have

[116] See Section 7.12, Blake Archer Williams, *Creedal Foundations of Waliyic Islam* (Forthcoming from Lantern Publications).

> taken into consideration what is best for you." At this point, Abu-Bakr came to and told 'Uthmān to read what he had written so far. After 'Uthmān read the will, Abu-Bakr recited the *takbīr* (*allāhu akbar*; God ﷻ is greater; God ﷻ is the greatest) and added, "I think you feared that if I died in my unconscious state that the people would be divided [as to who should succeed me]." 'Uthmān said, "Yes!" [And] Abu-Bakr said, "May God ﷻ reward you [for what you have done] for Islam and its people," and signed the will that 'Uthmān had written [during Abu Bakr's delirium]." [117]

The will was then brought to the mosque, where 'Umar was seated among the people [gathered there], and whilst holding a stick in one hand, he said, "O people! Listen to and obey the successor (*khalīfa*) of the Prophet of God ﷻ! He says that he has not stinted in the way of that which is best for you!" Now notice how when he is the beneficiary, there is no talk of Abu-Bakr being delirious or that the pain of death has overcome him. In no wise does he take refuge behind the phrase *hasbunā kitāb-allāh* (sufficient unto us is the Book of God ﷻ). No; these qualms he reserves exclusively for the will of his Prophet ﷺ.

> وَمِمَّنْ حَوْلَكُم مِّنَ الْأَعْرَابِ مُنَافِقُونَ ۖ وَمِنْ أَهْلِ الْمَدِينَةِ ۖ مَرَدُوا عَلَى النِّفَاقِ لَا تَعْلَمُهُمْ ۖ نَحْنُ نَعْلَمُهُمْ ۚ سَنُعَذِّبُهُم مَّرَّتَيْنِ ثُمَّ يُرَدُّونَ إِلَىٰ عَذَابٍ عَظِيمٍ ﴿١٠١﴾

> [9:101] … and among the people of the [Prophet's] City there are those who have grown insolent in [their]

[117] Tabarī, *at-Tārīkh*, (Leiden: vol. 1, p. 2138 and *Dār al-Ma'ārif*: vol. 3, pgs. 429-431); *al-Kāmil fi't-Tārīkh*, (*Dār al-Kitāb al-Arabī*: vol. 2, p. 292); *Tārīkh al-Khamīs* (vol. 2, pgs. 240-241).

> hypocrisy. Thou dost not [always] know them, [O Muhammad - but] We know them. We shall cause them to suffer doubly [in this world]; and then they will be given over to awesome suffering [in the life to come].

Indeed, the very letter of the Quran tells us that these types of people dwelt in Madīna among the believers and were so cunning in their duplicity that even the Prophet ﷺ dost not [always] know them. The only way to root them out is by reliance on revelation and the words of the Prophet ﷺ who posited Imām Ali ؑ as the Criterion between belief and unbelief.[118] Ultimately, this is the reason why the words of the Prophet must not be redacted and narrated and why "the Book of God ﷻ is sufficient unto us" – lest in between those sacred words, specific facts will be revealed which will raise the curtain and expose and disgrace a certain party. That is why it was necessary that the prophetic hadīth, i.e. the second of the two sources of Islam, be eliminated from public discourse and the everyday lives of Muslims, and naught but those *ahādīth* which were not detrimental to the ruling party were allowed to be redacted and distributed. This situation started from the very first caliph and continued throughout the Omayyad and Abbāsid periods, with the exception of the two years (95-97 HQ) of the reign of Abdul-Azīz, and of course, with the major exception of Sh'īa narrations which took place covertly and on pain of death.

Commentary on the Hadīth *of the Scroll and Inkpot*

It was not difficult for the opponents to Ali's ؑ succession to imagine what it was that the Most Noble Prophet ﷺ wanted to write. They could see that his Eminence was on his deathbed and that he wanted to

---

[118] See Section 6.8: "Whoever obeys Ali ؑ has obeyed me", Blake Archer Williams, *Creedal Foundations of Waliyic Islam* (Forthcoming from Lantern Publications).

write his will in these last moments of his life, and that this will was not about material affairs and inheritance issues and such, because his Eminence ﷺ had stated, "...so that you will not go astray." This was sufficient reason to believe that the last will of the Apostle ﷺ of God ﷻ concerned the future leadership of the Islamic community because the *sharīa'* (sacred law) of Islam had been perfected as announced by Almighty God ﷻ:

لْيَوْمَ يَئِسَ الَّذِينَ كَفَرُوا مِن دِينِكُمْ فَلَا تَخْشَوْهُمْ وَاخْشَوْنِ ۚ الْيَوْمَ أَكْمَلْتُ
لَكُمْ دِينَكُمْ وَأَتْمَمْتُ عَلَيْكُمْ نِعْمَتِي وَرَضِيتُ لَكُمُ الْإِسْلَامَ دِينًا ﴿٣﴾

> [5:3] This day have I perfected for you your religion, and have bestowed upon you the full measure of My blessings, and willed that self-surrender unto Me i.e. Islam shall be your religion.

Comparing the words of the Most Noble Prophet ﷺ where he said, "...so that you will not go astray" with his words in the Hadīth of the Two Weighty Trusts: "As long as you hold fast unto these two [Trusts], you will not go astray", one can conclude quite unequivocally that the Apostle ﷺ of God ﷻ wanted to will the Members of his own Household to the succession, Imām Ali ؑ being its vanguard.

At this point, the opponents strove with all their might to obstruct this plan of the Prophet's ﷺ and at one point even claimed that the Apostle of God ﷻ was delirious from his illness and was (God forbid!) speaking nonsense!!

Confronted with this insolence and audacity, the Most Noble Prophet ﷺ did not find any way to diffuse his anger other than to order all present to get up and leave his bedside: "Get up and leave [me alone]!"

This is not a matter that we have pieced together and arrived at from various pieces of circumstantial evidence. To the contrary! 'Umar b. al-Khaṭṭāb has expressly stated the matter himself. Ibn Abbās narrates:

"I entered upon 'Umar['s presence] during the early part of his caliphate. There was a stalk of dates beside him. He invited me to have some, and I went and ate one. He continued eating the dates until he finished the dates on the stalk. He then leaned back on his pillow and continually recited the invocation *alhamdᵘ li'llāh* (praise be to God 🌸). After a while, he asked, 'Where have you come from, O Abdullāh?'

I said, 'From the mosque.'

He said, 'How is it that you have left your [paternal] cousin [the reference is to Ali 🌸] alone?'

I thought he was referring to Abdullāh b. Ja'far. Thus, I said, 'I left him to play with [children of] his own age. He said, 'I didn't mean him, but rather the elder of you, [the elder of] the *Ahl al-Bayt* 🌸.'

He asked, 'Does he believe that the Apostle 🌸 of God 🌸 designated him to the succession?'

I said, 'Yes. Furthermore, I asked my father concerning his claim and he said that Ali 🌸 was right.'

'Umar said, 'The Apostle 🌸 of God 🌸 had said things concerning him by way of hints and insinuations which neither prove anything nor leave room for any excuses. He used to speak about his [Ali's 🌸] succession, and during his illness, he decided to expressly designate him as his successor, but I prevented him from this for the sake of the preservation of Islam. No, by God 🌸! The Quraysh would never have accepted the succession of Ali, and if he were to take on [the reins of] the caliphate, all of the Arab [tribes] would have broken their covenants and treaties. The Apostle ﷺ of God ﷻ understood that I was aware of what it is that he wanted to stipulate; that is why he became silent, and God ﷻ did not will anything other than signing off on that [which occurred] with certainty.'"[119]

[119] Ibn Abī'l-Hadīd, Abdul-Hamīd, *Sharh-e Nahj al-Balāgha*, 12:20-21, who has stated that Ahmad b. Abī-Tāhir, the author of the book *Tārikh al-Baghdād*, has entered this hadīth report in his book as a *musnad* hadīth. A *musnad* (uninterrupted) *hadīth* is a category of *wāhid hadīth* whose chain of transmitters is continuous or uninterrupted and is juxtaposed in contradistinction to a *munqate'* (interrupted) *hadīth*.

3 - The Seeds of Shīʿa Islam

Standing in opposition to those who considered it legitimate to practice *ijtihād* against the express will of the Apostle ﷺ of God ﷻ, and who were not willing to surrender to and obey him in everything that he said, were a number of people who believed that one's self-surrender and obedience to the Apostle ﷺ of God ﷻ must indeed be absolute and considered the prescriptive and proscriptive imperatives (*awāmir wa nawāhī*) of the Most Noble Prophet ﷺ to be commands. These commands were religious duties which are to be obeyed at all costs, be these imperatives which had to do with rites and rituals and matters of the sacred law, or whether they concerned the issue of succession and the social order after his passing. Initially, the number of people who believed in total obedience and absolute devotion to the express will (*nass*) of the Prophet ﷺ was minimal and in the order of tens of people, but this number increased in time.

Naturally, those who believed in total obedience and absolute devotion to the express will (*nass*) of the Prophet ﷺ would have asked him in the ordinary course of how events unfold about the issue of religio-political succession, so that they would know that they were acting in accordance with his will. Their position was not one of a personal decision arrived at through an individualistic striving (*ijtihād*), or one which was affected by personal desires, tribal and clannish proclivities and commitments, or other such external dynamics. In addition to the express will (*nass*) of the Prophet ﷺ, those with this mindset or religious posture saw in Ali's ؑ character certain attributes and excellences and merits which commended him to them as worthy of shouldering the perilous burden of this important office – an office upon which the sustenance of the ministry that the Prophet ﷺ had founded depended in order to be safe from the tempests of creedal deviance and to be anchored against the dangers of floating adrift.

It has already become evident that after the passing of the Most Noble Prophet ﷺ the situation had become ripe for any and all sorts of rebellion, relapse and apostasy. Factors that contributed to this condition included the fact that many of the Arab tribes and Bedouins had only recently converted to Islam so that the customs and norms of the Era of Ignorance were still deeply entrenched in them. The presence of hypocrisy and pretense to Islam as a factor after the migration to Medina was also a factor. Finally, the accumulation of animosity and hatred towards Islam on the part of the idolaters as a result of the intense warfare that they waged against the Most Noble Prophet ﷺ and his movement – a hatred whose flames were fanned especially by the falling of many of the great warriors and leaders of Quraysh in battle. There were many people who had accepted Islam as the only way to save their lives after their defeat in an unprovoked war which they had initiated and waged against the Muslim community; or had done so as a way to improve their material prospects (in order to receive war booty, for example). The Most Noble Prophet ﷺ had labeled these people as *tulaqā* (prisoners of war who had been freed) and hoped to win their hearts and minds by giving them a share of the war booty, and in this way, to rid Islam and the community of Muslims of the menace that they posed. For the Apostle ﷺ of God ﷻ well knew that these types of people had accepted Islam because no other viable option was available to them and that they would put aside their pretense if conditions changed. This posed a serious hazard to Islam. Additionally, Islam was threatened from outside the Arabian Peninsula, where powerful empires ruled the region that could not abide the rise of Islam and its increasing power and were biding their time for the right opportunity to destroy it.

Therefore, those who believed in total obedience to the express will (*nass*) of the Prophet ﷺ (and who were opposed by those who believed in the legitimacy of their personal *ijtihād* against this express will) on one hand strove to legitimize their position from the self-evident legitimacy of the Prophet's ﷺ position regarding Ali's ؑ succession. On the other hand, they saw that the Prophet's ﷺ position regarding Ali's ؑ succession and qualifications for leadership were coterminous with the specific attributes of Ali's ؑ character. This latter consideration was informed by such prophetic statements as:

"Whoever follows me has obeyed God ﷻ, and whoever disobeys me has disobeyed God ﷻ. Whoever obeys Ali has obeyed me, and whoever disobeys Ali has disobeyed me."[120]

When, therefore, the Prophet ﷺ proclaims to the community of Muslims that obedience to Ali ؑ is equivalent to obedience to himself, thereby granting Ali ؑ the same authority over them as himself, this, in effect, is a proclamation of Ali ؑ as the leader and successor to the Prophet's ﷺ comprehensive authority, and is a call to the community to render obedience to him.

And: "Ali and I are the *hujjatullāh* (the Proofs of God ﷻ) to His bondsmen."[121] And: "Three things have been revealed to me concerning

---

[120] al-Hākim, *al-Mustadrak*, 3:31 and 3:212. Al-Hākim reports this from Abū-Dharr and considers it to be *sahīh*. See also *ar-Riyāḍ an-Naḍra*.

[121] Khatīb al-Baghdādī, *Tarīkh al-Baghdād*, 2:88; Tabarī, Muhibbiddīn, *ar-Riyāḍ an-Naḍra*, 2:193; Tabarī, Muhibbiddīn, *Dhakhāer al-Uqbā*, p. 77.

Ali; that he is the Lord of the Muslims, the Leader of the Righteous, and the Chief of the Luminous."[122]

And: "Ali is with *al-haqq* (truth; justice; ultimate reality) and *al-haqq* is with Ali ; and these two shall not be separated from each other even up to the time that they come to me at the Pond [of Kawsar] on the Day of Resurrection."[123]

And the Apostle ﷺ of God ﷻ stated when Ali ؑ passed by him: "al-Haqq (truth; justice; ultimate reality) is with him! al-Haqq is with him!"[124]

The Companions understood from the above categorical scriptural imperatives (*nusūs*) that a fundamental declaration concerning the person of Ali ؑ was being communicated to them. And from what we have already mentioned concerning the hadīth of the Two Weighty

---

[122] Hākim al-Haskānī an-Neyshāpurī, *al-Mustadrak 'alā's-Sahīhayn*, 3:137, where he classifies this *hadīth* reports as sahīh; Muttaqī al-Hindī, *Kanz ol-A'māl*, 6:157; Khatīb al-Baghdādī, *Tarīkh al-Baghdād*, 13:122; Haythamī, *Majma' az-Zawāid*, 9:102; Munāwī's *Kunūz al-Haqāiq*, 4:358; Tabarī, Muhibbiddīn, *ar-Riyāḍ an-Naḍra*, 2:177; Esfahānī, Ahmad b. Abdullāh, Abū-Nu'aym, *Hilīat al-Awlīā*, 1:66; Ibn Abdul-Barr, al-Istī'āb, 2:657; etc. See also *Fayḍ al-Ghadīr*.

[123] Ibn Qutaybah, *al-Imāmah wa al-Siyāsa*, Vol. I, p. 68; al-Hamawinī, *Fara'id as-Samtayn*, Chapter 37. al-Khatīb al-Baghdadi, *Tarīkh al-Baghdad*, Vol. IV, p. 21; Fakhr ad-Din ar-Rāzī, *Fusul al-Muhimma*. The *Shī'a* version has it thus: "Wherever Ali is, the truth will incline to him."

[124] Khatīb al-Baghdādī, *Tarīkh al-Baghdād*, 14:321; Ibn Abī'l-Hadīd, Abdul-Hamīd, *Sharh-e Nahj al-Balāgha*, 3:119 & 3:124; Tirmidhī, Jami', 2:298; Haythamī, *Majma' az-Zawāid*, 9:134 & 7:235. The great Sunni *mufassir* (Quranic exegete) Fakruddīn ar-Rāḍī has stated: "Ali b. Abī-Tālib used to pronounce the *bismillāh* (The "In the Name of God ﷻ" opening) with vehemence [of belief], and that anyone who defers to him has in fact [been rightly-] guided; and the reason for this is the word of the Most Noble Prophet ﷺ who said, 'O Lord! Cause *al-haqq* to be with Ali wherever he is.'" (Fakruddīn ar-Rāzī, *at-Tafsīr al-Kabīr*, 1:204, under the heading of *bismillāh*).

Trusts,[125] it will be recalled that the Prophet ﷺ posited the Members of his Household and the Quran as supplements of each other. Moreover, it has been reported that after he said these words, he pointed specifically to Ali ﵇ and said, "Ali is with the Quran and the Quran is with Ali, and these two shall never be parted until they enter into my presence at the Pond of Kawthar."[126] Now if we grant that the Quran is a Divine Book in which there can be no doubt and into which no falsity is allowed to enter, and accept the Prophet ﷺ at his word that Ali ﵇ is always with the Quran, it clearly follows that Ali ﵇ is with the truth and that as long as he is with the truth, it is a religiously incumbent duty (*wājib*) to follow him and to defer to him, because it is categorically necessary to follow that which is right (*al-haqq*).

These were the most important reasons for those who believed themselves to be bound by the categorical scriptural imperatives of the Prophet ﷺ (*nusūs*) also to believe themselves to be bound to follow Ali ﵇ and to obey his commands. What is interesting and important to note is that this deference on their part to Ali ﵇ was evident even during the lifetime of the Most Noble Prophet ﷺ.

Muhammad Kord-Ali writes: "Some of the great Companions were known for their amity toward and deference to Ali ﵇, such as

---

[125] "The first is the Book of God ﷻ … and the other is my Family (*itrati*), the Members of my House (*ahl al-bayti*), and Almighty God ﷻ has informed me that these two shall never be parted until they enter into my presence at the Pond of Kawthar."

[126] Hākim al-Haskānī an-Neyshāpurī, *al-Mustadrak 'alā's-Sahīhayn*, 3:124; Haythamī, *Majma' az-Zawāid*, 9:124; Muttaqī al-Hindī, *Kanz ul-U'mmāl*, 6:153; Munāwi, *Fayḍ al-Ghadīr*, 4:356.

Salmān the Persian, who said, 'We pledged fealty to the Apostle ﷺ of God ﷻ in order to [be among the ranks of those who] wish the Muslims well and in order to accept the leadership (*imāmaʿ*) of Ali b. Abī-Ṭālib ؇ and to have [and to hold] love for him [in our hearts].'"

Similarly, Abū-Saʿīd al-Khiḍrī used to say, "The people [i.e. Muslims] had been ordered to [obey] five things, four of which they followed and one which they laid aside." When he was asked about the four, he said, "*salāt* (the mandatory ritual worship of Islam), *zakāt* (the purifying alms-due), *sawm* (mandatory fasting), and the Hajj pilgrimage. They asked what had been set aside, to which he replied, "the *walāyat* of Ali b. Abī-Ṭālib ؇ (giving a pledge of fealty to the *walī* or Imām, the leader of the community, in acknowledgement of his regency over them), as did Abū-Dharr al-Ghaffārī, Ammār b. Yāsir, Hudhayfaᵗ b. Yamān, Khuzaymaᵗ b. Thābit, Abū-Ayyūb al-Anṣārī, Khālid b. Saʿd b. ʿĀs, and Qays b. Saʿd b. ʿAbāda."¹²⁷

And Subḥī Ṣāleh, a martyr of the Sunni rite acknowledges this truth when he writes, "Among the Companions of the Apostle ﷺ of God ﷻ there were partisans of Ali ؇ (*shīʿaᵗ ali*) even during the lifetime of the Prophet ﷺ, including Abū-Dharr al-Ghaffārī, Miqdād b. Aswad, Jābir b. Abdullāh, Abī b. Kaʿb, Abū'l-Faḍl ʿĀmir b. Wāthala, Abbās b. ʿAbdul-Muṭallib and all of his children, Ammār b. Yāsir, and Abū-Ayyūb al-Anṣārī."¹²⁸

Use of the Expression "Shʿīa" by the Prophet ﷺ

Use of the expression "Shʿīa" is not one that was inaugurated after the passing of the Apostle ﷺ of God ﷻ, as some would like to have us believe. The truth is that the Most Noble Prophet ﷺ occasionally used this expression for the followers of Ali ؇ and would give them glad

---

¹²⁷ *Khaṭat ash-Shām*, 5:251.
¹²⁸ Subḥī Ṣālih, *an-Naẓm al-Islāmīa*, Beirut, p. 69.

tidings that they were on the right path, and that they will be among those who attain salvation and are among the best of men.

It is reported that when the following *āya* was revealed [98:7] *Verily, those who have attained to faith and do righteous deeds - it is they who are the best of all creatures* (*khayr al-barīya*); the Prophet ﷺ said, "O Ali! This revelation refers to you and your followers (*shī'a*)."[129]

The Companions who were the followers (*shī'a*) of Ali ؑ believed that the matter of the succession and the leadership of the community would be taken out of the hands of the Banī -Hāshim and the elders from among Ali's ؑ progeny, because the Most Noble Prophet ﷺ had been very adamant about this, and constantly encouraged and urged the believers to adhere to Ali ؑ and to the Members of his House (*ahl al-bayt* ؑ). But the events that took place

---

[129] Tabarī, *at-Tafsīr*, 3:171; and Suyūtī, *ad-Durr al-Manthūr*, in which he states, "Ibn Asākir relates from Jābir b. Abdullāh: 'We were with the Most Noble Prophet ﷺ when Ali approached. The Apostle ﷺ of God ﷻ said, "I swear upon He in Whose hands my soul rests! Verily this man and his followers are among those who will attain to felicity on the Day of Resurrection." And [because] the revelation [98:7] *Verily, those who have attained to faith and do righteous deeds - it is they, they who are the best of all creatures had been revealed* [and the Apostle ﷺ of God ﷻ had said that it was revealed about Ali ؑ], whenever Ali ؑ approached, the Companions of the Prophet ﷺ would say, 'Here comes the best of all [God's] creatures (*khayr al-barīya*).'" It is also related from Ibn 'Adī, from Ibn 'Abbās, that when the āya [98:7*] Verily, those who have attained to faith and do righteous deeds - it is they who are the best of all creatures* (*khayr al-barīya*) was revealed, the Apostle ﷺ of God ﷻ said, "You [O Ali ؑ] are this [who this revelation refers to], and on the Day of Resurrection, your Sh'īa will be [well] pleased, [just] as [God ﷻ] will be [well] pleased with them." And he goes on to write that Ibn Mardūya has commented on this āya that the Most Noble Prophet ﷺ said, "My appointment with you and your Sh'īa (followers) is at the Pond [of Kawthar, which is a pond in Heaven], and at that time, when the nations are brought forth to account [on the Day of Reckoning, the faces of] you and your Sh'īa (followers) shall be luminous [with the light of those who have attained to salvation]."

at the Saqīfa[130] (portico or pavilion) of the Banī -Sā'ida, completely changed things for the worse. This incident took Ali ﵇ and his followers by surprise as it never occurred to them that such an event could have taken place, even though there were, certainly, indications that the followers of the line of *ijtihād* from among the tribe of Quraysh would not bow to the will of the Most Noble Prophet ﷺ with respect to the issue of the succession. In fact, one of the notables of this line ['Umar] expressly stated as much to Ibn Abbās after the fact: "The Quraysh did not like to allow both prophethood and the caliphate to be combined in your House, for with this you would feel arrogant and rejoice."

On this basis, then, all of the measures taken by Ali ﵇ opponents were in order to prevent these two offices (prophethood and the imāmate) from being united in the House of Hāshim (the House of the Prophet ﷺ), and the effects of these measures saw their first manifestations in the Saqīfa of the Banī-Sā'ida. It would appear that the measures taken by those who believed in the legitimacy of their personal *ijtihād* against the express will of the Apostle ﷺ of God ﷻ did not remain wholly hidden from those who believed in total obedience to the express will (*nass*) of the Prophet ﷺ. The historical reality is that some of Ali's ﵇ followers felt that the Quraysh had hatched some plan for the eventuality of the passing of the Apostle ﷺ of God ﷻ in order to usurp

130 The Saqīfa was a portico of the Banī Sā'ida where the Ansār (the clans of Yathrib/ Medina who had entered into Islam and were its "Helpers") had gathered immediately upon the death of the Prophet ﷺ in order to determine who was to rule their city. It became the scene of the first manifestation of a carefully planned plot according to which six chieftains of Quraysh were to succeed, one after another, in taking the reins of leadership of the community after the Prophet's passing. While Ali ﵇ was seeing to the burial of the Prophet and while his burial shroud was not yet completely dry, 'Umar pledged allegiance to Abū-Bakr, and the two of them made most of the rest of the community fall in line, often by force of arms or the threat thereof. See *Creedal Foundations of Waliyic Islam*, Chapter Seven.

the succession from Ali ﷷ and his progeny. Barā'a^{t} b. 'Āzib explains these events as follows:

> "I am still a devotee of the Banī-Hāshim. After the Apostle ﷺ of God ﷻ passed, I feared that the Quraysh would take the office of the leadership of the community (*khilāfat*) from the Banī-Hāshim. I had become like someone who is afraid of something and sits in wait of it, while [at the same time] I was very distraught and saddened by the illness of the Apostle ﷺ of God ﷻ. I would go to the Banī-Hāshim, who were beside the Prophet ﷺ in his chambers. At the same time, I kept an eye on the leaders of the Quraysh. I was in this state when I noticed that Abū-Bakr and 'Umar were not among them. Then suddenly I heard someone saying that they have gathered in the Saqīfa of the Banī-Sā'eda. And another one said that pledges of allegiance have been sworn to Abū-Bakr. Before long I saw Abū-Bakr approaching, accompanied by 'Umar and Abū-'Ubayda and a group of those gathered at the Saqīfa. They were wearing the garb of those from San'ā (of the Yemen) and would grab the hand of everyone they approached and place it in Abū-Bakr's hand as [in the gesture of] a pledge of allegiance, irrespective of whether or not they were willing to make such a pledge! I could not believe what I saw. I hurried at speed to get to the door of the House of Hāshim. The door was closed. I knocked loudly and said, 'What are you sitting around for? Verily, the people are pledging allegiance to Abū-Bakr b. al-Ghaffān!' [At this juncture,] al-Abbās said, 'You have been condemned to black earth for all eternity! I ordered you to do something, but you did not listen.' A time passed and I suffered greatly at what had taken place. At night, I would see Miqdād b. Aswad, Salmān the Persian, Abū-Dharr al-Ghaffārī, 'Abāda^{t}

> b. Sāmit, Abol-Haytham b. Tayhān, Ammār b. Yāsir, and Hudhayfa^{t} b. Yamān who wanted to take the [issue of] the succession to the Council of the Emigrants (*muhājirūn*)."[131]

The activities of the Sh'īa of Ali ؑ after the incident at the Saqīfa and the abrupt pledging of allegiance to Abū-Bakr gained momentum by the minute and became more open. This short meeting that Barā'a^{t} b. 'Āzib mentioned was one such instance. After that, other measures were taken, and protests were made about the pledge of allegiance that had taken place suddenly and without due consideration of the interests of the community. One such protest of Salmān's was the following:

> "You pledged allegiance to the oldest person among yourselves and turned your back on the Members of the Household of the Prophet ﷺ. If you gave them the right [that was theirs], never would two of you have disputed [concerning this matter] and you would have reaped the benefits of it."

When many of the people spoke of Ali's ؑ refusal to pledge allegiance to Abū-Bakr and that Abū-Bakr and 'Umar had put pressure on him to pledge his allegiance, Umm Mastah b. Athātha came out of his house, stood by the grave of the Apostle ﷺ of God ﷻ and said, "Something untoward has taken place, and unfortunate things have happened [since your passing], which, if you were now present, such events would never have taken place. We lost you, just as the earth loses its rain and springtide verdure; the thread of the work of your House ruptured; would that you were present to witness this [tragedy]."[132]

In another of Barā'a^{t} b. 'Āzib's reports, we read about the beginnings of the incident at the Saqīfa: "I had left my house to see

131 Ibn Abī'l-Hadīd, *Sharh-e Nahj al-Balāgha*, 1:219.
132 Ibn Abī'l-Hadīd, *Sharh-e Nahj al-Balāgha*, 1:49-50.

some of the Companions... I was saddened and grief-stricken at what had happened. When night fell, I went to the mosque. When I had entered the mosque, the sound of the Prophet's ﷺ murmuring when he recited the Quran came into my mind. I got up from where I was seated and reached a place outside the mosque, the area of the Banī-Bayāḍa. There I saw a few people who were talking closely in low voices and who fell silent when I got close to them. [When] I came back [passing] in the same direction, they recognized me while I did not recognize them, and they called to me to come join them.

"I went to them and I saw Miqdād b. Aswad, Abāda[t] b. Sāmit, Salmān the Persian, Abū-Dharr al-Ghaffārī, Hudhayfa[t] b. Yamān, and 'Abul-Haytham b. Tayhān. Hudhayfa said, 'I swear [upon my oath] to God! That which I am telling you about will come to pass. I swear [upon my oath] to God ﷻ! I have not been lied to and I am not lying. This group wants to reconvene the Council of the Succession among the Emigrants (*muhājirūn*).' Hudhayfa then said, 'Let us go to 'Ubayy ibn Ka'b. He knows that which I know. We went toward the house of 'Ubayy ibn Ka'b and knocked on his door.

He came to the door and asked, 'Who is it?' Miqdād answered.

He asked, 'What is it that you want?'

[Miqdād] said, 'Open the door. We have important business that we cannot discuss behind the door.'

He said, 'I will not open the door! I know why you have come. You want to reconsider the pledge of allegiance that has taken place!'

We said, 'Yes!'

He asked, 'Is Hudhayfa among you?'

We said, 'Yes.'

He said, 'Whatever he says, that is what it shall be. By God ﷻ! I will only open this door after these events have taken their course, and [the situation] gets [even] worse than what it already is. I take my complaint to God ﷻ concerning these matters."[133]

It seems that ʻUbayy ibn Kaʻb did not disclose this secret until years later when he decided to do so, but at which time death did not give him the chance to do so, having caught up to him before he could disclose the secret.

It is reported from ʻAtbaᵗ b. Sakhra: "I told ʻUbayy ibn Kaʻb, ʻWhy don't you do something [about this situation], for you are, [after all,] a Companion of the Apostle ﷺ of God ﷻ. We have come from a long way into your presence, and harbor the hope of [seeing] good deeds from you; but you ignore us!' ʻUbayy ibn Kaʻb replied, 'I swear [upon my oath] to God ﷻ that if I am still alive by this Friday, I will tell of a matter, and I will not have any concern as to whether I live or die [as a consequence of it].' When Friday arrived, I came out of my house and saw the people of Medina thronging the streets in waves. I asked, 'What has happened?' And I was told that the Prince of the Muslims, ʻUbayy ibn Kaʻb, has departed this world."[134]

Ibn Saʻd has said: "I said, 'I swear [upon my oath] to God! I do not know of a more covert secret than the one which that man had [in his breast] that day [and which he took to the grave with him].'"[135]

In the hadīth compilations of Hākem an-Neyshābūrī it is reported: " ʻUbayy ibn Kaʻb said, 'If I am alive by Friday, I will tell [the public] that which I heard from the Apostle ﷺ of God ﷻ, and I shall not fear the retribution or reprisal of anyone.'"[136]

Yaʻqūbī writes, "A number of the *muhājirūn* (Emigrants) and the *ansār* (Helpers) refrained from pledging allegiance to Abū-Bakr and inclined to Ali b. Abī-Tālib ؑ, including the following: Salmān the

---

[133] Ibn Abī'l-Hadīd, Abdul-Hamīd, *Sharh-e Nahj al-Balāgh*, 2:51-52.

[134] Dhahabī, *Sayr I'lām al-Anbīyā*, 1:399.

[135] Ibn-Saʻd, *Tabaqāt al-Kubrā*, 3:501.

[136] Hākim al-Haskānī an-Neyshāpurī, *al-Mustadrak ʻalā's-Sahīhayn*, 3:305.

Persian, Abū-Dharr al-Ghaffārī, Ammār b. Yāsir, Khāled b. Sa'd b. 'Ās, Abbās b. 'Abdul-Mutallib, Faḍl b. Abbās, Zubayr b. 'Awwām, Miqdād b. 'Amr, Barā'a b. 'Āzib, and 'Ubayy ibn Ka'b."[137]

Perhaps this is what has caused some historians to conclude that Sh'īa Islam came into being after the incident at the Saqīfa! Jawlad Tasīhr says, "From the very beginning of the problematic issue of the succession, a party was formed among the great Companions of the Prophet ﷺ which objected to the way in which the first three caliphs, i.e. Abū-Bakr, 'Umar and 'Uthmān, were selected and who did not accept these [methods]. They said that in the selection as to who was to succeed the Apostle ﷺ of God ﷻ, the degree of kinship to the Prophet ﷺ had not been taken into account. This party preferred to suggest Ali ؑ to the succession on the basis of his close ties of kinship to the Apostle ﷺ of God ﷻ, because he was the Prophet's ﷺ cousin and Lady Fātima's ؑ husband. But this party was not given the opportunity to have their voice reach the whole community and [to be able] to persuade them of the veracity of their position."[138]

Khāled b. Sa'īd b. 'Ās had been sent by the Apostle ﷺ of God ﷻ on a mission outside of Medina, and returned after his passing. The people had already pledged their allegiance to Abū-Bakr, who called him to do the same, but he refused. 'Umar said, "Leave him to me so that he will have no choice but to pledge fealty [to you]." But Abū-Bakr refrained 'Umar until a year had passed. After that, one day Abū-Bakr passed by Khālid's house, outside of which Khālid was seated. Khālid called to him and said, "O Abū-Bakr, Will you still accept my pledge of allegiance?" When Abū-Bakr answered in the affirmative, Khālid said, "Then come on over here!" And Abū-Bakr went over to him and Khālid took his hand and pledged allegiance while [Khālid] was still seated![139]

---

[137] Ya'qūbī, *at-Tārīkh*, 2:124.

[138] *al-Aqīda wa'l-Sharī'a fī Islām*, p. 186; Amin, Ahmad, *Fajr al-Islām*, p. 266.

[139] Ibn Abī'l-Hadīd, *Sharh-e Nahj al-Balāgha*, 6:41.

The struggle of those who supported Ali ﷺ continued to the six-man council appointed by 'Umar. When the result of the vote of the council ended in the selection of 'Uthmān to the caliphate, the Companions stated their position openly and unambiguously. In the third day, which 'Umar had set as the final day for selecting the caliph, Abdur-Rahmān b. Awf said, "O people! Guide me and tell me which one to choose between Ali and 'Uthmān!"

'Ammār b. Yāsir said, "If you want to avoid schism, then pledge your allegiance to Ali."

After him, Miqdād said, "Ammār is right! If you pledge allegiance to Ali, we will accept him and obey him."

Abdullāh b. Abī-Sarh[140] said, "If you want to preclude a rift among the Quraysh, then pledge your allegiance to 'Uthmān." Abdullāh b. Abī-Rabī'a[t] al-Makhdhumī seconded him, saying, "He's right! If you pledge allegiance to 'Uthmān, we will accept him and obey him."

Ammār insulted Abdullāh b. Abī-Sarh and cried, "Since when have you been concerned for Islam and the [fate of] the Muslims?"

The discussion between the Banī-Hāshim and the Banī-'Umayya heated up.

'Ammār said, "O people! Verily, God ﷻ blessed you with His prophet and graced you with His religion. How much longer, then, will you continue to deprive the Members of the Household of your Prophet of this right of theirs?"

A man of the Makhdhūm clan said, "O son of Sumayya! You have exceeded your bounds. What business is it of yours to interfere in the choosing of the leader by the Quraysh?"

---

[140] A renowned hypocrite and apostate. Upon the conquest of Mecca, the Prophet ﷺ wanted to put him to death for everything he did against Islam when he had the upper hand, but he took refuge with 'Uthmān, who interceded on his behalf.

Sa'd said, "O Abdur-Rahmān! Finish the task before people fall out in dispute."

At this point Abdur-Rahmān said to Ali ؑ, "I will pledge allegiance to you on the condition that you act in accordance with the mode of conduct of the *shaykhayn* (i.e. Abū-Bakr and 'Umar). Ali ؑ said, "I shall act in accordance with my own judgment." He then offered the caliphate to 'Uthmān on the same condition and pledged allegiance to him after he accepted his condition.

Ali ؑ said, "This is not the first day upon which you have allied with each other against us. I shall adopt a posture of patience and forbearance and take refuge with God ﷻ concerning what will come [of this]. I swear [upon my oath] to God ﷻ! You did not pledge allegiance to 'Uthmān other than [for the reason that you know] he will return it [the favor of bestowing the caliphate] to you. Verily, each day God ﷻ has a certain disposition."

Abdur-Rahmān said, "O Ali! Do not place yourself in danger's way." This was an allusion to the fact that 'Umar had ordered Abū-Talha to sever the neck of anyone of the six members of the council who objected to any part of the procedure or to its outcome. After this, Ali ؑ rose and left the proceedings, saying, "Soon shall come the death that has been written."

'Ammār said, "O Abdur-Rahmān! I swear [upon my oath] to Godﷻ! Ali ؑ is a person who judges according to that which is right and would establish justice and equity."

And Miqdād said, "I swear [upon my oath] to God ﷻ! I have not seen anyone be subject to injustice like the Members of the Household of the Prophet ﷺ after the passing of their prophet. Woe unto Quraysh! They have put aside a man compared to whom I do not know of anyone who is more just, more learned and more pious. I swear [upon my oath] to God ﷻ! If some people would help me ..."

Abdur-Rahmān interjected, saying, "Fear God ﷻ, O Miqdād! I fear that you will cause sedition."[141]

After the matter had been settled in 'Uthmān's favor, on the following morning Miqdād left his house and came upon Abdur-Rahmān b. Awf. He went toward him, took his hand and said, "If you did what you did with the intention of seeking the pleasure of God ﷻ, I pray God ﷻ reward you with the benefits of this world and the world to come; and if your intention was worldly [gains], I hope that God ﷻ increases your wealth."

Abdur-Rahmān said, "Listen! May God ﷻ have mercy on you! Listen!"

Miqdād said, I swear [upon my oath] to God ﷻ! I cannot abide listening to you!" And he withdrew his hand quickly and left to join Ali ؑ, where he told him, "Arise and fight these people, for we are with you!"

Ali ؑ said, "May God ﷻ have mercy on you! With what force am I to fight them?"

Then 'Ammār b. Yāser came, while singing in a loud voice: "O ye who gives voice to the troubles of Islam! Arise and announce that the doing of that which is right has been set aside and the doing of that which is wrong has seen the light of day. I swear [upon my oath] to God ﷻ! If there are people to help me, I will rise up to fight them. I swear [upon my oath] to God ﷻ! If anyone rises up in rebellion against them, I will be the second person [after him]."

Ali ؑ said, "O Abū-Yaqzān! I swear [upon my oath] to God ﷻ! I do not see any allies with whom to wage war, and it would not please me to place on your shoulders a weight that is too heavy for you."[142]

This conversation makes it clear that the dispute between Ali's ؑ supporters and the ruling power took on a more intense form such

---

[141] Ibn Abī'l-Hadīd, Abdul-Hamīd, *Sharh-e Nahj al-Balāgha*, 1:193-194.
[142] Ibn Abī'l-Hadīd, Abdul-Hamīd, *Sharh-e Nahj al-Balāgha*, 9:55.

that their members invited each other to open rebellion. And if Ali ﷺ had given their requests a positive answer, a bloody war would have ensued. But his Eminence was more far-sighted than that, and he foresaw the end result of such a course of action and the dangers that it would have posed to Islam. He was completely aware of the intentions of the supporters of the caliphs and the objectives of those who represented the majority position and clearly expressed what motivated some of them to fall behind and support the caliphs.

Another example of this can be seen in the report of Jandab b. Abdullāh al-Azdī: "I entered the mosque of the Prophet ﷺ. I saw a man seated in a kneeling position who was speaking in such a way that it was as if the whole world had been his and they had taken it away from him. He said, 'Woe unto Quraysh! How could they have deprived [the office of] the succession to the Prophet ﷺ from the Members of his House, while there is in their midst the first believer [in the Prophet ﷺ] and the cousin of the Apostle ﷺ of God ﷻ, and [the person who is] the most knowledgeable and most learned in the religion of God ﷻ, and the one who has the greatest insight as to what the correct path is, and who is the best guide to the straight path? I swear [upon my oath] to God ﷻ! They took this office away from one who was a [true] guide [and who was himself] guided [from Above], one who was pure and immaculate. Their purpose was not [to serve] the interests of the community of Islam; rather, they preferred [the goods of] this world to [those of] the hereafter, and that is what they were after; so, would that you be far from the mercy of God ﷻ, and would that you be afflicted with the fires of Hell!'

"I approached him and asked, 'Who are you? And who is this man of whom you speak?' He replied, 'I am Miqdād b. 'Amr and the man is Ali b. Abī-Tālib ﷺ.' I asked, 'Will you not rise in insurrection so that I can be your helper?' He said, 'My brother: this is not a task that can be accomplished with one or two people.'

"I then left the mosque and saw Abū-Dharr. I related to him what Miqdād had said. He said, 'My brother [in faith] Miqdād has spoken the truth.' I then went to Abdullāh b. Mas'ūd and explained the situation to him. He said, 'We knew all this but were not able to do anything about it."[143] Ibn Abī'l-Hadīd has also related this hadīth report with slight variations.[144]

The events that occurred during the caliphate of 'Uthmān and which caused the people to rise up in insurrection against him opened their eyes further. Protests against the mistaken policies of 'Uthmān became more widespread by the day, and people recognized that all of these problems and injustices were the result of the community's having ignored the commendations and express commands of the Apostle ﷺ of God ﷻ and of their having deprived the Members of the Household of his Eminence of what was rightfully theirs.

Elders of the Sh'īa such as 'Ammār, Ibn Mas'ūd and Abū-Dharr were at the forefront of those who wanted to correct the deviation that had occurred and to return that which had been usurped to its rightful owners. The protests against the policies of the third caliph were initially verbal, but the caliph's insistence on the implementation of his wrong-headed policies laid the groundwork for armed rebellion. Hudhayfa[t] b. Yamān was one of the first Sh'īa of Imām Ali ؑ and was on his deathbed by this time. Haythamī relates that when they gave the news of the uprising of the people against the third caliph and asked him what they were to do in this situation, he said, 'Constantly attend to what 'Ammār does [and follow his lead]."

They said, "Ammār never leaves Ali's ؑ side."

He replied, "Verily, envy destroys a person. Will you [then] allow 'Ammār's closeness to Ali ؑ to turn you away from him?" I swear [upon my oath] to God ﷻ!" Haythamī concludes, "Ali ؑ is superior to

[143] Ya'qūbī, *at-Tārīkh*, 2:57.

[144] Ibn Abī'l-Hadīd, Abdul-Hamīd, *Sharh-e Nahj al-Balāgha*, 9:57-58.

'Ammār and the distance between them is [as] the distance of the earth to the sky. Verily, 'Ammār was a friend. He [Hudhayfa^{t} b. Yamān] knew that if they were at 'Ammār's side, they would necessarily be supporting Ali عليه السلام."[145]

When they gave Hudhayfa^{t} b. Yamān the news that Ali عليه السلام had entered the area known as Dhī Qār and that the people have accompanied him in support, he gathered his supporters and acquaintances and, after giving a brief sermon of exhortations and advice against being enamored with the bounties of this world, and commending the people for focusing their attention to the higher ideals and values that bring felicity in the hereafter, Hudhayfa told them, "Join [forces] with [Ali,] the Commander of the Faithful عليه السلام and the *wasī* (legatee, executor and successor) of the Prince of the Apostles ﷺ. That which is right (*al-haqq*) is that you [join and] support him."[146]

Hudhayfa^{t} b. Yamān was a person who cautioned the believers against sedition, and throughout the time that the Sh'īa of Imām Ali عليه السلام had charge of the affairs of the community, he would invite people to stick with Ali عليه السلام. He would always say, "See which group invites people towards [supporting] the Commander of the Faithful عليه السلام and join that group, because these people are the ones who are [rightly-] guided."[147]

And Abū-Dharr would sit in the mosque and say, "... And Muhammad ﷺ is the inheritor of the knowledge of Adam عليه السلام and is endowed with all of the excellences and virtues (*faḍāil*) of all of the prophets ﷺ. And Ali b. Abī-Tālib عليه السلام is the *wasī* (legatee, executor and successor) of Muhammad ﷺ and the *wasī* (inheritor) of his knowledge

---

145 Heythamī, *Majma' az-Zawāid*, 7:243. Haythami has stated in the margin that this report is related by Tabarānī and that its narrators are *thaqa* (reliable).

146 Ibn Abī'l-Hadīd, Abdul-Hamīd, *Sharh-e Nahj al-Balāgha*, 2:187-188.

147 Heythamī, *Majma' az-Zawāid*, 7:236; where Heythami states that this report has been related by Bazzāz and that its narrators are *thiqa*. Ibn Hajr al-Asqalānī, *Fath al-Bārī*, 13:45.

and learning. O [ye of the] community who is at a loss after [the passing of] your prophet! If you had preferred the person whom God ﷻ had preferred, and had relegated to the back the person whom God ﷻ had relegated to the back, and had accepted the *walāya*^{t} (regency, dominion) and succession of the Members of the Household of the Prophet ﷺ, your daily sustenance would be provided for you from Heaven at every moment [of need]. In that eventuality, no problems [would occur] and no question would arise concerning the ordinances and injunctions of God ﷻ which the Members of the Household of the Prophet ﷺ, who are [fully] aware of the Book [of God ﷻ] and of the *Sunna*^{t} (the way of the Most Noble Prophet ﷺ as exemplary model and paradigmatic example), would not be able to answer. But now that you have done this, then taste the consequence of what you have wrought yourselves, and know that [26:227] *those who are bent on wrongdoing will in time come to know how evil a turn their destinies are bound to take! Those who have done wrong will soon come to understand the place to which they will be consigned!*"[148]

Adī b. Khātam reports, "If the criterion for attaining to the office of the succession is knowledge of the Book [of God ﷻ] and the Sunna^{t} of the Prophet ﷺ, then Ali b. Abī-Tālib عليه السلام is the most knowledgeable person about these two matters; and if [the criterion] has to do with one's priority and [spiritual] station in Islam, then Ali is the first Muslim and the brother of the Prophet ﷺ [in faith] and the best Muslim; and if [the criterion] has to do with one's piety and devotion, Ali عليه السلام is the most pious and most devoted [of the believers], and if [the criterion] has to do with one's intellect and temperament, Ali عليه السلام is the most intelligent and best-natured person [among the Muslims]."[149]

---

[148] Ya'qūbī, *at-Tārīkh*, 2:67-68.
[149] *Muhra*^{t} *al-Khutab*, 1:379, #267.

At the Pledge of Allegiance to Ali

The continual call of the partisans of Ali increased the awareness of the people every day, making the delineation between the Islam of the Sh'ia of Ali and [the Islam of] the followers of the caliphs clearer and more distinct. Those who were the early followers (*shī'a*) of Ali played an essential role in this regard. Thus, we see that Mālik Ashtar says on the day the pledge of allegiance was given to Imām Ali by the people: "O people! This [leader] is the *wasī* (inheritor, legatee, executor and successor) of the *awsīā* (plural of *wasī*), and the inheritor of the knowledge and learning of the prophets; [he is] the resolver of problems [for which he is] not in need [of the help] of anybody, for God has testified to his faith and His prophet has given the glad tiding that he is of those who shall attain to heaven. He is one in whom the virtues have been perfected, and [nobody] doubts that he is the *alpha* and *omega* (*awwalīn wa ākhirīn*) of knowledge and learning, or doubts the priority of his virtue and his Islam."

Mālik Ashtar pledged allegiance to Imām Ali as the representative of the people of Kūfa, and Talha and Zubayr did so as representatives of the Emigrants (*muhājirūn*). Abul-Haytham b. Tayhān, Abū-'Ayyūb al-Ansārī and 'Aqabaʿ b. 'Amr arose and said, "We pledge allegiance to you on the understanding that the allegiance of the Helpers (*ansār*) and the remainder of the Quraysh rests with us."

After this, a number of people got up and spoke, and the first of these was Thābet b. Shammās al-Ansārī. He was the spokesman of the Ansār (the Muslims domiciled in Medina; i.e. those who had not emigrated from Mecca), and he said, "O Commander of the Faithful ! I swear [upon my oath] to God ! If they surpassed you in [de facto] authority (*walāyaʿ*), they did not surpass you in religion; and if yesterday they set you aside, [that is the reason as to why] today they have become entangled in these troubles and difficulties. You were present among them and [the preeminence of] your competence and merit was not hidden from anyone. They were in need of you in every matter, while you, with your overflowing knowledge, were in need of no one."

Then Khudhaymaᵗ b. Thābet al-Ansārī, who was a *dhū'l-shahādatayn*,[150] said, "O Commander of the Faithful ﷺ! We have not found anyone other than you who can take on the [burden of] responsibility of this important office, and we had no other option but to return to you. If we are to be honest with ourselves, we must admit that you are the person who has the most priority in terms of his faith, being conscious of God ﷻ (i.e. piety and devotion), and the person who is closest [in spirit] to [the spirit of] the Apostle ﷺ of God ﷻ. The virtues that others have, you have more of; and there is much that you have which others do not have."

And then Sa'sa'aᵗ b. Sawhān arose and spoke, saying, "O Commander of the Faithful ﷺ! I swear [upon my oath] to God ﷻ! [By accepting this responsibility] you adorned the office of the succession (i.e. the caliphate, *khilāfaᵗ*) and the caliphate did not adorn you. You raised its rank and station and the caliphate did not elevate your rank and station; and verily, the caliphate is more in need of you than you are in need of it."[151]

Another Deviation

After 'Uthmān's reign came to its abrupt end with his murder, the people turned to Ali ﷺ in droves, such that his Eminence has described the people's pledge of allegiance to him in these terms: "After the murder of 'Uthmān, the people came up to me, bumping up against

---

[150] This title, which the Prophet ﷺ bestowed on him, literally means 'possessed of two testimonies.' What occasioned the bestowal of this title was a case where there was a dispute concerning a matter of trade concerning which Khudhayma gave testimony, and whose testimony was accepted as the testimony of two witnesses of sound moral character by the Prophet ﷺ.

[151] Ya'qūbī, *at-Tārīkh*, 2:75.

each other and thronging [me], like the thronging of a thirsty camel at the water trough whose bridle and reins have come apart and who has been let loose by its driver, such that I thought they were going to kill me, or that some of them intended to kill others among them in my presence."[152]

However, things gradually started to reverse direction. When a number of the Companions understood that Imām Ali ﷺ was intent on governing the affairs of state as did the Prophet ﷺ and was going to treat everyone as equal [under the law], they began their enmity against him and started to sabotage his government. They had been the beneficiaries of many endowments – a custom which 'Umar had started and which 'Uthmān had expanded. Additionally, Imām Ali ﷺ replaced governors and mayors who abused their positions of authority or who did not have the necessary competence for the position. In this way, the flames of war were fanned and continued to blaze until the martyrdom of his Eminence.

The five-year reign of Imām Ali ﷺ was spent fighting the hypocrites. The insubordination and mutiny of opponents, and the devastating battle of the Camel and the war of Siffin consumed the purest and most devoted Sh'īa of Imām Ali ﷺ and cast doubt and uncertainty in the faith and beliefs of his followers, to the point that only a few remained steadfast.

The situation was very grave indeed. Those [who had survived three battles and] who had remained loyal to his Eminence until the end did not have the faith and devotion of his true Sh'īa, such as Ammār and Salmān and Miqdād and Abū-Dharr. At the same time, war had exhausted them and had sapped their spirit. This explains why they surrendered quickly when confronted with the ruse of the son of Abū-

[152] Ibn Abī'l-Hadīd, Abdul-Hamīd, *Sharh-e Nahj al-Balāgha*, 4:6.

Sufyān,[153] and wanted to strike a peace at all costs When Imām Ali ﷺ told them that this offer of arbitration is nothing but a sham and that they have put these fragments of the Quran on the end of their spears in an attempt to deceive you, they objected and even threatened to kill him if he failed to accept the demand for arbitration.

And so, Ali ﷺ had no choice but to accept the arbitration; but those same people who had forced him to accept the arbitration immediately regretted their choice and understood the enormity of the mistake they had made. They wanted to make up for their mistake by committing an even bigger one: they turned on Imām Ali ﷺ and demanded that he annul every provision of the armistice agreement and start hostilities anew. This vacillation in itself suffices to inform us that these people had no vision of forethought and that their following of Imām Ali's ﷺ lead was superficial, and that they did not have a firm and deeply-rooted faith in his sovereignty (*walāyat*). These folk were no different to those who believed in the legitimacy of their personal *ijtihād* against the express will of the Apostle ﷺ of God ﷻ, who thought of insubordination and defiance of the will of the Imām ﷺ to whom they had pledged allegiance to be acceptable, just as they believed disobedience to the will and express commands of the Apostle ﷺ of God ﷻ to be a norm that was possible and somehow acceptable.

The defiance of these people of the will of Ali ﷺ made matters more complicated. The occurrence of certain incidents left no choice for Imām Ali ﷺ but to fight them. They had broken out in open insurrection, spread corruption in the land, and killed several innocent

---

[153] The reference is to Mu'āwīya, the son of Abū-Sufyān, who was the arch-enemy of the Prophet ﷺ in Mecca, and who was the chief of the Hypocrites after the conquest of Mecca, whereupon he was forced to accept Islam, if only superficially. The ruse refers to the offer of arbitration at Siffīn, when Mu'āwīya's forces were finally being routed, but which Imām Ali ﷺ was forced to accept due to the threat of mutiny on the part of his forces. See Jafri, *Origins and Early Development of Sh'īa Islam.*

people. The points of contention between them and Imām Ali ﵇ increased daily until the war of Nahrawān broke out where Imām Ali ﵇ was forced to route the Khawārij schismatics. This tragic event reached its climax when a member of the Khawārij who had escaped with his life from Nahrawān decided to murder Imām Ali ﵇ as he was praying in the prayer-niche (*mihrāb*) of the mosque of Kūfa, where his Eminence ﵇ attained to martyrdom after five long years of perseverance and forbearance in the attempt to revive the way in which the ordinances of the Book of God ﷻ and the *Sunna*^{t} of the Apostle ﷺ of God ﷻ were meant to be implemented.

This event had a huge impact on the world of Islam, completely changing its course. Imām Ali's ﵇ son, Imām Hasan al-Mujtabā ﵇ intended to continue his father's path in this turbulent and perilous situation, which was the path of his grandfather, the Apostle ﷺ of God ﷻ. However, he did not have a sufficient number of supporters to do so, and even the rank and file of the forces that remained loyal to him did not have the proper belief and faith in his leadership and authority (*imāma*^{t} *wa wilāya*^{t}). Thus, many of them abandoned him and joined Mu'āwiya's forces, leaving Imām Hasan ﵇ no choice but to negotiate a peace with Mu'āwiya.

The hardest and most painful period for Sh'īa Islam started after Mu'āwiya was ensconced in power, because he started on a course of vengeance against the Sh'īa which was unmatched in its brutality and ruthless cruelty. Nor did it take long for him to decimate the ranks of the Sh'īa to the point that only a handful of the true Sh'īa of Imām Ali ﵇ remained. Mu'āwiya martyred people such as Hajr b. 'Adī and his supporters and committed torture and all sorts of other atrocities throughout his twenty-year reign against the Sh'īa. Ibn Abī'l-Hadīd, the Mu'tazalite scholar, relates from the book *al-ihdāth al-īmadāinī*: "In an edict to all of his agents, Mu'āwiya wrote, 'I hereby remove my protection [of the force of law] from anyone who relates any hadīth report concerning the virtues of Abū-Turab [reference to Imām Ali عليه السلام] and his House.' After this, the preachers in every town and village started to vilify Ali عليه السلام and cursed and maledicted him from the pulpit."

In these times, the people of Kūfa were the most oppressed because the Sh'īa of Ali عليه السلام were mostly here and Mu'āwiya had appointed Zīād b. Sumayya as the governor of the town and had added Basra to its administrative prefecture. Zīād, who at one time was thought of as one of Ali's followers and was a commander during his caliphate, knew all of his Sh'īa and special aides and would hunt them down no matter where they were able to hide themselves and martyr them. He is known to have severed the hands and feet of a large number of the Sh'īa and to have blinded many using a hot needle or sword and crucified many others and generally to have routed them from the Irāq. Thus, it did not take too long before there were no renowned Sh'īa left in the Irāq.

Mu'āwiya had ordered all of his operatives not to accept the testimony of any Sh'īa in any law-court. In another edict, he wrote, "Look out for those who were the followers of 'Uthmān. Any who supported 'Uthmān prior [to Mu'āwiya's ascension to power] should be respected and honored in the councils and assemblies. Any virtue concerning 'Uthmān that they narrate should be written down and sent to me." The vassals of Mu'āwiya continued [to foster] this act [of hadīth fabrication] up to the point where there was a superfluity of hadīth reports singing the praises of 'Uthmān. This was because a monetary reward was given each time to anyone who produced a "hadīth" which contained a virtue of 'Uthmān's, and many of the elders of the community who enjoyed being lavished with honors and accolades strove to produce such reports.

After this, Mu'āwiya told his operatives, "There are plenty of hadīth reports singing the praises of 'Uthmān and everyone now knows about them. When this edict reaches you, ask the people to relate reports concerning the Companions and the first and second caliphs, and to come up with reports concerning the Companions which are similar in their content to any hadīth reports which mention [the virtues of] Abū-Turāb [= Imām Ali ﷺ]. Verily, this task is more pleasing to me [now] and will put a sparkle in my eyes and will disturb Abū-Turāb ﷺ and his Sh'īa and make them distraught and will be harder for them than the relaying of reports concerning the virtues of 'Uthmān!"

After his directive reached the hands of his administrators and was read to the people, a large number of hadīth reports started to circulate which were utterly baseless. The people went to such extremes in the fabrication of hadīth reports concerning the Companions that compilations of these were gathered in many volumes. These same fabrications were then taught in a systematic fashion to school-children and students so that they would be transmitted by rote from breast to breast, thereby entering into the oral tradition and marrow of the culture. In another directive, Mu'āwiya then ordered: "For whomsoever there exists evidence or a reason [to suppose] that he or his dependents have a liking for Ali ﷺ, his name shall be erased from the roster and his stipend from the treasury shall be cut off!" He followed this with an addendum, ordering "Anyone who is accused of amity toward the Members of the Household of the Prophet ﷺ shall be dealt with harshly and their houses destroyed!"

As was stated earlier, this pain and suffering was inflicted most acutely on the people of the Irāq and of Kūfa in particular. The situation had become so bad that even if a trustworthy person came to one of the followers of Ali ﷺ, the latter would be afraid to talk to him in the privacy of his own home because it was possible that a servant or handmaiden might report the meeting so that such meetings could only take place in conditions of absolute secrecy and only after having obtained the interlocutor's promise to keep his being a Sh'īa of Ali ﷺ a secret.

Fabricated hadīth reports had been disseminated everywhere. The *fuqahā* (doctors of religious jurisprudence or sacred law) and judges and governors acted on them as sources for the derivation of Islamic law. The worst of the people were the reciters and scribes of these supposed scriptural sources who would recite and write down these fabrications in order to gain access and proximity to the courts and lobbies of the agents and administrators that did the bidding of the Umayyads. These scoundrels attained to their immediate worldly goals, but the helpless people who came on the scene later following in the wake of this wretched deception (and who had no idea about the historical realities that went before them) equated these fabricated reports with the genuine article despite their efforts at wanting to arrive at the truth. Having bought into the authenticity of these reports, [the masses] attained to faith in their substance and acted on their provisions and implications.

The trials and tribulations of the Muslim peoples inflicted at the hands of the administrators appointed by the Umayyads increased daily until Hasan b. Ali ﷺ was martyred in the fiftieth year of the Hijra (or Muslim calendar). At this time, all of the Sh'īa feared for their lives, living under the very real possibility that they could at any moment be arrested and executed.

After the uprising of Husayn b. Ali ﷺ in the year 61 HQ,[154] and the martyrdom of that august person, the situation became even more serious. After Abdul-Mālik b. Marwān (the fifth Omayyad caliph, reigned 65-86 HQ) came to power, he appointed Hajjāj b. Yūsuf ath-Thaqafī as governor of the Irāq, who exceeded even the outrageous limits of Zīād b. Sumayya in his blood-lust, brutality and extermination of the people of the Irāq. It is recorded in the books of history that an individual whom it is said was the forefather of Abdul-Mālik b. Qurayb al-Asma'ī, told Hajjāj b. Yūsuf ath-Thaghafīi, "O Prince! My parents

[154] The 61st lunar year after the migration from Mecca to Medina.

have renounced me and have chosen the name "Ali" for me. Now I am impoverished and indigent, and look with hope to an association with and a reward from the prince!"

Hajjāj laughed and said, "I hereby appoint you the governor of such and such a place on account of your being such a sweet-talker!"

Ibn 'Arfa, known as Naftūya, who is one of the great and most learned of the *muhaddithūn* (the scholars of the science of hadīth), reports a matter that relates to our topic. He states, "Most of the hadīth reports about the goodly attributes and virtues of the Companions were forged during the reign of the Banī-'Umayya. They wanted to legitimize their reign in this way, and believed that they could [= needed to] humiliate the Banī-Hāshim [in order to do so]."[155]

Additionally, Ibn Abī'l-Hadīd relates another report from Imām al-Bāqir ﵇ with the same purport, via some of the companions of his Eminence that he said: "O So and so! What have we suffered at the hands of the Quraysh and their conspiring against us? What have our followers (*Sh'īa*) and devotees suffered? The Apostle ﷺ of God ﷻ passed while having stipulated the succession of the Members of his Household, but the Quraysh conspired against us in order to derail this wagon from its path. And this was while in their argumentation with the Ansār, the Quraysh resorted to the right which the Apostle ﷺ of God ﷻ had stipulated for us in their attempts at proving their [supposed] right to the office of the succession relative to the Ansār! The Quraysh occupied the office of the caliphate one after the other until it eventually returned back to its rightful owner, but [even then] they broke their pledges of allegiance and fanned the flames of [internecine] war and preoccupied Ali ﵇ with war to the extent that they eventually martyred him. They then pledged allegiance to his son [Imām] Hasan ﵇, only to break their pledges and to abandon him,

[155] Ibn Abī'l-Hadīd, Abdul-Hamīd, *Sharh-e Nahj al-Balāgha*, 11:44-46.

forcing him to accept the peace which the Banī-Ummaya imposed on him with cunning and guile. The people of the Irāq showed such insolence toward him and they eventually entered the dagger into his side and fragmented his army, and the anklets of the mothers were taken off their feet by their sons.

"Perforce he made peace with Mu'āwiya so as to prevent the additional shedding of the blood of his followers and of the Members of the Household of the Prophet ﷺ, who were a small group of people who lived under strenuous conditions. After this, twenty-thousand people of the 'Irāq pledged allegiance to Husayn b. Ali ؑ, but they broke their pledge and attacked him and martyred him while they were still bound by the obligation of their pledge to him. After that, we, the Members of the Household of the Prophet ﷺ, were always [kept] under pressure and [imposed] hardships. We were not left at peace for a single moment, and we had no sense of security concerning our property or our persons. Alongside this, the liars in every town and village were engaged in the fabrication of hadīth reports and spreading lies and misinformation about us in order to defame and vilify us.

"The height of this conspiracy and plot occurred at the time of Mu'āwiya who, after having martyred Imām Husayn ؑ, would cut off the limbs of every Sh'īa he could find and [then] murder him. Anyone who was accused of amity toward us would be imprisoned or killed, and would have their property confiscated and their house destroyed. These calamities and barbarities increased daily until 'Ubaydullāh b. Ziād martyred Husayn b. Ali ؑ in Karbalā in the most heinous way imaginable. After that, Hajjāj b. Yūsuf came to the Irāq and carried out an atrocious bloodbath. The situation had reached a point that if they accused someone of being an atheist or an unbeliever, it would have been better for him than if he were accused of being a follower (*Sh'īa*) of Ali ؑ, because [in this latter case] he would be arrested and executed immediately.

"And what is interesting is that the *muhaddithūn* (the scholars of the science of hadīth) would relate bizarre hadīth reports about the Companions and the [early] caliphs, none of which had any factual basis, but because the narrators [of these reports] were not [known] liars or people of a low [quotient of] piety, people deemed what they said [to be true] and accepted [what they said]."[156]

These two reports describe the situation of the Sh'īa during the Omayyad era. The tribulations of the supporters of the Members of the Household of the Prophet ﷺ did not end even after the collapse of the 120-year reign of the Umayyads and the coming to power of the Abbāsids. The Abbāsids had attracted people to their cause and mustered their armies by resorting to slogans in support of the House of the Prophet ﷺ, but no sooner had they taken over the reins of power that they changed their tune and adopted the way of the Umayyads. They subjected the Members of the Household of the Prophet, who were their paternal cousins, to the harshest torments and the most brutal torture, and poisoned them one after the other or martyred them in some other way.

During this time, the Members of the Household of the Prophet ﷺ and their Sh'īa were only able to breathe a sign of relief during the interregnum where the Umayyads and Abbāsids were busy fighting each other. But this situation changed for the worse before too long, gaining pace, especially during the reign of al-Mansūr (the second Abbāsid Caliph, reigning from 136 to 158 HQ), who had become acutely aware of the dangers of the expansion of Sh'īa activity. The Abbāsids witnessed the people gathering around the Members of the Household of the Prophet ﷺ in support of their cause and establishing emotional bonds of amity with them. Thus, as a preventive measure for

[156] Ibn Abī'l-Hadīd, Abdul-Hamīd, *Sharh-e Nahj al-Balāgha*, 11:43.

ensuring the foundations and longevity of their dynasty, they tried to prevent the expansion and development of Sh'ia Islam.

They increased the repressive measures against the descendants of the Prophet ﷺ and against the Members of his House to such a degree that it caused the Ālids (descendants of Imām Ali ؑ) to rise up in insurrection against their injustices. One such instance was the insurrection of Muhammad b. Abdullāh b. al-Hasan b. Ali ؑ, known as the Pure Soul (*an-Nafs az-Zakīya*) who rose in rebellion against al-Mansūr the Abbāsid. In a letter addressed to al-Mansūr, an-Nafs az-Zakīya reminded him how the Banī-Abbās gathered the people around them and brought down the Omayyad dynasty by abusing the station and rank of the Members of the Household of the Prophet ﷺ and by using the false pretext of wanting to avenge the blood of the Ahl al-Bayt ؑ. He continues, "Verily, this right is our right. At first, you claimed that you have risen in rebellion for our sake, recruited our Sh'ia into your ranks by means of this [ruse], and achieved your objective on our account. Verily our [fore-] father, Ali b. Abī-Tālib ؑ was the *wasī* (legatee, inheritor, executor and successor) of the Prophet ﷺ and the legitimate leader (*imām*); so how could you inherit his regency (*welāya*[t]) while his progeny are still alive? You are well aware that nobody has our [priority of] ancestry and cannot [legitimately] place [a stake on] such a claim. We are not the progeny of those who were accursed of the Prophet ﷺ, those who have been outcast [by him] or those who have been freed [after having been prisoners of the wars they waged against Islam – reference to the Umayyads] by the Most Noble Prophet ﷺ, and none among the Banī-Hāshim has the closeness of kinship, virtue and competence that we have… Verily, God the Sublimely Exalted selected us and appointed certain excellences and virtues for us. Verily, our forefather is his Eminence Muhammad ﷺ, the Seal of the Prophets ﷺ, and our forefather is Ali b. Abī-Tālib ؑ, the first Muslim; and of the wives of the Prophet ﷺ, the most virtuous is Lady Khadīja[t] al-Kubrā, the first person to pray toward the Ka'ba; and our mother, Lady Fātema[t] az-Zahrā ﷺ, the Lady of the Women of Both Worlds and the Lady of the Women of Heaven, and among those born into Islam, al-Hasan ﷺ and al-Husayn ﷺ, the Lords of the Youth of Paradise."[157]

With the receipt of this letter, al-Mansūr decided to arrest an-Nafs az-Zakīya, but was unable to do so. He thus took out his vengeance on those of the progeny of Ali ﷺ that he could get his hands on. Jāhez writes about these activities as follows: "Al-Mansūr the Abbāsid went after the sons of al-Hasan ﷺ in Kūfa and imprisoned them in the palace of Ibn Hubayra. He ordered Muhammad b. Ibrāhīm b. al-Hasan to be brought forth, and while he was still alive, he ordered that a column be built around him and left him in this state to die of hunger and thirst. He then killed most of the Banī-Hasan (the progeny of al-Hasan ﷺ). And Ibrāhīm b. Ghamar b. Hasan b. Hasan b. Ali b. Abī-Tālib was among those who were taken in shackles and chains from Medina to the town of Anbār. He would tell his two brothers Abdullāh and Hasan, "We prayed that one day the government of the Umayyads would fall and we would give glad tidings to each other that the Banī-Abbās have acceded to power; but now our situation is even worse than it was before."[158]

After the defeat of the uprising of an-Nafs az-Zakīya and his martyrdom in Medina, his brother Ibrāhīm b. Abdullāh, who had risen in rebellion in Basra, was also martyred in an area called Bākhmarī in the vicinity of Kūfa in a war which has been called the Lesser Badr (*al-badr as-sughrā*).[159]

---

[157] Tabarī, *Tārīkh ar-Rusul wa'l-Mulūk*, 7:567.
[158] *An-Nizā' wa'l-Takhāsom*, p. 74.
[159] Isfahānī, Abī'l-Faraj, *Maqātil at-Tābi'īn*, p. 364.

Insurrections against the Abbāsids continued unabated. During the reign of al-Mahdī,[160] the son of al-Mansūr, Ali b. Abbās b. Hasan b. Hasan b. Ali b. Abī-Tālib ؏ also rose in rebellion, but al-Mahdī arrested and imprisoned him. He was released after Hasan b. Ali ؏ interceded on his behalf, but because they had given him a poisoned tincture to drink, his body was gradually weakened such that when he arrived in Madina he had lost all of his muscle mass and his bones were visible. He attained to martyrdom three days after having reached Medina.[161]

During the reign of al-Hādī (the 4th Abbāsid caliph, reigned 169-170 HQ), Husayn b. Ali b. Hasan b. Ali b. Abī-Tālib ؏ rose in rebellion. He attained to martyrdom in an area known as Fakh outside of Mecca and is therefore known as the Sheykh of Fakh.

When Hārūn ar-Rashīd (the 5th Abbāsid caliph, reigned 170 – 193 HQ) took on the reins of power after al-Hādī, he arrested Yahyā b. Abdullāh b. al-Hasan and ordered that a wall be built around him and left him to die of hunger and thirst within that wall.[162]

Moreover, when Maʿmūn (the 7th Abbāsid caliph, reigned 198 – 218 HQ) took on the reins of power after having defeated al-Amīn (the 6th Abbāsid caliph, reigned 193 – 198 HQ), he feigned amity and friendship with the Members of the Household of the Prophet ﷺ. He called Imām ar-Riḍā ؏ (the 8th Imām, 182 – 203 HQ) from Medina and forced the position of the crown prince on him as a public relations stunt, after which he poisoned him.

The foul measures of the Abbāsids against the Imāms of the Shʿīa continued to where they even disrespected the dead bodies of the Imāms ؏. Al-Mutawakkil (the 10th Abbāsid caliph, reigned 232 – 247

---

[160] Muhammad b. Abdullāh al-Mansūr, better known by his regnal name al-Mahdī, the third Abbāsid Caliph who reigned from 775 to his death in 785.
[161] Esfahānī, Abī'l-Faraj, *Maqātil ot-Tābi'īn*, p. 403.
[162] Ibid.

HQ) ordered the shrine of Imām Husayn ؑ destroyed and ordered water to be poured on his grave and to prevent the people from making pilgrimage to it. He had appointed a group to inspect the travelers to Karbalā (the site of Imām Husayn's ؑ martyrdom and burial place) and to arrest anyone who had come there as a pilgrim.

Al-Mutawakkil instituted a policy of the economic strangulation of the Members of the Household of the Prophet ﷺ. He appointed 'Umar b. Faraj as the governor of Mecca and Medina in order to institute measures that would bring about economic hardships for the Members of the Household of the Prophet ﷺ. He prevented any sort of help on the part of the people to the Members of the Household of the Prophet ﷺ and would punish anyone who was intent on helping them. In this way, the Prophet's ﷺ household was kept under conditions of extreme economic hardship. Indeed, it has even been related that their womenfolk used to have to make their prayers sharing the same clothes, as they did not each have suitable prayer attire of their own.[163]

After al-Musta'yūn (the 12th Abbāsid caliph, reigned 247 – 252 HQ) came to power, he ordered Yahyā b. 'Umar b. al-Husayn to be put to death. Abul-Faraj al-Isfahānī writes about him as follows: "He (Yahyā b. 'Umar b. al-Husayn) was a strong and courageous man. When they brought him to Baghdād, the people cheered and rejoiced. Abū-Hāshim Ali Muhammad b. Abdullāh b. Tāhir entered the court of al-Musta'yūn and said, 'I have come to pay my condolences to you concerning the death of this man for whose sake the Apostle ﷺ of God ﷻ would have been condoled if he were alive.' After this, they brought in the prisoners who were the companions of Yahyā and tortured them with a severity that was unprecedented. They marched them bare-

[163] Ibid.

footed and disrobed in a long line, and if anyone fell behind, they would sever his neck."[164]

Thus, the Sh'īa were never privy to any peace and security throughout the centuries until in the year 320 HQ when the Būyids came to power. Theirs was a better approach to statesmanship, and Islamic culture and civilization bloomed during their reign. This changed when the Seljūqs conquered Baghdād in the year 447 HQ and Tūghrīl Beyk ordered that the library of the Shaykh at-Tā'ifa at-Tūsī, the chief religious authority of the era for the Sh'īa, be burned together with the pulpit from which he taught.

Similarly, the Seljūqs burned the library that had been founded by Abū-Nasr Shāpūr b. Ardeshīr, the vizier of Bahā ad-Dawla. This vizier built a large and important building in the Karkh district of Baghdad, which was situated between the Tigris and Euphrates rivers and which was similar in its usage to the House of Wisdom (*Dār al-Hekma*) which Hārūn or-Rashīd had built. This vizier who was a friend of the sciences had gathered many different books in Persian, Arabic, Hindi, Chinese, and Latin which added up to more than ten thousand manuscript volumes, all of which were important references which had been penned by the hands of their original writers. Among the books that went up in the flames of ignorance and bigotry were Qurans written in the calligraphy of Ibn Muqla, the inventor of many modes of inscription.[165]

The renowned biographer and geographer Yāqūt al-Hamāwī has described this library as follows: "There was not a better library in the whole world. All of the books were in the manuscript of the most learned scholars and on the basis of correct principles."[166]

---

[164] Ibid.

[165] Ibn Athīr, *al-Kāmil fi't-Tārīkh*, 10:3; *Khatat ash-Shām*, 3:185.

[166] Hamāwi, *Majma' al-Būldān*, 2:342.

During the era of the Ottomans the Sh'īa did not see any peace and security either. During the reign of Sultan Selīm (r. 918–26/1512–20), he had been informed that some of the teachings of the Sh'īa had been disseminated among his subjects, and that some of his subjects had inclined to this rite. He ordered everyone who had become a Sh'īa to be put to death![167] After this, approximately forty thousand men were massacred and the *sheikh al-islām* (the highest officially-appointed religious authority of the land) of the Ottoman state issued a *fatwa* (authoritative religio-legal opinion) which stated that the killing of the Sh'īa and the declaration of war against them had *thawāb* (rewards in this world and in the hereafter)![168]

Consequently, they marched thousands of the Sh'īa to a slaughterhouse which they had improvised in the city of Aleppo (in present day northern Syria) and slaughtered them all. This action followed as a consequence of a fatwa issued by Shaykh Nūh al-Hanafī in reply to the question of someone who had asked what the basis of the religious obligation to wage war on the Sh'īa and the lawfulness of their killing was. Shaykh Nūh had written in response, "Know that these are morally corrupt unbelievers who have [at once] gathered unbelief, obstinacy, corruption, rebellion, and atheism in their persons. Anyone who harbors any doubt concerning the religious obligation to fight them or concerning the lawfulness of the shedding of their blood is a heretic (*kāfir*) like them! ... The killing of these evil miscreants (*ashrār*) and heretics is a religious imperative (*wājib*), irrespective of whether or not they repent! Additionally, their womenfolk and children should be taken into slavery!"[169]

---

[167] Ibid.
[168] Haydar, Asad, *al-Imām as-Sādiq wa-l-madhhab al-arba'a*, 1:244.
[169] *al-Fatāwā al-Hāmedīya*, 1:104, Quoted in Sharafuddīn, Sayyid Abdul-Husayn, *al-Fusūl al-Imāmīya fī Ta'līf al-Umma*, pgs. 195-196; Muzaffar,

This was a vignette of the pain and suffering that the Sh'īa of Imām Ali ﷺ have endured throughout their turbulent history, whose outline we sketched very briefly. It is hoped that the reason is by now clear to the gentle reader as to why the dominant powers were intent on vilifying the Sh'īa and presenting an unpalatable image of them to their subject peoples: the Members of the Household of the Prophet ﷺ and their Sh'īa (adherents) have been a thorn in the side of despots and tyrants throughout the course of history, and this is why they were subject to their hatred and ire.

The above history also lays the groundwork for the explanation as to why and how conflict and schism occurred between various factions of the Sh'īa. During all this upheaval, deviant sects would appear whose beliefs were far removed from the authentic path of Sh'īa Islam. Moreover, it was a common occurrence that agents provocateurs or 'agents of incitement' would infiltrate the ranks of the Sh'īa and assert false and deviant statements in order to portray a false image of what Sh'īa Islam actually is, thereby laying the groundwork and providing the opportunity for the tyrants and oppressors of the day to eradicate the Sh'īa. The oppressive authorities wanted to sow division among the ranks of the Sh'īa by any means necessary and to have them fight each other so as to preclude them from preserving the true values of Islam and the *Sunna*^{t} (the way of the Most Noble Prophet ﷺ as an exemplary model and paradigmatic example), and in order to preclude the proper implementation of the ordinances and injunctions of the Quran, because the Most Noble Prophet ﷺ equated the Members of his Household as one of a perfect pair with the Noble Quran.

Shaykh Muhammad Riḍā, *Tārīkh ash-Sh'īa*, p. 147; *at-Taqīya fī Fiqh Ahl al-Bayt*, 1:51.

4 - The Continuation of the Path of Sh'ia Islam

After the martyrdom of Imām Husayn ﵇ the Imāms of the Household of the Prophet ﷺ knew that the first generation of the Sh'ia, whose devotion to their beliefs was unparalleled, has been lost and that the generations which followed have not reached a stage where they were ready to put their lives on the line for the sake of their faith and their beliefs. They therefore worked to strengthen the faith and creedal bases of what remained of their followers in order to inoculate them from the deviant beliefs which were introduced under different names from the time of the Umayyads. This is what is now referred to as the cultural front or taking the fight to the cultural arena.

After the martyrdom of his father, Imām Zayn al-Ābidīn ﵇ (known as as-Sajjād) started this path and strove to preserve the straight path of Islam and the prophetic *sunna*[t] by disseminating the correct and true teachings of Islam. However, the oppressive and suffocating environment that followed in the wake of the martyrdom of Imām Husayn ﵇ and the intense pressures that the Umayyads brought to bear on the House of the Prophet precluded the possibility of Imām as-Sajjād from being able properly to enter this cultural field of battle.

After his son, Imām Muhammad al-Bāqir ﵇ took on the responsibility of the *imāmate* (the religio-political leadership of the community which adhered to the teachings of the House of the Prophet (ﷺ), the atmosphere had improved a little. The grip of the Umayyads on power had weakened, and they did not have complete control over everything. Claimants to their throne would show up from every nook and cranny claiming their right to the caliphate. Thus, Imām Muhammad al-Bāqir (ع) could maintain better contact with his followers and use these occasions for the dissemination and expansion of the true teachings of Islam.

When Imām Ja'far as-Sādiq (ع) became the Imām after his father's death, the Omayyad dynasty was breathing its last breaths. All of their energies were spent trying to suppress the various uprisings occurring on a continual basis, so they could not pay much attention to the Sh'īa. Imām Ja'far as-Sādiq (ع) considered this a golden opportunity and expended all of his efforts on the development and dissemination of the correct Islamic sciences.

Imām Ja'far as-Sādiq (ع) would sit in the mosque of the Prophet (ﷺ) and thousands of people from all over the realm of Islam came to sit at his feet and to learn from him. That period of time provided for an excellent opportunity for the followers of the Imām to establish relationships with him and to be nurtured and fortified both intellectually and in terms of correct beliefs, together with their scriptural and rational proofs. In this way, they could stand their ground against apologists of the other rites within Islam that were crystalizing at that time, as well as against aberrant sects which had been fostered by the Umayyads.

The Imāms (ع) refrained from any sort of armed insurrection because they saw that their Sh'īa were not at the stage where they were able to take on the responsibilities that go along with such an insurrection and to be able to hold on to its gains. At the same time, they did not have either the personnel or the materiel in sufficient quantities to enable them to go against the military might of the ruling establishment. Thus, the focus was placed on the cultural front, which [at that time] entailed the building of the intellectual infrastructure [in preparation] for the next phase.

The veracity of this fact (of the prematurity of armed revolt) was proved by the armed insurrection of Zayd b. Ali (Zayn al-Ābidīn ﷺ) b. Husayn ﷺ b. Ali b. Abī-Tālib against Omayyad rule and his subsequent tragic martyrdom. The people of Kūfa abandoned Zayd, just as they had abandoned his grandfather because they lacked sufficient understanding to be able to endure the consequences of an armed rebellion.

At the beginning of the founding of Abbasid rule, there was relative calm and security for the Members of the Household of the Prophet ﷺ, and this relative peace provided a sufficient opportunity for the Sh'īa to learn the Quranic sciences from their Imāms, and especially from Imām Ja'far as-Sādiq ﷺ. This is why the rite (*madhhab*) of the *imāmīya* (i.e. the Twelver Sh'īa) got to be known as the "Ja'farī" rite: the relatively open space of that period in time allowed Imām Ja'far as-Sādiq ﷺ to fortify the creedal and intellectual pillars of Sh'īa Islam.

However, it was not long before the repressive pressures of the Abbāsids started. The Abbāsids would see the people's love for the Members of the Household of the Prophet ﷺ and were unable to tolerate it. They had initially started with sloganeering in order to obtain the approval of the House of Muhammad ﷺ for their rebellion against the Umayyads but once they had the reins of power in hand, they started their repression of the Members of the House of the Prophet ﷺ. This duplicity of theirs caused the people to turn away from them and to turn to the Ahl al-Bayt ﷺ.

Fearing insurrections against their authority under the banner of the Ahl al-Bayt ﷺ, the Abbasid power increased their repression of them, putting them under more pressure. Popular uprisings headed by any Ālid were severely suppressed. At the same time, they closely monitored and controlled the activities and movements of the Members of the Household of the Prophet ﷺ to the point of keeping them imprisoned for long periods of time. For example, according to one report, Hārūn ar-Rashīd imprisoned Imām Mūsā al-Kāzim ؑ for fourteen years. Another tactic they used was to exile the Members of the Household of the Prophet ﷺ from Medina to Baghdād, the capital of the Abbāsid state, where they could keep a closer eye on them; all of the Imāms ؑ after Imām ar-Reḍa ؑ (i.e. all those who followed Imām Mūsā al-Kāzim ؑ) to Imām Hasan al-Askarī ؑ were exiled from Medina.

The Abbāsids had created extremely difficult conditions for the Ahl al-Bayt ؑ. The Sh'īa could not easily meet with their Imāms, and these conditions of strict monitoring and control continued until the imāmate of Imām Hasan al-Askarī ؑ. The Lesser Occultation of the twelfth Imām lasted seventy years, and during this time, contact of the Sh'īa with their Imām could be made only through a series of four successive deputies (*nā'ib*, plural *nuwwāb*), after which the Greater Occultation began and the most learned magisters (*fuqahā*; doctors of sacred jurisprudence) who had the necessary competence and qualifications (i.e. were *jāma' osh-sharāyit*) gradually took on the mantle of the religio-legal and de jure political authority of the Sh'īa community. These were the general deputies of the occulted Imām ؑ (just as the four successive deputies were his specifically-appointed deputies during the Lesser Occultation). They acted to derive the ordinances of the sacred law as well as the ethical norms and injunctions of the sacred canon from the scriptural sources of the law (i.e. the Quran and the *hadīth* report corpus), using principles and protocols that the purified Imāms ؑ had established for such derivations.

Sects within Islam and the Deviations of the *Ghulāt* (Extremists)

The continuation of the path of Shʿīa Islam throughout the rest of its history was not free of difficulties either. The Omayyad and Abbāsid rulers constantly held the Shʿīa under pressure, plundering their property, subjecting them to torture, and murdering them. This caused the Imāms ﷺ to have to resort to prudential dissimulation (*taqīya*), as they were not able to tell the truth openly and in an explicit manner. The Imāms would recommend their followers adopt prudential dissimulation (*taqīya*) in order to save their lives so that the sapling of Shʿīa Islam would stay alive and, when the conditions allowed, would be able to grow, thrive, and to bear fruit.

These pressures and the prudential dissimulations which necessarily followed as the logical reaction to them caused doubt and uncertainty in the hearts of some of the Shʿīa. Certain ill-intentioned and opportunist elements took advantage of this situation and tried to use these circumstances to arrive at their delusional objectives. Additionally, the ignorance of the general populace concerning the true beliefs of their religion caused deviant beliefs to take root and to grow rapidly within those who followed the Members of the Household of the Prophet ﷺ, just as this phenomenon occurred in the other rites (*madhāhib*) within Islam, wherein sects such as the Khawārij, the Muʿtazelites, the Jahmīya, the Murjiʿa and so on appeared in rapid succession because of the differences they had in the interpretation of the Quranic revelations and of the prophetic ḥadīth corpus.

Furthermore, adherents of the other Abrahamic faiths (*ahl al-kitāb*) as well as those from other faiths who had become Muslim in appearance only, played a critical role in the initiation and promulgation of these deviant sects. In addition to the fabrication of false ḥadīth reports, these agents of disinformation disseminated *isrāīliāt* (misconceived accretions and syncretisms of Judaic provenance).

The rise of these different sects meant that each one of them resorted to the Quranic revelations and the prophetic hadīth corpus for the validation and vindication of their respective creed and rite, and in order to prove that it is only their sect that is informed of the truth, and that the rest of the sects are aberrant and false.

With this narrow-minded view, which was adopted by some of the denominations or rites (*madhāhib*), the rest of those who self-identified as Muslim were considered to be unbelievers or to have apostatized (i.e. *takfīr* was pronounced on them; they were considered to have become *kāfir*), and the shedding of their blood was considered to be licit, as was the taking of their womenfolk and children into slavery or as personal property! Concurrently, the fervor and vehemence of debates in apologetics or dogmatics between sects increased, in which each party would reject and deny the positions of their counterparts. Prejudice and blind bigotry caused confusion in the exact meanings and definitions of terms and beliefs, which in turn caused accusations to be made which were not worthy of a Muslim believer.

The rite (*madhhab*) of the Members of the Household of the Prophet ﷺ suffered and bore the worst brunt of the fallout from this sectarian milieu. The problem was that many of the false prophets and their followers, all of whom harbored false and deviant beliefs, attached themselves to the true rite (*madhhab*). What is interesting to note is that the beliefs and practices of some of these deviant sects were completely different to those of the rite of the Members of the Household of the Prophet ﷺ, but this did not stop them from claiming that they were their devotees; and of course, their goal was to deceive the ignorant masses and to gain a foothold for themselves by way of this false, unsolicited and unrequited association. All of those who moved in the sectarian milieu that consisted of cliques and cults and micro-factions fell under the general identification of the *Ghulāt* (extremists), and considered themselves to be "followers" of the Members of the Household of the Prophet ﷺ. Reason and the variations of their beliefs and practices from the sacred canon would dictate, however, that this was not the case; and the Imāms, too, of course, disassociated themselves from them, had disowned some of their supposed followers and devotees, and would expose the latter's self-interested objectives for what they were. The reason why these Ghulāt sects and cults were associated with Sh'īa Islam is that they pretended to be the devotees of the Members of the Household of the Prophet ﷺ whereas in fact what gave rise to their deviant beliefs was their proclivity to extremism.

The above factors, together with other reasons, not the least of which was the tension with the ruling powers and its multiple dynamics which were at play, brought about a general confusion and gave rise to much misunderstanding. Heresiographers exacerbated the confusion with their gross errors in the descriptions of the various sects they wrote about. The grossest of their errors were reserved for the Sh'īa, such that there is not even any consensus about the number of Shī'ī sects, let alone on what they are each supposed to believe.

Some of the sects that they named did not even have an objective existence. Some writers would at times refer to the beliefs of a given individual as a "sect". For example, Shahristānī refers to the "Hāshimīya", "Yūnusīya" and "Zarārīya" as "Sh'īa sects", whereas no such sects or movements exist nor have any particular theses or beliefs concerning them been proffered.

Among other examples of gross biases in the heresiographical works of the majoritarian strains, the following instance can be mentioned, where, due to their prejudices, some of these writers deprive all other sects of every possible virtue! Take Baghdādī, for example:

"Thanks to the grace of God ﷻ, in the sects of the Qadrīya, Mujassama, Khawārij, Rawāfiḍ, Jahmīya, and all other sects, there exist no scholars of great stature in *fiqh* (sacred jurisprudence), *hadīth* science, lexigraphy, grammar, etc. and they are bereft of any [competent] biographers who are able [properly] to write a moral biography (*sīra*) of the Prophet ﷺ, or a religious leader (*imām*) who can deliver a [righteous] sermon, [discuss] ethics or carry out a [serviceable] exegesis [of the Quran], and all of the religious leaders of these sciences [who have any stature worthy of note] both in general terms and as specialists belong to the *ahl as-Sunnaᵗ wa'l-Jamā'aᵗ* (i.e. are of the Sunni sect)."

This is a position that is totally prejudicial to everyone else! Moreover, anyone who has any inkling about the literary heritage of Islam, which is brimming with books written by scholars from all sorts of sects, will not find such claims to be creditable.

An example that demonstrates the conceptual confusion in the minds of certain writers is the categorization architecture employed by Abul-Hasan Ali b. Ismā'īl al-Ash'arī (d. 324 HQ) in his book *al-maqālāt al-Islāmīīn wa'l-ikhtilāf al-musallīn.* At first, he divided the Sh'īa into three main headings. He then goes on to mention sub-tier categories and branches. And then, he divides the *Ghulāt* sect into fifteen sub-divisions. He then mentions the *Imāmīya*, which he calls "*Rāfiḍī*" and divides them into no less than 24 sects. The *Kaysānīya* he classifies as a sect of the *Imāmīya*, whereas they are a *Ghulāt* sect which have no connection with the *Imāmīya.*

Ash'arī then describes the Zaydīya, dividing them into the three sub-sects of the Jārūdīya, Batrīya and Sulaymānīya, subdividing these grouping further still. What is interesting to note is that many of these heresiographers of a majoritarian bent have classified the Sulaymānīya as a sub-sect of the Zaydīya, whereas in point of fact, their beliefs are similar in every way with the belief of the majority Sunni position, as we shall explain. It is truly dismaying to see that a number of contemporary authors have followed these footsteps and have bought wholesale everything that appears in the books of the ancients without having troubled themselves to carry out any research of their own. In an age where such things are readily and freely available at the touch of a button, these types of people have not even bothered to do the most basic rudiments of research, which of course requires one to refer to the texts of each sect in order to read what it is that they believe from their own mouths. Absurdly, they content themselves with seeing what the enemies of a given sect have written or said about them!

What is essential for the purposes of our discussion here is to investigate the genesis, growth and development of each of the Sh'īa sects that bear on our discussion and to juxtapose our findings with the historical and temporal factors at play so as to arrive at an understanding of what evolutionary phases Sh'īa Islam has undergone in order to arrive at where it is today. Then we can proceed to bring to the light of day and to elucidate the fallacies and errors which these authors have been subject to, and to disentangle groupings and sects which have been identified as Sh'īa which are not in fact Sh'īa, and those which have not been identified as Sh'īa, which in fact are.

Thus, we shall at first discuss the meaning of Shī'ā Islam, and then proceed to a typology of the most important divisions within Sh'īa Islam, and shall end with a summary of the *Imāmī* (Twelver) position on the *Ghulāt* extremists.

The Meaning of Sh'īa Islam

Writers have provided many descriptions of Sh'īa Islam. We shall explicate the definitions of the more important ones among them:

- **Abul-Hasan al-Ash'arī** has stated, "They are referred to as Sh'īa because they followed and supported Ali ﷺ and believed him to have priority over the other Companions of the Apostle ﷺ of God ﷻ."

- **Ibn Hazm** has stated, "Anyone who holds the same beliefs of the Sh'īa, that Ali عليه السلام is the most preeminent person after the Apostle ﷺ of God ﷻ and most deserving of [the office of] the imāmate, and that this competence is vested in Ali's عليه السلام progeny after him, is a Sh'īa, even if such a person does not hold the same views as them in other matters; but if a person does not hold the above-mentioned views, he is not a Sh'īa."

- **Shahristānī** has stated, "A Sh'īa is one who stipulates that they follow Ali عليه السلام specifically and that he is the leader (*imām*) and successor (*khalīfa*) of the Apostle ﷺ of God ﷻ based on the express will (*nass*) and testament of the Prophet ﷺ, irrespective of whether this imāmate and succession is overt or covert… They believe that [tenure to the office of] the imāmate is restricted to the progeny of Ali عليه السلام, and that if it [the office] is [occupied] by anyone other [than said group], it is [occupied] by way of the oppression of others, or on account of the prudential dissimulation (*taqīya*) of the Imām himself… They say that [tenure of the office of] the imāmate is not a matter of expedience whose criterion is the acceptation of the general populace, and that the leader (*imām*) is not appointed by the people, but that it is a creedal matter [belief in which] is a pillar of the religion, neglecting [the appointment to] which [office] on the part of prophets is not permissible, and neither is it permissible for them to relegate this decision to the will of the people… [Shahristāni continues:] The Sh'īa believe that the explicit appointment of the leader (*imām*) [on the part of God ﷻ by way of His prophet] is a categorical imperative and that the prophets ﷺ and Imāms عليه السلام must necessarily be immune to major and minor

[sins], and believe in *tawallā*[170] and *tabarrā*,[171] in words, deeds, and belief, except in cases where prudential dissimulation (*taqīya*) [must be practiced]."

❖ **Muḥammad-Farīd Wajdī** states, "The Shʿīa are those who follow Ali ؉ and consider him to be their Imām, and that [tenure to the office of] the imāmate is restricted to the progeny of Ali ؉. They say that [tenure of the office of] the imāmate is not a matter of expedience whose criterion is the acceptation of the general populace, and that the leader (*imām*) is not appointed by the people, but that it is a principle and pillar of the religion, and that it is necessary for the Apostle ؉ of God ؉ to make an explicit statement in this regard. The Shʿīa believe that the Imāms ؉ must necessarily be immune to major and minor [sins], and believe in *tawallā* and *tabarrā*, in words and deeds, except in cases where prudential dissimulation (*taqīya*) [must be practiced] in order to secure [their persons] from the evil of the oppressors."

Among the Shʿīa writers who have described the meaning of Shʿīa Islam, we can mention Nowbakhtī, who states, "The first sect in Islam is the sect of the Shʿīa. This is the sect of Ali b. Abī-Ṭālib ؉ which was named "Shʿīa" during the lifetime of the Apostle ؉ of God ؉ and after his passing. They believed in [the priority of] the imāmate of Ali ؉ and some of their great leaders consisted of Miqdād b. Aswad, Salman the Persian, Abū-Dharr Jandab b. Janāda al-Ghaffarī, ʿAmmār b. Yasser, etc. Ali ؉ is the first person in this community whose name is associate with "Shʿīa" (follower, partisan, devotee); this epithet had always existed in the past, and was used in cases such as "the Shʿīa of Abraham", "the

---

[170] The religiously obligatory duty to love and befriend those who love God ؉, his Prophet ؉, and the Members of the Household of the Prophet ؉.
[171] The religiously obligatory duty to repudiate and consider as enemies those who repudiate God ؉, his Prophet ؉, and the Members of the Household of the Prophet ؉ and have enmity towards them.

Sh'īa of Moses", "the Sh'īa of Jesus" and of the other prophets, may God's ﷻ peace be with all of them."

Shaykh Mufīd says, "Anyone who follows Ali ؑ and considers him to have preeminence over the other Companions of the Apostle ﷺ of God ﷻ and who believes that he was appointed to be the Imām of the people by the explicit will and testament of the Apostle ﷺ of God ﷻ and at God's ﷻ behest is a Sh'īa."

Shaykh Tūsī has spoken about the *nass*[172] (a scriptural source containing an injunction or burden of duty whose meaning is clear and self-evident) and about the Prophet's ﷺ testament concerning Ali's ؑ succession and defines Sh'īa Islam as the belief that "Ali ؑ is the Imām of the Muslim community by way of the testament of the Prophet ﷺ and the will of God ﷻ the Exalted. He then divides *nass* into the two categories of *jalī* and *khafi*, defining *jalī* as "a category of *nass* which only the Imāmī Sh'īa believes in despite the fact that some hadīth historians have related the report as a *wāhid*[173] report"; and *khafi* as "a *nass* which the whole of the community accepts, despite the fact that there are differences of opinion in their interpretations, allegorical or archetypal exegeses, or implication, and [despite the fact that it is a *nass*] which is not denied by anyone whose opinion [on these kinds of matters] within the community is given any credence."

Shaykh Tūsī considers the Sulaymānīya sect to be a branch of the Zaydīya, which he does not consider to be Sh'īa on the grounds that they do not believe in the principle of divine investiture to succession (*nass* or *tansīs*), and that they state that [the tenure of the office of] the imāmate is determined by means of a consultative council (*shurā'*), and that this council is vested with formal validity given the presence of two select Muslims, and that the tenure to the office of one less worthy and

[172] See footnote #102 on page 87.

[173] *Wāhid ahādīth* are reports that have been transmitted solely on the authority of a single narrator or single chain of narrators.

less preeminent over one who is more worthy and more preeminent is acceptable. Shaykh Tūsī continues and concludes that in so far as the positions of the Sālihīya and Batrīa concerning the issue of the imāmate are the same as that of the Sulaymānīya, they similarly fall outside the bounds of Sh'īa Islam.

The above was a presentation of the most important classical and contemporary opinions concerning the meaning of Sh'īa Islam from both Sunni and Shī'ī sects. What we can conclude from these words is that there are two meanings to the word "Sh'īa": Sh'īa in a general sense and Sh'īa in a specific sense.

Almost all of the people who have engaged the subject have confused these two meanings, conflating them and failing to distinguish between them. Now the definitions of the authors which we have presented above are ones which have the specific sense of the definition of Sh'īa Islam in mind and have not discussed the general meaning. This is the topic to whose subdivisions we now direct your attention.

The Meaning of Sh'īa Islam in its General Sense

1. A sub-category within this general category is the position of those who maintain the preeminence (*afḍalia'*) of Ali b. Abī-Tālib ﷺ over 'Uthmān b. Affān rather than over Abū-Bakr and 'Umar. A very large number among the Companions and the Followers (*tābe'īn*, or the generation that followed that of the Companions) believed in Sh'īa Islam as so defined.

In his biographical portrayal of Abān b. Taghallub and in his refutation of those who disputed his reliability as a transmitter of hadīth reports, Shams od-Dīn adh-Dhahabī says, "Reprehensible innovation (*bid'a*) is of two types: the lesser reprehensible innovation, like the hyperbole of the Sh'ia; and the greater reprehensible innovation [which puts a given person outside of the fold of religion]. We see a great number of the followers of the Sh'īa who are religious, God-fearing, and honest. If the hadīth reports transmitted by people such as these are rejected, then what would in fact happen is that a large portion of the prophetic hadīth corpus will have been laid aside [to waste], and this is a manifest evil. The Sh'īa who exaggerated [the rank of Ali and his progeny] during the time of the Forefathers (*salaf*) and according to their custom, were people who engaged in arguments with 'Uthmān, Zubayr, Talha, Mu'āwiya, and anyone who fought Ali and cursed them."

2. Those who believe in the preeminence of Ali over all of the Companions, including Abū-Bakr and 'Umar, but nevertheless accept the caliphate of these two shaykhs and do not believe that any divinely-sanctioned investiture to succession (*nass*) has taken place in favor of Ali's succession or in favor of anyone else.

Some of the Mu'tazila of Baghdad and some of those from Basra fall into this group. We will end this section with a rather lengthy passage from Ibn Abī'l-Hadīd, the great Mu'tazelite scholar of the Shāfi'ī rite, writing in his commentary on the *Nahj al-Balāgha* concerning the issue of preeminence (*afḍalia*):

> "All of our religious leaders – may God's mercy be with them all – be they among the ancients or the contemporaries, or be they from [the school of] Baghdad or Basra, have a consensus on the belief that the pledge of allegiance to Abū-Bakr was a pledge that was proper and licit [according to the sacred laws of Islam], and that this pledge was not on account of a divinely-sanctioned investiture to succession (*nass*), but was [executed]

and established by a choice [which had the support] of consensus or otherwise; and this is a [legitimate] means [for the determination of the tenure of the office] of the imāmate.

"They differed concerning [the issue of] preeminence (*tafḍīl*). The older scholars among the Basrans such as Abī-'Uthmān Amr b. 'Ubayd, Abī-Ishāq Ibrāhīm b. Yassār an-Niẓām, Abī-'Uthmān 'Amr b. Bahr al-Jāhiz, Abī-Ma'n Thumāma b. Ashras, Abī-Muhammad Hāshim b. Amūr al-Fawtī, Abī-Ya'qūb Yūsuf b. Abdullāh ash-Shahām and a group of others maintain Abū-Bakr's preeminence over Ali ﷺ. This group maintains [the order of preeminence] in accordance with [the sequence of their accession to] the caliphate.

"In opposition to these, all of those from [the school of] Baghdad, be they among the ancients or the contemporaries, such as Abī-Sahl Bashr b. Mu'tamir, Abī-Mūsā b. Sabīh, Abī-Abdullāh Ja'far b. Mubashshir, Abī-Ja'far al-Iskāfī, Abī'l-Husayn al-Khayyāt, Abul-Qāsim Abdullāh b. Mahmūd al-Balkhī and their pupils maintain Ali's ﷺ preeminence over Abū-Bakr.

"Some among the Basrans such as Abū-Ali Muhammad b. Abdul-Wahhāb al-Jubāī have recently owned to this latter position. He used to be among those who were undecided (*mutawaqqifīn*), and inclined toward the preeminence of Ali ﷺ over everyone else but did not expressly state his position, preferring to keep his silence in his writings, and would not say anything. In many of his writings he has said, 'If the hadīth report of the Tāir[174] (a roasted chicken) is sound (*sahīh*), then Ali ﷺ is preeminent.'

[174] This famous hadīth report appears in Tirmidhī's Jāmi' (one of the *as-sihāh as-sitta*) from Anas with Tirmidhī's own chain of transmitters. Anas reports: "One day I was at the service of the Most Noble Prophet ﷺ and a chicken had

"Similarly, Qāḍī al-Quḍāt has stated in his commentary on Abul-Qāsim al-Balkhī's book al-Maqālāt, "Abū-Ali al-Jubbāī did not leave the world before he owned to Ali's ﷺ preeminence. He adds that he has heard this [assertion] from him [personally] and that he has not expressly stated this [position of his] in his writings." Qāḍī al-Quḍāt adds, "On the day that Abū-Ali al-Jubbāī passed from the world, he called his son, Abū-Hāshim, to his side and told him a matter in a weak voice, which included his owning to Ali's ﷺ preeminence.

"Among the Basrans who owned to Ali's ﷺ preeminence was Shaykh Abū-Abdullāh Husayn b. Ali al-Basrī. He was adamant about this matter and insisted upon it and has composed a lengthy book on the subject. Another Basran who owned to Ali's ﷺ preeminence was Qāḍī al-Quḍāt Abul-Hasan Abduj-Jabbār b. Ahmad. Citing the *al-kifāya*, which is a book of dogmatic or creedal theology (*kalām*), Mattūya writes, 'He was initially among those who were undecided (*mutawaqqifīn*) on the question of [the preeminence of] Ali ﷺ or Abū-Bakr, for which [position] he had made extensive arguments.'

"Many of the religious leaders – may God's ﷻ mercy be with them all – were undecided (*tawaqquf*) on the question of [the preeminence of] Ali ﷺ or Abū-Bakr, such as Abū-Hudhayfa Wāsil b. Atā and Abī'l-Hudhayl Muhammad b.

---

been roasted. His Eminence ﷺ raised his hands up in supplication and prayed: 'O Lord! Send me your most beloved of servants to eat this roasted chicken with me!' Then Ali ﷺ came and ate the chicken with the Prophet ﷺ." The hadīth report appears with many different chains of transmission in many different sources, including Tabarī's *Tafsīr* 1:226, 7:96 & 10:343; Dhahabī, *Mīzān al-I'tidāl*, 2280, 2633, 7671 & 8506; Ibn Hajar, *Lisān al-Mīzān*, 1:71 & 1:85; as well as many others, such as *Kanz ul-U'mmāl, al-Mishkāt, Majma' az-Zawā'id, Tārīkh ad-Damishq*, etc.

Hudhayl al-Allāf, from among the early scholars. And even though these two were undecided as to the question of preeminence when it concerned Ali ﷺ, Abū-Bakr and 'Umar, they had certainty concerning Ali's ﷺ preeminence over 'Uthmān.

"Among others who maintained the position of uncertainty (*tawaqquf*) were Shaykh Abū-Hāshem Abd os-Salām b. Abī-Ali and Shaykh Ab'ul-Husayn Muhammad b. Ali b. Tayyib al-Basrī.

"But we [i.e. Ibn Abī'l-Hadīd] hold the same position that our Baghdādī masters maintained and who said that Ali ﷺ is preeminent [among all men after the Prophet ﷺ]. We have mentioned in our books on dogmatic or creedal theology (*kalām*) what we mean by preeminence, and whether by this is meant [one whose piety and nobility of character warrants] a greater amount of *thawāb* (rewards given by God ﷻ for performed good deeds and oblations), or, one whose [personality is endowed] with the benefits of virtue and a greater share of the temperance of character; and we stated in our books that Ali ﷺ is preeminent in terms of both definitions."[175]

The Meaning of Sh'ïa Islam in its Specific Sense

The position of Sh'ïa Islam in its specific sense (i.e. as a formal denomination) is that Ali ﷺ has preeminence over all of the people of the community after the Prophet ﷺ. Additionally, the Sh'ïa believe that there is scriptural evidence of a specific designation on the part of the Most Noble Prophet ﷺ of the divine investiture of Ali ﷺ to his succession (*nass*); that this designation was vested in Ali ﷺ by divine

[175] Ibn Abī'l-Hadīd, Commentary on the *Nahj al-Balāgha*, 1:7.

command; and that tenure to the office of the imāmate resides in Ali's ؑ progeny.

This is a definition that had widespread applicability and to which a number of the close Companions of the Apostle ﷺ of God ﷻ had attained to faith in and conveyed to others. This creed has continued from that time to the present and has become more pronounced with each passing generation. This is the creed of Twelver Sh'īa Islam, which we shall proceed to summarize below.

The Creed of Twelver Sh'īa Islam

Twelver Sh'īa Muslims believe in the imāmate of the Twelve Imāms that are mentioned in the chart at the beginning of the book.

For proving this belief of theirs, the Sh'īa rely on categorical scriptural imperatives (*nusūs*) from the Prophet ﷺ which are acceptable to both sects concerning the divine investiture to succession and the regency (*walāya*ʾ) of Ali b. Abī-Tālib ؑ by the Apostle ﷺ of God ﷻ. Some of these scriptural imperatives have already been discussed, the most important of which is the hadīth reporting the Sermon of Ghadīr Khumm. Additionally, there is the Hadīth of the Two Weighty Trusts, in which the Apostle ﷺ of God ﷻ explicitly states the necessity of adherence to the Members of his Household.

"There will be Twelve Imāms after me."

In our previous discussions, we also discussed who the Members of the Household of the Prophet ﷺ are, and how the rest of the Imāms and the fact that they are twelve in number is referenced not just in the prophetic hadīth corpus that is explicitly accepted by the Sh'īa but also appear in sound Sunni hadith reports.

These hadith reports have been narrated by the great *muhaddithūn* (the scholars of the science of hadīth) of the majoritarian sect, including Bokhārī and Muslim, let alone the rest of the compilers of the *sihāh* and *masānīd* (authoritative compilations of books of hadīth). In these authoritative compilations, it is reported from Jāber b. Samara as follows (the wording is as it appears in Bokharī): "I heard the Apostle ﷺ of God ﷻ say, 'There will be twelve *amīrs* (leaders; rulers).' He then said some words that I did not hear. My father said [that the Prophet ﷺ said,] 'they will all be from the Quraysh [tribe].'" This hadīth report has been narrated by compilers of hadīth reports with slightly differing variations such as "There will be twelve caliphs;' and 'There will be twelve men;' and 'There will be twelve guardians (*qayyim*).'

Sunnī scholars are bewildered as to who these twelve people are! Ibn Kathīr has stated:

> "What is meant by this [hadīth report] is not the twelve people which the *rawāfiḍ* [a pejorative term for the Sh'īa] believe in because the people whom they count [as leaders] never had responsibility for administering the affairs of the people, other than Ali b. Abī-Tālib ﵇ and his son Hasan ﵇. The last of the people whom they consider [to be the subject of the hadīth report] is the Awaited Mahdī (Guided One) who, according to the beliefs of the *rawāfiḍ*, disappeared in a cellar in Sāmarrā and has no existence, presence or trace. Rather, what is meant by these twelve people [which have been referred to] in the hadīth report are the four rightly-guided caliphs (Abū-Bakr, 'Umar, 'Uthmān and Ali ﵃), and then, 'Umar b. Abdul-Azīz [who] is [also] one of them; and there is no conflict between the imāms [referred to] in the hadīth report on the basis of both versions of the report [which appear in] Sunnī [sources] concerning the interpretation of [who it is to which the hadīth of] 'the twelve [emirs]' refers."

And then, after having presented the texts of the hadīth report, Ibn Kathīr relates the positions of different scholars on the possible meaning of the hadīth, such as Bayhaqī, but ultimately, cannot make the number work. This is because these scholars attempt to marry the Omayyad sultans to the Rightly Guided Caliphs in order to come up with the number twelve, and in so doing, they are forced to include such people as Yazīd b. Mu'āwiya and Walīd b. Yazīd b. Abdul-Malik in their count sequence. This they do while Ibn Kathīr has stated about Walīd b. Yazīd b. Abdol-Malek elsewhere that "He is a morally corrupt degenerate concerning whom we have brought hadīth reports to bear wherein he is cursed and condemned." In addition to this, if the sultans of the Umayyads are to be counted in the equation, the total number will exceed twelve. Thus, they are forced into arbitrarily eliminating some of them on the pretext that "they were not acceptable to everyone" (as if the rest were)! At all events, they do not arrive at any definitive conclusions.

Ibn Kathīr concludes, "The position of Abī'l-Jald is closer to the truth because Abī'l-Jald has studied old books and has found the following meaning in the Tawrāt: 'Verily God ﷻ gave the glad tiding of Ishmael to Abraham, telling him that he will increase his progeny and will select twelve great men from among his seed.'" After this, Ibn Kathīr relates his teacher Ibn Taymīya al-Harrānī's position, the essence of which is as follows: "... And these are persons concerning whom glad tidings have been given in the hadīth report of Jābir b. Samara, and it has been established that these [twelve] appear in the community sporadically [!] and that the Day of Resurrection will not arrive until all of them have made their appearances [at random!] And [it is the case that] many of the Jews who have inclined to Islam have made the mistake of thinking that these [twelve] are the self-same persons about whom the *rawāfid* sect (i.e. the Twelver Shī'a) make their call and whom they follow."

It has been admitted in the above words that the scripture of the People of the Book (i.e. recipients of earlier revelations; the reference here is to the Jewish converts and to their *Tawrā'*) informs them that these twelve people are Members of the Household of the Prophet ﷺ, which is of course what the Sh'īa believe, and that that is why they converted to Islam and adopted its Sh'īa form or denomination.

Of course, one cannot pay any attention to the words of Ibn Taymīya where he says that "these [twelve] appear in the community sporadically", for no such thing appears in the text of the hadīth report! Furthermore, the number of these alleged "sporadic [or random] appearances" has not reached twelve to date, despite the fact that the Islamic caliphate was brought to an end in 1924.[176]

Ibn Hajar al-Asqalānī also weighs in on this subject, relating the position of some other scholars such as Ibn Jawzī and others. Ibn Jawzī states, "There has been much discussion concerning the content and meaning of this hadīth report. I have investigated the various speculations and conjectures and have consulted with countless individuals concerning this matter, but I was not able to reach my purpose because the wordings of the reports vary, and there is no doubt that this confusion is due to the narrators [themselves]."[177]

Clearly, the differences of opinion concerning the interpretation of the hadīth report of the Sunnī scholars and their anxieties have to do with the presence of words such as caliph and emir.

---

[176] On March 3, 1924, the first President of the Turkish Republic, Mustafa Kemal, constitutionally abolished the institution of the Caliphate as part of his secular reforms. Its powers within Turkey were transferred to the Grand National Assembly of Turkey, the parliament of the newly formed Turkish Republic. The title was then claimed by King Hussein bin Ali of Hijaz, leader of the Arab Revolt, but his kingdom was defeated and annexed by Ibn Saud in 1925.

[177] Ibn Hajar al-Asqalānī, *Fath al-Bārī fī Sharh Sahīh al-Bokhārī*, 13:181.

They per force believed that the Prophet ﷺ referred to the Omayyad and Abbāsid caliphs and other such illegitimate ruling powers (*tāghūt*) and failed to understand that the Prophet's intended meaning by words such as "emirate" and "caliphate" is none other than the imāmate or the Islamic form of government whose ambit is very wide and can include imāms who do not have de facto powers, just as the Prophet ﷺ himself did not have any de facto power in Mecca prior to his emigration to Medina.

The Sh'īa Creed in Brief[178]

Tawhīd: the Unicity of Creatorship

Tawhīd means that there is only one God ﷻ; that He has no co-equal partners; that he is the Necessary Being in His essence; that He is not begotten, and that He does not beget; He is perfect and flawless, is not bound by the limits of time or place, and there is nothing like unto Him; He is uncreated and unsubstantial (being the cause and originator of all of the realities which we refer to as creation and substance); He cannot be seen by the physical eye, either in this world or in the world of the hereafter; and all of his essential Attributes such as 'the all-living', 'the all-powerful', 'the all-knowing', and 'will' are exactly equivalent to and no different from His Essence.

'Adl (Justice)

Shaykh Mufīd has summarized this principle as follows: "Verily, God ﷻ is Just and Benevolent (*karīm*), and has created His bondsmen in order that they might worship Him, and has ordered them to obey Him, and has prohibited them from transgressing [His bounds]. Everyone has been given guidance by Him and everyone is the beneficiary of His beneficence, munificence and grace.

[178] Based on Muzaffar, Shaykh Muhammad Reḍā, *'Aqāid al-Imāmīa*, p. 36 ff.

لَا يُكَلِّفُ اللَّهُ نَفْسًا إِلَّا وُسْعَهَا ۚ لَهَا مَا كَسَبَتْ وَعَلَيْهَا مَا اكْتَسَبَتْ ۗ
رَبَّنَا لَا تُؤَاخِذْنَا إِن نَّسِينَا أَوْ أَخْطَأْنَا ۚ رَبَّنَا وَلَا تَحْمِلْ عَلَيْنَا إِصْرًا كَمَا
حَمَلْتَهُ عَلَى الَّذِينَ مِن قَبْلِنَا ۚ رَبَّنَا وَلَا تُحَمِّلْنَا مَا لَا طَاقَةَ لَنَا بِهِ ۖ وَاعْفُ
عَنَّا وَاغْفِرْ لَنَا وَارْحَمْنَا ۚ أَنتَ مَوْلَانَا فَانصُرْنَا عَلَى الْقَوْمِ الْكَافِرِينَ
﴿٢٨٦﴾

[2:286] God ﷻ does not burden any human being with more than he is well able to bear: in his favor shall be whatever good he does, and against him whatever evil he does.;

الَّذِي خَلَقَ سَبْعَ سَمَاوَاتٍ طِبَاقًا ۖ مَّا تَرَىٰ فِي خَلْقِ الرَّحْمَٰنِ مِن تَفَاوُتٍ ۖ
فَارْجِعِ الْبَصَرَ هَلْ تَرَىٰ مِن فُطُورٍ ﴿٣﴾

[67:3] He created seven heavens in full harmony with one another: no fault will thou see in the creation of the Most Gracious. He is not in need of any partner. He does not punish anyone other than for his sin,

إِنَّ اللَّهَ لَا يَظْلِمُ مِثْقَالَ ذَرَّةٍ ۖ وَإِن تَكُ حَسَنَةً يُضَاعِفْهَا وَيُؤْتِ مِن لَّدُنْهُ
أَجْرًا عَظِيمًا ﴿٤٠﴾

[4:40] Verily, God ﷻ does not wrong [anyone] by as much as an atom's weight; and if there be a good deed, He will multiply it, and will bestow out of His grace a mighty reward.

[All of this is part of the Sh'ïa creed] while most of the other sects within Islam hold that it is possible for God ﷻ to punish a righteous believer without his having committed a sin! To reward a sinner and to enter him into heaven! This is an injustice that is attributed to God ﷻ while he is innocent of such charges. The Mu'tazelites are of the same opinion with the Sh'īa on this issue, which is why they are at times referred to as the *'Adlīya* (justice-centered)."

3. Nubuwwa^t (Prophethood)

The Sh'īa believe that the sending of prophets for the guidance of humanity and as deliverers of warning is a necessity, and that God the Sublimely Exalted has indeed sent His prophets to mankind from the time of Adam ﷺ and has brought this cycle of prophecy to a close with the Seal of the Prophets, the Prophet Muhammad ﷺ. The *sharīa^t* (revealed law) brought by Prophet Muhammad ﷺ, who is personally immaculate (defined as being immune to errors of judgement as well as to being immune to sin and vice and any ignobility) prior to his commission to prophethood as well as after it, shall be in effect until the Day of Resurrection, Prophet Muhammad ﷺwords and deeds of the Prophet ﷺ are not motivated by bodily desires and urges or by base emotions; rather, his words and deeds are a form of revelation, prophets being theophanies but never incarnations of God ﷻ. The Sh'īa also believe that the Prophet Muhammad ﷺ executed his mission completely and perfectly and explicated the bounds of the revealed law which define the bounds of the 'broad path' (*sharīa^t*) within which Muslims have the leeway to travel on their path back to God ﷻ, and believe that the Quran, which descended from heaven unto him, is not uncreated (*qadīm*), because only God ﷻ the Exalted is uncreated; and that no falsity can enter into His book (the Quran), which is immune to any and all distortion and corruption until the Day of Judgement.

4. *Imāma*[t] (The Imāmate or the religio-political leadership of the community)

The *Imāmī* (Twelver) Sh'īa believe that the imāmate is a grace from God concerning the proclamation of which it would be improper for a prophet to neglect. Our Prophet did indeed appoint Ali b. Abī-Tālib as the Imām of the community after him in his last sermon at Ghadīr Khumm and, as has been reported in a large number of hadīth reports, called upon all the believers to entrust in him and to follow his lead, just as he called upon all the believers to entrust and follow the lead of the Members of his Household (the *ahl al-bayt*).

5. *Ma'ād* (The Return [back to God]; Escatology)

Ma'ād means that all of God's creatures will be raised from the dead on the Day of Resurrection in order that God reward or punish them in accordance with their deeds: anyone who has done good shall be rewarded for it, and anyone who has been wicked shall be punished for their wickedness. Intercession is real and is a privilege reserved for Muslims who have committed major sins. The unbelievers (*kuffār*) and the idolaters (*mushrikūn*) shall have their place in the eternal fire.

The foregoing was a very concise summary of the creed of the Imāmī (Twelver) Sh'īa, which we mention in passing as a method to disabuse people of false notions and accusations which have been levelled against the Sh'īa. Some have accused the Sh'īa of the sin of belief in incarnation and other such deviant beliefs, and their objective is simply to paint an ugly picture of what Sh'īa Islam really is.

5 - Disambiguation from Deviated and Extremist Sects

Deviated Sects

The events that occurred after the death of the Prophet ﷺ resulted in the victory of those who considered it legitimate to practice *ijtihād* against the express will of the Apostle ﷺ of God ﷻ, and their accession to power and to the caliphate. This fact simultaneously caused the Sh'īa to be turned into a protestant group or a group arrayed in opposition to the ruling power; this opposition was especially evident during the reigns of the Umayyads and Abbāsids. The ruling powers attempted to destroy and eliminate the Sh'īa but were unsuccessful, despite the intensity and violence of their efforts, the Sh'īa continued to remain a threat to their dominion by both overt and covert means. Faced with the failure of brute force as their first line of attack, the authorities decided to enter the Sh'īa citadel by way of deception and cultural penetration and by painting a false picture of what true Sh'īa beliefs are. To this end, they entered penetration agents into the ranks of the Sh'īa so that they could inseminate poisonous ideas and deviant beliefs in the midst of the unsophisticated and uninformed masses. In this way, they would attain to their objectives because the masses would turn away from the Sh'īa and, as a consequence of this, there would be an inverse increase in the power and standing of their illegitimate powers. Or at a minimum, in this way, the Shī'a could be portrayed as a deviant and hence declawed sect, thereby rendering it incapable of threatening their reign.

This is why we see the phenomenon of the rise of groups or individuals who averred deviant and corrupt beliefs which had no bearing whatever on Islam and its teachings, and who claimed, despite this, that they were the "followers" of the Members of the Household of the Prophet ﷺ. By thus undermining the credibility of the Ahl al-Bayt ؑ in the eyes of the unwitting masses, the popular base and support of the Household of the Prophet ﷺ could be weakened, paving the way for their marginalization and eventual destruction.

Of course, the Imāms of the Household of the Prophet ﷺ were fully cognizant of the situation and continually warned their devotees against falling into the traps of these deviant individuals and groups. However, their warnings notwithstanding, due to the enforced isolation of the Imāms and the vast distances that lay between Medina where the they were domiciled (usually under house arrest) and the far reaches of the newly-acquired realms of Islam where some of their followers were, sometimes these psychological operations met with relative success and these false-flag charmers were able to muster up a following. Meanwhile, the authentic path of the Twelver Shī'a continued with their teachings despite all of the various false theses and *shubahāt* (intentional misdirection; confounding or discombobulating memes; misconceptions; misunderstandings; spurious arguments; distractions; dubious positions; erroneous or faulty thoughts or beliefs; calumnies) levelled at and against them, and deviant groups such as the Ghulāt were unable to tarnish their lustrous image.

As was stated earlier, entrusting in the twelve Imāms of the Ahl al-Bayt ؑ is a practical application of total obedience to the express will (*nass*) of the Prophet ﷺ, who made adherence to the Members of his House a categorically incumbent religious duty. This categorical imperative of the Prophet's ﷺ causes those who abide by it to follow the true path of Islam and prevents the inclination toward the path of *ijtihad* (those who believed in the legitimacy of their personally-derived opinions to stand against the express will of the Apostle ﷺ of God ﷻ); but some among the ranks of the Sh'īa did not remain steadfast on this path and inclined toward others mid-stream, such as the Zaydīs and Ismāīlīs, who share many beliefs in common with the Sh'īa, but who differ on others. We shall summarize their beliefs briefly.

The Zaydīs

The Zaydīs believe in the preeminence of Ali ؑ over all of the Companions of the Prophet ﷺ but nevertheless own to the legitimacy of the caliphates of Abū-Bakr and 'Umar, considering the priority of one who is less preeminent over one who is the most preeminent to be legitimate and proper. They also maintain that tenure to the imāmate after the martyrdom of Husayn b. Ali b. Abī-Tālib ؑ can reside in the person of anyone who is born in the line of Lady Fatema ؑ and who is learned, courageous, and pious, and who rises up in insurrection with a sword against the illegitimate ruling power of the age.

The Jārūdīya are among the sub-groups of the Zaydīya. They believe in the preeminence of Ali b. Abī-Tālib ؑ and do not believe that anyone has the right to usurp the station to which this preeminence entitles him. According to their beliefs, anyone who does not admit to this station of Ali's ؑ is an unbeliever (*kāfir*), and that by failing to pledge allegiance to him, the community of Muslims has in fact apostatized and deviated from the true path. They believe that the imāmate after Ali ؑ resided in Hasan b. Ali ؑ and after him, in Husayn b. Ali ؑ, after which it passes to the progeny of these two by way of consultative councils, and that anyone from among their progeny who rises in insurrection and who has the competence for the office and receives the support of his piers becomes the Imām.[179]

The important point to note is that the beliefs of the Zaydīs are close to the meaning of Sh'īa Islam in its general or broad sense, as was held by the Mu'tazelites of Baghdad and by some of the Basran Mu'tazelites (see above, in this same chapter).

The Ismāīlīs

After the death of Imām Ja'far as-Sādiq ﵇, this sect came to believe in the imāmate of his son Ismāīl who predeceased him. They claimed that Ismāīl had not died and shall not die until he becomes the master of the world.

Among their beliefs is that the Quran has an outward and an inward aspect, according to which the Quranic expression [17:44] *The seven heavens extol His limitless glory, and the earth, and all that they contain*; refers to the seven Imāms. In the book *The Principles of the Beliefs of the People of Muhammad* ﷺ it is stated that the revealed law of Islam has an inner aspect which is hidden from all but the Imām or his deputy (*nāyib*), and that everything that appears in the Quran concerning the Gathering on the Day of Judgement and other matters are symbolic of the mysteries of the Quran's true inner meaning.

For example, *ghusl* (a form of ritual ablution of the entire body in accordance to directions provided by the revealed law) is thought to be symbolic of the renewal of one's vows; the ritual devotions and prayers are thought to be symbolic of supplications for the Imām; *zakāt* (the purifying poor due) is thought to stimulate the knowledge of the one for whose purification the *zakat* is paid, and who is deserving of this knowledge; and ritual fasting (*sawm*) is thought to be the hiding of knowledge from those who only understand the superficial aspects of reality; the Hajj pilgrimage ritual is thought to be symbolic of the quest

[179] Baqdādī, Abdul-Qāher b. Tāhir, *al-Farq bayn al-Firaq*, 39.

for knowledge; the Ka'ba is thought to be symbolic of the Prophet ﷺ; the door of the Ka'ba is thought to be symbolic of Imām Ali ؑ, *Safā*[180] is thought to be symbolic of the Prophet ﷺ; and *Marwā* is thought to be symbolic of Imām Ali ؑ, and the *Mīqāt* (the appointed place) is thought to symbolize the Imām, the *talbīya* (requesting) is thought to mean the compliance with the call towards God ﷻ; and the seven *tawāf* (circumambulations around the Ka'ba) are thought to mean the circumambulation around Muhammad ﷺ in the number corresponding to the seven Imāms, and so on.[181]

Having thus reviewed these beliefs, we can now see that these sects do not represent the Shʿīa Islam that was founded by the Prophet ﷺ and which has survived to the present day. We can also see that the denomination which represents the mission and the teachings of the ministry of the Most Noble Prophet ﷺ and which has observed and heeded his instructions is the Twelver Shʿīa denomination of Islam.

Extremism and the Extremists (*Ghulū wa Ghulāt*)

What has occasioned our including this subject in our discussion is the fact that the beliefs of the Ghulāt are oftentimes conflated with those of Twelver Shʿīa Islam in the minds of a large number of the general public and in the minds of many researchers as well, both contemporary and among the earlier generations, in all of whose minds a general confusion reigns between the two. This is despite the fact that most of the Ghulāt and their sub-sect offshoots have been extinct for centuries; nonetheless, a number of people, either deliberately or out of their utter ignorance of the facts, ascribe the beliefs of the Shʿīa to those of the Ghulāt.

---

[180] This term and the few others that follow in italics refer to specific places or practices which are part of the greater Hajj pilgrimage ritual.
[181] The Principles of the Beliefs of the People of Muhammad ﷺ, page 8.

Unfortunately, some employ the word *rāfeḍī* (plural, *rawāfeḍ*; refuser(s), rejector(s)) in order to demean and denigrate the Sh'īa and as a technique to continue their conflation with extremist Ghulāt views and with the views of other deviant sects, all of which they put in one basket and refer to as *rāfiḍī* and *rawāfiḍ*; all of which is just another part of their underhanded efforts to continue their marginalization and ostracism of the Sh'īa. For example, Ibn Taymīya produces a series of bizarre and morally corrupt beliefs and attributes them wholesale to "the *rāfiḍa*", thereby making the reader believe that these beliefs are subscribed to by all of the Sh'īa. After having filled several pages with his poisoned pen in this vein, he then says, "What is important to remember is that the reprehensible words and deeds of the Sh'īa variety that exist are several times more numerous than what we have been able to describe, but that not all of these [beliefs] obtain in the Twelver Imāmīya or Zaydīya [factions], but [rather,] much of these [beliefs] are held by the Ghulāt and their laity."[182]

The main difficulty that is the cause of these unwarranted ascriptions to the Twelver Sh'īa is that many of the deviant sects and Ghulāt claim amity and affinity with the Ahl al-Bayt ﷺ. What exacerbated the confusion was that many of these sects and cults originated in the town of Kūfa, which was the center of Sh'īa Islam, it having been the garrison town which Imām Ali fought all of the internecine wars that were imposed on him out of, and so became the de facto capital of his caliphate. This town was the epicenter of the exchange of imported sectarian and syncretic views and of heated debates between various factions such as the Manicheans and other dualist forms of belief which grew out of the Magian culture. These dualists believed in the incarnation of God ﷻ in human form, in pantheism, and/ or in the transmigration of souls or reincarnation and other such Hindu accretions which had found widespread acceptance in

[182] Ibn Taymīya, *Minhāj as-Sunna' an-Nabawīya*, 1:57.

the minds of the naïve and gullible masses among certain sectors of the population. And because the Members of the Household of the Prophet ﷺ held a special place of honor and respect among the Muslims and especially among the Kūfan Sh'īa, the Ghulāt would claim that they are associated with the Ahl al-Bayt ﷺ of the Prophet ﷺ and are among their devotees and followers, in order to ingratiate themselves and gain the hearts and minds of the people, paving the way for the propagation of their bogus beliefs.

The Imāms of the Ahl al-Bayt ﷺ would point to these wayward groups and would warn all of the Muslims and especially those who were their followers away from their deceptions and shenanigans, as we shall describe below.

One of the difficulties in the discussions on the topic of the extremists is the absence of a clear definition of their views which sometimes caused a general confusion between certain concepts and beliefs. Thus, it is necessary to provide some clarifications.

The word *ghulū* literally means "leaving the [original] purpose" or "transgressing the bounds [of something]". Thus, any deviation from moderation is a form of *ghulū*. Ibn Manzūr writes, "*ghulā fi'd-dīn wa'l-amr; yaghlū ghulū*[an]", which means that he transgressed the bounds of his religion. And we find in the Quran, *lā taghghlū fī dīnikum*: [4:171] *Do not overstep the bounds [of truth] in your religious beliefs*. Nevertheless, we do not find a comprehensive definition for the word when it is used as an idiomatic expression that refers to a sect or a group of sects with extremist beliefs. However, by referring to the extant scholarly materials which talk about the beliefs of this extinct sect, we can arrive at a definition that describes *ghulū* as a deviation from the original purpose in the belief concerning certain individuals, elevating them to a status or rank that does not belong or apply to them.

And so, *ghulū* or extremist tendencies can start off with the exaggeration of the virtues of a person, and gradually degenerate to the point where the person is believed, in turn, to be a prophet and, ultimately, to be the incarnation of God ﷻ, and be turned into an object of worship. Thus, we can say that exaggeration of the virtues of a person is a form of *ghulū*. Given that, we can then go on to say that the authoritative sources of Sunnī hadīth scripture are full of the fabricated, exaggerated virtues of some of the Companions which were contrived during the Omayyad period for the purpose of destroying the virtues of Ali ﷺ and putting an end to the station of honor in which the Banī-Hāshim were held, as has been admitted to by some of the reliable memorizers and transmitters from among the Sunnites, such as Madāinī and Naftūya. An example of such a hadīth report is: "God ﷻ appears in epiphanies (*mutijallī*) to people generally and to Abū-Bakr and 'Umar specifically, and the angels feel belittled and ashamed (*hayā'*) [compared] to 'Uthmān." There are also such reports of the supposed virtues and excellences of 'Āisha, Talha and Zubayr in the Sunnī *hadīth* corpus, and these are people who arose in insurrection against the Imām of their time to whom they had pledged allegiance and obedience to whom was categorically incumbent upon them.

Some of the Sufis among the Sunnite sect have also committed exaggerations (*gholū*) about their shaykhs and have made some outrageous claims about them, at times raising their rank to above that of the Prophet ﷺ! Similarly, some of the adherents of the four Sunnite rites have made some exaggerated claims about their respective Imāms, taking their claims to extremes.

The Rāwandī sect, which goes back to its eponymous founder Abdullāh ar-Rāwandī, has taken their exaggerations about the Abbāsids to the limits of unbelief (*kufr*). This sect has claimed that Abū-Hāshim has made a testamentary will (*wasīa'*) concerning the succession of Muhammad b. Ali b. Abdollah b. Abbās b. Abdul-Muttalib, basing their claim on the allegation that he left this world in the area of Sharā in Shām (the Levant) while at his side, and that the testamentary will reached him by way of his father, Ali b. Abdullāh. The Rāwandī sect believes that "He was an Imām! He was God ﷻ!! And was omniscient. And so, anyone who recognizes him [as such] will be able to achieve whatsoever feat [he desires]!"

Thereupon, Muhammad b. Ali made a testamentary will in favor of his son Ibrāhīm b. Muhammad, known as "the Imām". He was the first among the children of Abbās in whom the imāmate was vested. Abū-Muslim of Khorāsān called the people to [obey] him. Thereupon, Ibrāhīm b. Muhammad made a testamentary will in favor of his brother Abul-Qāsim Abdullāh b. Muhammad, known as "as-Sifāh". He was the first caliph of the Banī-Abbās (the Abbāsids) to make a testamentary will in favor of Abū-Ja'far Abdullāh b. Muhammad, known as "al-Mansūr" to succeed him, as well as to his son Muhammad b. Abdullāh al-Mahdī, but the Abbāsid al-Mahdī denied the fact that the Prophet ﷺ had made a testamentary will in favor of Muhammad b. al-Hanafīya, but rather, claimed that the Prophet ﷺ had made a testamentary will in favor of Abbās b. Abdul-Muttalib because Abbās was his uncle and his heir and his closest kin. It is further alleged that after the passing of the Prophet ﷺ Abū-Bakr, 'Umar, 'Uthmān and Ali ؑ usurped the caliphate from the progeny of Abbās! And that in fact, the caliphate had been vested in Abbās after the passing of the Prophet ﷺ, after whom it is vested in his son Abdullāh b. Abbās, and then it is vested in his son Ali b. Abdullāh, and then in Ibrāhīm b. Muhammad al-Imām, and then to his brother Abdullāh, and then to his brother Abul-Qāsim, and then to his brother Abū-Ja'far Abdullāh b. Muhammad al-Mansūr, etc.

The Rāwandī sect believe that the Imām is omniscient and is in fact Almighty God ﷻ Himself! He gives life and takes life, and Abū-Muslim of Khorāsān had been sent by Him as His prophet and had knowledge of the unseen. He had been sent by Abū-Ja'far Abdullāh b. Muhammad al-Mansūr who is none other than God ﷻ Himself! He was privy to all of their secrets and openly proclaimed their call, inviting the people to [obey] them!

When these claims reached al-Mansūr, he rounded up a number of the Rāwandīs, who confessed to their beliefs. Al-Mansūr ordered them to repent and to turn their backs to such beliefs, but they said, "Verily, al-Mansūr is our God ﷻ! And it is He who shall take our lives while we shall become martyrs! Just as he takes the lives of his apostles and prophets and whomsoever he wills! Some of them he puts to death by way of accident, and some he takes by way of attacks by wild beasts, and he takes the spirits of some [back to himself] in a manner that is sudden or for reasons known [only] to him! All of this is in accordance with his will and he does whatsoever he wills concerning his creatures, and it is not meet to question his will![183]

The *ghulū* phenomenon of exaggeration to the point of extremism existed in the religions of the past as well. The Jews claimed the status of prophethood for Ezra, a prophet concerning whom Almighty God ﷻ has stated:

أَوْ كَالَّذِي مَرَّ عَلَىٰ قَرْيَةٍ وَهِيَ خَاوِيَةٌ عَلَىٰ عُرُوشِهَا قَالَ أَنَّىٰ يُحْيِي هَٰذِهِ
اللَّهُ بَعْدَ مَوْتِهَا ۖ فَأَمَاتَهُ اللَّهُ مِائَةَ عَامٍ ثُمَّ بَعَثَهُ ۖ قَالَ كَمْ لَبِثْتَ ۖ قَالَ لَبِثْتُ
يَوْمًا أَوْ بَعْضَ يَوْمٍ ۖ قَالَ بَل لَّبِثْتَ مِائَةَ عَامٍ ﴿٢٥٩﴾

[2:259] Or [art thou, O man, of the same mind] as he who passed by a town deserted by its people, with its roofs caved in, [and] said, "How could God ﷻ bring all this back to life after its death?" Thereupon God ﷻ caused him to be dead for a hundred years; where after He brought him back to life [and] said: "How long hast thou remained thus?" He answered: "I have remained

183 Nowbakhtī, *Feraq osh-Sh'ia*,46-50.

> thus a day, or part of a day." Said [God ﷻ]: "Nay, but thou hast remained thus for a hundred years!

The Noble Quran describes the abhorrent statements of the Jews concerning Ezra as follows:

> وَقَالَتِ الْيَهُودُ عُزَيْرٌ ابْنُ اللَّهِ وَقَالَتِ النَّصَارَى الْمَسِيحُ ابْنُ اللَّهِ ۖ ذَٰلِكَ
> قَوْلُهُم بِأَفْوَاهِهِمْ ۖ يُضَاهِئُونَ قَوْلَ الَّذِينَ كَفَرُوا مِن قَبْلُ ۚ قَاتَلَهُمُ اللَّهُ ۚ أَنَّىٰ
> يُؤْفَكُونَ ﴿٣٠﴾

> [9:30] And the Jews say, "Ezra is God's ﷻ son," while the Christians say, "The Christ is God's ﷻ son." Such are the sayings which they utter with their mouths, following in spirit assertions made in earlier times by people who denied the truth! [They deserve the imprecation:] "May God ﷻ destroy them!" How perverted are their minds!

The reason for these claims is that miracles emanated from him, and they took this to mean that he was a deity. The same situation also occurred in the case of the Christians, who exaggerated the rank of Jesus and claimed his divinity, which is why the Quran follows the reprimand of the Jews with one of the Christians.

> يَا أَهْلَ الْكِتَابِ لَا تَغْلُوا فِي دِينِكُمْ وَلَا تَقُولُوا عَلَى اللَّهِ إِلَّا الْحَقَّ ۚ إِنَّمَا
> الْمَسِيحُ عِيسَى ابْنُ مَرْيَمَ رَسُولُ اللَّهِ وَكَلِمَتُهُ أَلْقَاهَا إِلَىٰ مَرْيَمَ وَرُوحٌ مِّنْهُ ۖ
> فَآمِنُوا بِاللَّهِ وَرُسُلِهِ ۖ وَلَا تَقُولُوا ثَلَاثَةٌ ۚ انتَهُوا خَيْرًا لَّكُمْ ۚ إِنَّمَا اللَّهُ إِلَٰهٌ
> وَاحِدٌ ۖ سُبْحَانَهُ أَن يَكُونَ لَهُ وَلَدٌ ۘ لَّهُ مَا فِي السَّمَاوَاتِ وَمَا فِي الْأَرْضِ ۗ
> وَكَفَىٰ بِاللَّهِ وَكِيلًا ﴿١٧١﴾

> [4:171] O Followers of the Gospel! Do not overstep the bounds [of truth] in your religious beliefs, and do not say of God ﷻ anything but the truth. The Christ Jesus, son of Mary, was but God's ﷻ Apostle - [the fulfilment of] His promise which He had conveyed unto Mary - and a soul created by Him. Believe, then, in God ﷻ and His apostles, and do not say, "[God ﷻ is] a trinity". Desist [from this assertion] for your own good. God ﷻ is but One God ﷻ; utterly remote is He, in His glory, from having a son: unto Him belongs all that is in the heavens and all that is on earth; and none is as worthy of trust as God ﷻ.

Thus, it is not too far-fetched to hypothesize that extremisms of belief concerning human beings (*ghulū*) entered into the thinking of the Muslims by way of their contact with the People of the Book, just as other false beliefs gained currency among the Muslims by way of their contact with other religions such as Zoroastrianism, Mithraism, Manicheism, Hinduism and Buddhism. Furthermore, some of the People of the Book, inclusive of those who pretended to have accepted and entered into Islam, promoted such extremist beliefs within the minds of the uninformed and naïve masses of the Muslim populace in order to weaken their creedal pillars from within.

As stated earlier, none of the sects within Islam remained immune to the plague of extremist views, and each one has been guilty of extreme exaggeration of the virtues and excellences of their imāms to a point that far surpasses any rational standard. But what is strange is that it is a very rare occasion indeed when otherwise sober historians and experts ascribe ghulū extremism to any Muslim sect other than to the Sh'īa, which perennially stands accused of these charges as if it is the only sect who is saddled with this problem This is due, of course, to the lasting effect of the enmity and hatred of the sultans of the illegitimate Omayyad and Abbāsid powers with the rite of the Ahl al-Bayt ﷺ of the Prophet ﷺ who used every means within their power to inflict blow after blow to the creedal edifice of the Sh'īa.

The Sh'īa Position with respect to the Ghulāt

1. The Position of Twelver Sh'īa Scholarship

We have briefly reviewed the Twelver Sh'īa creed, noting that the unicity of God ﷻ and His transcendence are among the most basic of Sh'īa beliefs. These matters are nothing new and are readily available to anyone who has a genuine interest in understanding the Twelver Sh'īa creed. Nonetheless, a number of people continue to lump the Twelver Sh'īa in with the Ghulāt and classify the Sh'īa as idolaters and heretics. Thus, in the section that follows, we shall discuss the position taken by some of the Twelver Sh'īa scholars, both from among the ancients as well as from contemporary scholarship with respect to the Ghulāt, so that the Sh'īa position becomes clear.

Shaykh Mufid: "The Ghulāt are people who pretend to be Muslim. They are people who believe that Ali b. Abī-Tālib ﷺ and his immaculate progeny are deities and prophets and claim virtues for them in terms of religion and worldly [powers] which are extreme and go beyond all bounds [of reason and decency]. They are people who are wayward and who are heretics, and the Commander of the Faithful (Ali b. Abī-Tālib) ﷺ has ordered that they be killed and [that their bodies be] burned; and the Immaculate Imāms ﷺ have stated that the Ghulāt are heretics and are beyond the pale of Islam."[184]

---

[184] Mofīd, Shaykh, *Tashīh al-I'teqādāt al-Imāmīa*, p. 63.

Shaykh Saddūq: "Our belief concerning the Ghulāt and the Mafūḍa (a sub-sect of the Ghulāt) is that in comparison to the Jews, the Magians, the Qadrīya and Harwarīya and compared to all of those who have deviated and who hold deviant views, they are the worst."[185]

Muhaqqiq al-Hillī: "The Ghulāt are beyond the pale of the religion of Islam, irrespective of the fact that they pretend to be Muslims."[186]

Narāqī: "There is no doubt that the Ghulāt are anathema (*nijāsaʿ*); they believe that Ali ﷺ or some other people are deities."[187] Narāqī also states that "Holding prayer services for the dead of the *nawāsib*, *khawārij* and *ghulāt* is not permissible according to the consensus [of Twelver Shʿia scholarship], even if they feigned Islam [while alive]."[188]

Shaykh Muhammad Hasan Najafī: "The *ghulāt*, *nawāsib*, and *khawārij*, and others who necessarily deny the religion [of Islam due to the nature of their beliefs] do not [= are not legally permitted to] inherit from Muslims."[189]

Āqā Reḍā Hamadānī: "... concerning certain sects which are condemned as heretics. Among these is the Ghulāt [sect], for whose heresy there can be no doubt whatsoever, on the basis that they believe in the divinity of the Commander of the Faithful (Ali b. Abī-Tālib) ﷺ or another one of [God's ﷻ] creatures."[190]

---

[185] Saddūq, Shaykh, *al-Iʿteqādāt fī dīn al-Imāmīa*, 109.
[186] Muhaqqiq ol-Awwal, *al-Moʾtabar fī Sharh al-Moqtasar*, 1:98.
[187] Narāqī, Ahmad b. Muhammad al-Fāḍel, *Mustanad ash-Shʿia fī Ahkām ash-Sharʾīa*, 1:204.
[188] Ibid, 6:27.
[189] Najafī, Muhammad Hasan, Sāhib-e Jawāhir, *Jawāhir al-Kalām fī Sharh Sharāyeʿ al-Islām*, 39:32.
[190] Hamadānī, Hāj Āqā Reḍā, *Mesbāh al-Faqīh*, 2:568.

Sayyid Muhammad Riḍā Golpāyegānī: "Among the prerequisites of being a [legally sanctioned] butcher [for the ritual slaying of animals for meat in accordance with the sacred ordinances of Islam] (*dhābaḥ*) is that he be a Muslim or that he is considered to be a Muslim, as in the case of one who is born to Muslim parents. And a butcher who is an unbeliever is not legally sanctioned [to perform this task], whether he is an idolater, [heretic,] or otherwise [unqualified]; or whether he is one of the People of the Book (in all appearances (*al'al-aqwā*), as inward belief is not a precondition for a [legally sanctioned] butcher). Thus, [eating the meat of animals slaughtered by] butchers of all Islamic denominations is licit (*ḥalāl*), except for the *nawāseb* who are condemned as heretics, and these are people who are infamous [= known] for being the enemies of the Members of the Household of the Prophet (the Ahl al-Bayt 🌟), even though they [outwardly] feign to be Muslim. And this is also the case with other sects which feign Islam despite their having been condemned as heretics, such as the Ghulāt and *khawārij*."[191]

The above statements make it clear that the legally binding edicts (*ḥukm*) of the Twelver Shʿīa magisters (doctors of religio-legal jurisprudence, the ʿulamā) is for the anathematization (*nijāsaʿ*) of the Ghulāt and their condemnation as heretics, and that they are subject to all of the rulings that follow from and are consequent to this excommunication, such as their status as being ritually unclean (*najāsaʿ*), their inability to inherit from Muslims, the prohibition against the eating of meat that is ritually slaughtered by one of their number, and so on.

The position of the scholars whose expertise is the evaluation of the reliability of hadīth reports (*jarh wa taʿdīl*) is also very clear. For

---

[191] Golpāyegānī, Seyyed Muhammad Reḍā, *Hidāyat al-ʿIbād*, 2:217.

example, they have made the following statements concerning Abdullāh b. Sabā.[192]

Shaykh Tūsī and Ibn Dāwūd have stated that "Abdullāh b. Sabā was someone who became a heretic and who espoused extremist (*ghuluw*) views."

Allāma Hillī says, "He was one of the Ghulāt and is damned. He believed that Ali ﷺ is God ﷻ and that he was his prophet! May God ﷻ curse him!"[193]

Kashī relates the report of Abān b. 'Uthmān: "I heard Imām Sādiq say, '... I swear [upon my oath] to God ﷻ! Contrary to the exaggerated claims some ascribe to him,] The Commander of the Faithful Ali ﷺ was a humble and unassuming bondsman of God ﷻ the Exalted. May woe and damnation be upon any who tell lies about us! Verily, certain people say things about us which we ourselves do not say.

[192] Abdullāh b. Sabā is a fictitious character that was invented in the early years of Islam by the enemies of the Sh'īa in order to undermine the credibility of the rite (*madhhab*) of the Ahl al-Bayt. There have been many books written on the question itself, as to whether or not he was in fact a fabrication and invention, or whether he did in fact exist, and many well-meaning Sh'īa historians of high-stature have taken the position that he did in fact exist, and go on to say that he and his teachings had nothing to do with the teachings of the Ahl al-Bayt or of Sh'īa Islam. Fortunately, thanks to the priceless research of Allama Askarī, this issue was finally and definitively put to rest with the publication of his landmark book, *The Myth of Abdullāh b. Sabā and other Historical Fictions*. A serviceable translation of portions of the book can be found here: http://www.al-islam.org/abdullah-ibn-saba-and-other-myths-sayyid-murtadha-al-Askari. In the passages that follow, what is important to bear in mind is that although the opinions of these scholars concern a person who is actually a clever and very successful hoax, this does not detract from their opinions themselves, which have validity for anyone who falls under the general Ghulāt rubric.

[193] Hillī, Allāma, *al-Khulāsa*, p. 254.

We are weary of and fed up with these kinds of people! We take refuge with God ﷻ from these kinds of people.'"[194]

Kashī also relates from Abdullāh who reports that the Imām as-Sādiq ﵇ stated: "We, [the purified and immaculate] Members of the Household of the Prophet ﷺ are the *siddīqīn* (those who never deviate from the truth, and those who bear witness to the truth by virtue of the way they live), but we are not immune from being lied about by liars and having our honesty sullied in the minds of people with their lies. Verily, the Prophet ﷺ was the most truthful of [all] people, but Masīlama the Liar would invent lies about him. The Commander of the Faithful Ali ﵇ was the most truthful of creatures after the Apostle ﷺ of God ﷻ, [but people invented lies about him also]."[195] In the *Bihār al-Anwār* hadīth compendium this hadīth is continued: "Abū-Abdullāh Husayn b. Ali ﵇ had become burdened with the exaggerations and lies which Mukhtār [told concerning him]. Hārith ash-Shāmī and Banān would exaggerate [and lie] about Ali b. Husayn ﵇. Then, his Eminence ﵇ named Mughayra[t] b. Sa'īd, Bazī', Sarī, Abul-Khattāb, Mu'ammar, Bashār ash-Shu'īrī, Hamza[t] at-Tirmidhī and Sā'īd an-Nahdī and said, 'May God ﷻ curse them! We are not immune from liars who lie about us. May God ﷻ keep us secure from the evil of every liar and make them taste the heat of the iron [of the sword]."[196]

2. The Position of the Purified Imāms ﵇ and their Followers

The Most Noble Prophet ﷺ had prophesied the various intrigues and seditions which would befall his community. Among these phenomena which the Prophet ﷺ shared with Imām Ali ﵇ was the rise of sects and cults of personality which maintained a pretense of love and friendship toward Ali ﵇, but who would soon fall into extremes of exaggeration

---

[194] Kashshī, Shaykh Muhammad, *ar-Rejāl*, 1:324, H#171.
[195] Kashshī, Shaykh Muhammad, *ar-Rijāl*, 1:324, H#174.
[196] Majlisī, Allama Muhammad Bāqir, *Bihār al-Anwār*, 25:263.

about him to the extent that this would put them outside of the pale of Islam and make them revert to unbelief and heresy.

It is reported from Ahmad b. Shādhān with his own chain of narrators, from Imām Ja'far as-Sādiq ﵇, from his father … from Ali b. Abī-Tālib ﵇: "The Apostle ﷺ of God ﷻ said, 'O Ali ﵇! O Ali! Your example among this community of mine is like the example of Jesus, the son of Mary. His nation divided into three groups: the group which attained to faith in him who were the [Twelve] Disciples, the group which fought him, who were the Jews, and a group who exaggerated and went to extremes to the point of deifying him and going beyond the pale of faith [in his religion]. My community will also divide into three groups concerning you. There will be a group who will attain to faith in you and will be your Sh'īa; another group will become your enemies, and these are the doubters; and a [third] group will go to extremes [in the exaggeration of your virtues], and these are the deniers. O Ali ﵇! You and your Sh'īa shall have your place in Heaven, and your enemies and those who go to extremes shall have their place in Hell."[197]

3. The Position of the Commander of the Faithful ﵇

The Commander of the Faithful ﵇ dealt with the Ghulāt decisively, imprecating them and punishing them. It is reported by Ibn Nabāta that the Commander of the Faithful ﵇ said, "O Lord! I seek to be clear (*barā'a*) of the Ghulāt, just as Jesus the son of Mary wanted to be rid (*barā'a*) of the Nazarenes (*nasārā*). O Lord! Abject and humiliate them for all time and never come to their aid!"[198]

Imām Ali ﵇ said, "Beware not to exaggerate and go to extremes concerning us! Say that we are God's ﷻ bondsmen; and then [you may] put into words whichever [of our] virtues you please."[199]

---

[197] Ibid, 25:365.

[198] Tūsī, Shaykh at-Tāifa, *al-Amālī*, 2:54.

[199] Majlisī, Allama Muhammad Bāqir, *Bihār al-Anwār*, 25:270.

It is reported by Imām as-Sādiq ﷺ "A man who was a [Jewish] Rabbi came to the Commander of the Faithful ﷺ and asked, 'O Commander of the Faithful ﷺ, since when has God ﷻ existed?' The Imām replied, 'May your mother sit in mourning for your loss! [Tell me] since when God ﷻ has not existed, so that it can [then] be said since when He has existed! My Lord existed before [there was such a thing as] "before" and existed without [there being a] "before" and shall exist after [such a thing as] "after" and shall exist without [there being such a thing as] an "after". He has no limit and there is no limit to His purpose; all intentions end in Him and He is the purpose of all intentions.' [The rabbi] then asked, 'O Commander of the Faithful ﷺ, are you a prophet?' [Imām Ali ﷺ] replied, 'Woe unto you! Verily I am a servant among the servants of Muhammad ﷺ.'[200]

And elsewhere Imām Ali ﷺ has stated, "Verily, you must seek [the answers to your questions concerning that which is] licit and illicit from us, but you should not ask us concerning [matters that relate to the ambit of] prophethood [and the bringing of revealed law]."[201]

4. The Position of Imām Zayn al-Ābidīn ﷺ

Imām Zayn al-Ābidīn ﷺ stated, "May God ﷻ curse anyone who tells lies concerning us! I swear [upon my oath] to God ﷻ! Ali ﷺ was a righteous servant of God ﷻ and the brother of the Prophet ﷺ who did not attain from God ﷻ to any greatness [of spiritual rank] whatsoever except by way of his obedience to God ﷻ and to His Apostle; and verily the Apostle ﷺ of God ﷻ did not attain from God ﷻ to any greatness [of spiritual rank] whatsoever except by way of his obedience to God ﷻ.

"The Apostle ﷺ of God ﷻ informed Abū-Khālid al-Kābulī that extremist beliefs (*ghulūw*) will appear in the community of Muslims just

---

200 Koleynī, Shaykh, Shaykh Muhammad b. Ya'qūb, Thiqat al-Islam, *Usūl al-Kāfi*, 1:89.

201 Majlisī, Allama Muhammad Bāqir, *Bihār al-Anwār*, 26:83.

as they had appeared among the Jews and the Nazarenes. His Eminence ﷺ told him, 'Verily, the Jews adored Ezra ؑ [to excess], such that they said things about him that they should not have said. After this [state of affairs came to pass], neither was Ezra ؑ of them [= their prophet], nor were they [considered to be] the followers of Ezra ؑ. And verily, the Nazarenes adored Jesus ؑ [to excess], such that they said things about him that they should not have said. After this [state of affairs came to pass], neither was Jesus ؑ of them [= their prophet], nor were they [considered to be] the followers of Jesus ؑ. We are [caught] in this same predicament. Verily, a number of our followers (*Sh'iatunā*) adore us [to excess], such that they say things about us that the Jews said about [the prophet] Ezra ؑ and the Nazarenes said about [the prophet] Jesus the son of Mary ؑ. In this case, neither are we of them [= their Imāms], nor are they [considered to be] our followers.[202]

5. The Position of Imām al-Bāqir ؑ

It is reported by Zurāra that he heard Imām Bāqir ؑ say, "May God ﷻ curse Banān al-Bayān! Banān – May God's ﷻ curse be upon him! – used to exaggerate about my father. I [hereby] testify that my father Ali b. Husayn ؑ was a righteous servant [of God ﷻ]."[203]

6. The Position of Imām as-Sādiq ؑ

The number of the adherents of the Ghulāt increased during the time of Imām Ja'far as-Sādiq because the Imām had taken advantage of the increasing openness that had resulted for the Ahl al-Bayt ؑ due to the weakening of the grip of the Umayyads on the reins of power and their preoccupation with the Abbāsid claimants to the throne and had started to teach and thus to impart and to propagate the true knowledge of the Quranic sciences to his students, and to lay the foundation stones

---

[202] Kashshī, Shaykh Muhammad, *ar-Rijāl*, 2:336.
[203] Ibid, 4:590.

of the Islamic magisterium. This dissemination of the true teachings (*ma'āref*) of the Prophet ﷺ went through the territories of Islam like a juggernaut which carried the reputation of the Imām ﷺ to every corner of the realm, greatly increasing the number of his students and adherents. Imām Ja'far as-Sādiq ﷺ informed the people of much that they were ignorant of, drawing on knowledge which his forefathers going back to the Apostle ﷺ of God ﷻ had taught. Consequently, when some of the more gullible types among his devotees saw the vast extent of the Imām's ﷺ knowledge and saw that he was able to draw knowledge of the supra-sensible world (*ilm al-ghayb*) as if from some occult or hidden source [at will], they naively believed this necessarily to be a sign of his divinity, reasoning that only God ﷻ had access to knowledge of the unseen.

Some of the enemies of Islam took advantage of the opportunity this situation presented and used these gullible types to their own end, which was their desire to destroy the image of authentic or Sh'īa Islam. They focused their efforts especially on new converts to Islam who did not as yet have a proper understanding of correct Islamic beliefs and in whom their old beliefs and norms still had a foothold, as they were more readily able to leverage this naïveté to their advantage. Financial considerations and psychological proclivities also played their part as factors that were conducive to deviations from the straight path.

Thus, unwarranted claims were made for Imām Ja'far as-Sādiq ﷺ. Mālik b. 'Atya relates from some of the companions of the Imām that, "Imām Ja'far as-Sādiq ﷺ came to us while he was [visibly] perturbed and distressed and said, 'I had left [the house] a few moments ago on some business. Suddenly an African resident of Medina stopped me and accosted me and yelled, "I am at your command (*labbayk*), O Ja'far b. Muhammad! Labbayk! Labbayk!!" I returned home, overcome by the shivers. I prostrated myself to my Lord in my prayer niche, touching my forehead and face to the ground, seeking refuge [in my Lord of Providence] from what that man [implicitly] claimed. And if Jesus ❀ the son of Mary ❀ had disagreed with that which Almighty God ❀ had said concerning him, he would have become deaf to all sense of hearing and blind to all sense of seeing and would have become completely mute, such that he would not have been able to utter a single word.' [Mālik b. 'Atya continues the report:] He then said, 'May God ❀ curse Abul-Khattāb and destroy him!'"[204]

Abū-'Amr al-Kashī relates from Sa'd from Ahmad b. Muhammad b. 'Īsā from Husayn b. Sa'īd from Abī-'Umayr from Hāshim b. Hakam from Abī-Abdullāh [al-Husayn] ❀: "Imām Husayn ❀ said, 'May God ❀ curse Banān, Sarī and Bazī'. Satan appeared to them in the best of forms."

I said to him, "Would that I were sacrificed [for your sake = O my dearly beloved master], Banān interprets this revelation (āya), [43:84] *for [then they will come to know that] it is He [alone] who is God ❀ in heaven and God ❀ on earth, and [that] He alone is truly wise, all-knowing.* By saying that the God ❀ on Earth is different to the God ❀ in Heaven, and that the God ❀ in Heaven is greater than the God ❀ on Earth; and that those on Earth acknowledge the virtues and preeminence of the God ❀ in Heaven and defer and page homage to him.'

[Imām Husayn ❀] said, 'I swear [upon my oath] to God ❀ that He is One and has no partners. He is the Lord of Providence (*rabb*) of the creatures in the heavens and on earth. May God ❀ curse Banān for the lies which he espouses! He has belittled the grandeur of God ❀, the Most Glorious and Exalted.'"[205]

---

[204] Koleynī, Shaykh, Shaykh Muhammad b. Ya'qūb, Thiqat al-Islam, *Usūl al-Kāfī*, 8:226.
[205] Kashshī, Shaykh Muhammad, *ar-Rijāl*, 4:592.

Kashī relates by way of his own chain of narrators from Imām Husayn ﷷ who said concerning the following revelation:

هَلْ أُنَبِّئُكُمْ عَلَىٰ مَن تَنَزَّلُ الشَّيَاطِينُ ﴿٢٢١﴾ تَنَزَّلُ عَلَىٰ كُلِّ أَفَّاكٍ أَثِيمٍ ﴿٢٢٢﴾

> [26:221] [And] shall I tell you upon whom it is that those evil spirits descend? [26:222] They descend upon all sinful self-deceivers.

"There are seven of them: Mu'ghayra[t] b. Sa'īd, Banān, Sāid, Hamza[t] b. 'Ammār, Zubaydī, Hārith ash-Shāmī, Abdullāh b. 'Amr b. Hārith, and Abul-Khattāb."[206]

Kashī has also related from Hamdūya from Ya'qūb, from Ibn Abī-'Umayr from 'Abd as-Samad b. Bashīr from Masādaf: "When a delegation had come from Kūfa who believed in the divinity of the Imām ﷷ, I went to Imām Ja'far as-Sādiq ﷷ and informed him [of this]. His Eminence quickly prostrated himself, levelled his chest to the ground and began to weep. He continually pointed at himself, saying, 'I am an indigent slave of God ﷻ who is in need of Him [at every moment]!' He repeated this sentence several times, after which he raised his head, showing the tears that were running down his face. I regretted my having informed his Eminence ﷷ of this news, and I reproached myself. I told him, 'Would that I were sacrificed [for your sake], why are you in such a state? Has something [untoward] happened?' He said, 'O Masādaf, If Jesus ﷷ had remained silent in the face of what [exaggerations] they claimed about him, he would deserve to have been made deaf, dumb and blind. And if I remain silent in the face of what

[206] Kashshī, Shaykh Muhammad, *ar-Rijāl*, 4:591.

Abul-Khattāb says [about me], then God ﷻ has every right to make me deaf, dumb and blind [also].'"²⁰⁷

Kolaynī relates from Sadīr: "I mentioned to Imām Ja'far as-Sādiq ؑ that a number of people believe you to be God ﷻ and cite the following revelation (*āya*) in order to prove their claim:

$$ \text{وَهُوَ الَّذِي فِي السَّمَاءِ إِلَٰهٌ وَفِي الْأَرْضِ إِلَٰهٌ ۚ وَهُوَ الْحَكِيمُ الْعَلِيمُ ﴿٨٤﴾} $$

[43:84] for [then they will come to know that] it is He [alone] who is God ﷻ in heaven and God ﷻ on earth, and [that] He alone is truly wise, all-knowing.

[Imām Ja'far as-Sādiq ؑ] said, 'O Sadīr, my eyes and ears and skin and blood are weary and fed up with these [people]. God ﷻ is weary of them also. These [types of people] are not of my religion and of the religion of my forefathers. God ﷻ shall not gather these people with me on the Day of Resurrection, except [under the condition of His] being angry with them.'

I said, 'So what, then, is your nature?' He said, 'We are the treasuries of the knowledge of God ﷻ. We are [the vehicles which give] expression to God's ﷻ commands. We are the Immaculates (*ma'sūm*) whom God ﷻ the Exalted has made obedience to incumbent [upon every believer] and has prohibited disobedience to. [For] we are the perfect evidence [of all truth] and the conclusive argument and proof [against all falsehood] (*al-hujja' al-bāligha*) [sent] for all who are in the heavens and on earth.'"²⁰⁸

Mughayra' b. Sa'īd was one of the "poles" (*aqtāb* = central figures; pillars) of the Ghulāt who attracted gullible people to himself with trickery, deception, sorcery and magic, after which he would

---

²⁰⁷ Kashshī, Shaykh Muhammad, *ar-Rijāl*, 4:588.
²⁰⁸ Koleynī, Shaykh, Shaykh Muhammad b. Ya'qūb, *Usūl al-Kāfī*, 1:269.

proceed to inculcate extreme beliefs concerning the virtues and spiritual rank of Imām Jaʿfar as-Sādiq ؑ in the minds of his neophytes. Imām Jaʿfar as-Sādiq ؑ told his followers what Mughayraᵗ b. Saʿīd's motivations and objectives were, and exposed him for the fraud that he was.

One day his Eminence ؑ said, "May God ﷻ curse Mughayraᵗ b. Saʿīd. May God ﷻ curse the Jew who consorted with him and from whom Mughayra learned sorcery and magic and [the ability to perform] extra-ordinary feats. Mughayra would lie about my father, which is why Almighty God ﷻ deprived him of his faith. Verily, a number of people have lied about me [as well]. May God ﷻ destroy them for what they say! I swear [upon my oath] to God ﷻ that we are [aught] but servants who have been created and selected by God ﷻ. The control of whether something benefits or harms someone is out of our hands. If God ﷻ is merciful to us, it is due to His grace; and if he torments us, it is on account of our own sins. I swear [upon my oath] to God ﷻ that [like any other mortal,] we would have no [cause for any] argument against God ﷻ [were he to pass judgment against us]. We die and are buried and are raised up again and shall be brought before God ﷻ for questioning. What could possibly have caused such claims to be made against us? May God ﷻ curse them [all]! They molest God ﷻ and molest the Prophet ﷺ of God ﷻ in his grave, and have molested the Commander of the Faithful ؑ and Lady Fāṭima ؑ and al-Ḥasan ؑ and al-Ḥusayn ؑ and Ali b. al-Ḥusayn ؑ and Muhammad b. Ali ؑ. Verily, I who am in your midst am [of the same substance as] the flesh and bones of the Apostle ﷺ of God ﷻ. Yet, I go to bed with fear and dread; others are heedless while I weep and wail. Others sleep easy while I am in fear and tremble in awe of the grandeur of God ﷻ the Sublimely Exalted, wandering among the peaks and valleys of the earth.

"I seek refuge with God ﷻ concerning that which Ajdaʿ al-Barrād, the slave of the Banī-Asad, has said about me. May God ﷻ curse

Abul-Khattāb. I swear [upon my oath] to God ﷻ! If these [people] come to us and we order them to believe these things about us, it would be a religiously incumbent imperative (*wājib*) on them to reject [such a command]; and [this is all the more the case when, all the while,] they see how distressed and concerned I am from the things which they have said. Pray God ﷻ give me aid and succor against them. I seek refuge with God ﷻ against them and declare myself to be innocent of them [and of what they ascribe to me]. I hold you to bear witness that I am [nothing more or less than] the progeny of the Prophet ﷺ of God ﷻ. If I obey God ﷻ, He will show mercy toward me, and if I disobey Him, he will torment me severely or will impose the severest of torments on me."

Imām Ja'far as-Sādiq ؑ denied all which the Ghulāt ascribed to him. It is related from Abū-Basīr:

"I told Imām Ja'far as-Sādiq ؑ 'They say things about you.'

He asked, 'What do they say?'

I said, 'They say that you are aware of the [exact] number of raindrops, and the number of the leaves of the trees, and the number of the stars, and the weight of the waters of the seas, and the volume of the soils of the earth.'

He said, 'Glory be to God ﷻ, the Sublimely Exalted above all that which we might ascribe to him! Limitless is He in his Glory! (*Subhānallāh*!). I swear [upon my oath] to God ﷻ! None but God ﷻ know these things!'

They said to his Eminence ؑ, 'So and so says that you provide the daily sustenance (*rizq*) of the bondsmen.'

He said, 'None but God ﷻ the Exalted provides sustenance [to us all]. There was an occasion when I had a need to provide some food for my family, and because I had no money, I became despondent. My mind was constantly preoccupied [with the thought of how to provide for my family] until [at last] I was provided with a sufficient amount of food, after which my mind found relief.'"

It is related from Zurāra: "I told Imām Ja'far as-Sādiq 'Someone said that he believes in delegation (*tafwīḍ*).

He said, 'What is *tafwīḍ*?'

I said, 'They say that Almighty God created Muhammad ﷺ and Ali and then delegated [all] affairs to them. Thereafter, these two created [the world] and provide for its sustenance and [have the power to] give life and [to] take it away.'

He said, 'That enemy of God is a liar! If you go to him, recite this revelation to him:

قُلْ مَن رَّبُّ السَّمَاوَاتِ وَالْأَرْضِ قُلِ اللَّهُ ۚ قُلْ أَفَاتَّخَذْتُم مِّن دُونِهِ أَوْلِيَاءَ
لَا يَمْلِكُونَ لِأَنفُسِهِمْ نَفْعًا وَلَا ضَرًّا ۚ قُلْ هَلْ يَسْتَوِي الْأَعْمَىٰ وَالْبَصِيرُ أَمْ
هَلْ تَسْتَوِي الظُّلُمَاتُ وَالنُّورُ ۗ أَمْ جَعَلُوا لِلَّهِ شُرَكَاءَ خَلَقُوا كَخَلْقِهِ فَتَشَابَهَ
الْخَلْقُ عَلَيْهِمْ ۚ قُلِ اللَّهُ خَالِقُ كُلِّ شَيْءٍ وَهُوَ الْوَاحِدُ الْقَهَّارُ ﴿١٦﴾

> [13:16] Or do they [really] believe that there are, side by side with God, other divine powers that have created the like of what He creates, so that this act of creation appears to them to be similar [to His]? Say: "God is the Creator of all things; and He is the One who holds absolute sway over all that exists."

I went to see that man and told him what Imām Ja'far as-Sādiq had said. My words were so forceful that he didn't answer me and it was as if he had become a mute."

It is related from Mufaḍḍal: "Imām Ja'far as-Sādiq mentioned the followers of Abul-Khattāb and the Ghulāt and said, 'O Mufaḍḍal! Do not keep company with them, and do not journey with them, and do not shake hands with them, and do not bequeath to them any inheritance'."

7. The Position of Imām al-Kāẓim ﵇

Imām al-Kāẓim ﵇ was also entangled with the problem of the Ghulāt. The most dangerous of the Ghulāt during the time of Imām al-Kāẓim ﵇ was Muhammad b. Bashīr. Initially he was among the companions of Imām al-Kāẓim ﵇, but then began to harbor extremist views concerning the Imām ﵇, to the point that he came to believe in the divinity of Imām al-Kāẓim ﵇ after his death and proclaimed himself to be his prophet! Muhammad b. Bashīr was an initiate in the dark arts of sorcery and magic, and he was put to death for this reason. The Wāqifīya believed that he (Muhammad b. Bashīr) 'stopped' (*tawaqquf*) at Ali b. Mūsā al-Kāẓim ﵇ and believed in the divinity of Imām Mūsā al-Kāẓim ﵇ and proclaimed himself to be his prophet.[209]

A number of naïve people from among the masses followed Muhammad b. Bashīr and called themselves the Bashrīya. Included in their false beliefs was that only [the three pillars of] *salāt* (mandatory ritual worship), *khums* (the "fifth" of ones disposable income payable as religious dues to the Imām), and *sawm* (ritual fasting) were religiously incumbent upon them, and that the rest of the rites, rituals, ordinances and injunctions of Islam such as the Hajj pilgrimage and the *zakāt* poor due ceased to apply to them. They also believed in the reincarnation of the Imāms ﵇ and claimed that these were all the same Imām whose [spirit] is transferred from one body to the next!

They also held some other bizarre beliefs such as believing in communal property, including food and drink, and women! They also believed that sodomy was allowed, basing their belief on this revelation: [42:50] *or He gives both male and female [to whomever He wills], and causes*

[209] Kashshī, Shaykh Muhammad, *ar-Rejāl*, 6:777.

to be barren whomever He wills: for, verily, He is all-knowing, infinite in His power.

When Imām Mūsā al-Kāẓim ﷺ passed from this world, this group claimed that he had not died but had been occulted and was the Mahdī concerning whom glad tidings had been given, and that he has appointed Muhammad b. Bashīr as his replacement.

Kashī reports from Ali b. Hadīd al-Madāinī: "I heard that someone said to Imām Mūsā al-Kāẓim ﷺ, 'I have heard Muhammad b. Bashīr say that you are not the same [person] as Mūsā b. Ja'far, but that you are our *imām* and our *hujja*ᵗ (the perfect evidence of all truth and the conclusive argument and evidentiary proof against all falsehood on Judgement Day) between us and God ﷻ.'

"The Imām cursed him three times and then said, 'May God ﷻ subject him to the worst and harshest [of penalties].'

"I told him, 'Would that I were sacrificed [for your sake], now that I have heard such talk from him, is the shedding of his blood permissible for me, just as the shedding of the blood of one who curses the Prophet ﷺ and the Imām is licit.'

"He said, 'Yes. I swear [upon my oath] to God ﷻ that the shedding of his blood is licit, and I [hereby] pronounce this [to apply to] you and to whomever hears these words from you.'

"I said, 'Is this a blasphemy against you [personally]?'

"He said, 'It is a blasphemy against God ﷻ and against His Apostle ﷺ and blasphemy against my forefathers and blasphemy against myself. What blasphemy can be worse than this, and what possible [statement] can be more outrageous than this claim?'

"I said, 'If I come across him and I do not put him to death, would I have then committed a sin?'

"He said, 'His sins will fall upon your shoulders several-fold without his sins having been reduced [for him]. Do you not know that the greatest degree of martyrdom on the Day of Resurrection is reserved for one who has furtively come to the aid of God ﷻ and of His Apostle?'"[210]

"Kashī relates from Ali b. Hamza[t] b. Batāinī: "I heard Abul-Hasan Mūsā al-Kāżim ﷺ say, 'May God ﷻ curse Muhammad b. Bashīr and destroy him! He tells lies about me. God ﷻ is weary of him, and I seek safe refuge with God ﷻ from his [menace]. I am weary, O Lord, from the [false] claims that Ibn Bashīr makes about me, and seek refuge in you. Rid me of his [menace], O my Lord of Providence!'

"He then said, 'O Ali! Nobody purposefully lies concerning us but that Almighty God ﷻ makes him taste the heat of the iron [of the sword]. Verily, Abul-Mughayra b. Sa'īd lied about Abū-Ja'far [Mohammd al-Bāqir] ﷺ and Almighty God ﷻ made him taste the heat of the iron [of the sword]. And verily, Abul-Khattāb lied about my father [Imām Ja'far as-Sādiq] ﷺ and Almighty God ﷻ made him taste the heat of the iron [of the sword]. And now Muhammad b. Bashīr lies about me, and I seek safe refuge with God ﷻ from his [menace]. I am weary, O Lord, from the [false] claims that Ibn Bashīr makes about me, and seek refuge in Thee. Rid me of his [menace], O my Lord of Providence! I ask Thee, O my Lord of Providence, to rid me of this filthy abomination, Muhammad b. Bashīr! Truly, Satan has partnered with his father in [entering] his mother's womb.'

"Ali b. Hamza[t] b. Batāinī said that not long had passed that the prayer of Imām al-Kāżim ﷺ was answered, and I never saw anyone meet his end in a more heinous way than Muhammad b. Bashīr."[211]

8. The Position of Imām ar-Riḍā ﷺ

Imām ar-*Riḍā* ﷺ continued the path of his forefathers with respect to the struggle against the Ghulāt. He would expose them [as frauds] and warn people against them. It has been related from Husayn b. Khālid

---

[210] Kashshī, Shaykh Muhammad, *ar-Rijāl*, 6:778.
[211] Kashshī, Shaykh Muhammad, *ar-Rijāl*, 6:779.

as-Sārafī that Imām ar-Riḍā said, "Anyone who believes in reincarnation (*tanāsukh*) is a heretic (*kāfir*)." He then said, "May God's curse be upon the Ghulāt, be they Jewish, Nazarene, of the Magus religion, of the Qadrīya, Murji'a or Harwarīya." He then said, "Do not mix in their company. Do not acknowledge them, and stay clear of them and repudiate them, for God repudiates them."[212]

Imām ar-Riḍā considered the Ghulāt to be the worst of sects and the sect with the most morally corrupt and [theologically] deviant beliefs, stating: "O my Lord of Providence! I seek refuge in Thee from powers and strengths, and there is no power nor strength except by your leave, Lord! I seek refuge in Thee from people who make false claims about us. O my Lord of Providence! I seek refuge in Thee from people who make claims about us which we ourselves do not profess. O my Lord of Providence! [The entirety of] Creation and the Reign [over it] is all [in] your [hands]. [1:5] *Thee alone do we worship; and unto Thee alone do we turn for aid.* O my Lord of Providence! You are our Creator and the Creator of our forefathers, [from] the first to the last. O my Lord of Providence! No one is worthy of Providential Lordship (*rububīa'*) but You. O my Lord of Providence! Curse the Nazarenes who belittled Your grandeur, together with all those who make such claims! O my Lord of Providence! We are Your bondsmen and are the sons of Your bondsmen. The control of whether something benefits or harms someone is out of our hands. O my Lord of Providence! We are weary and wash our hands of any who claim Providential Lordship (*rububīa'*) for us, just as Jesus the son of Mary was weary of the Nazarenes. O my Lord of Providence! We did not call any of them to that which they believe in. Then do not hold us to account for what they say [concerning us], and indemnify us from what they believe. [71:26] "*O my Lord of Providence! Leave not on earth any of these heretics, for, behold,*

---

[212] Shaykh Saddūq, *Uyūn Akhbār ar-Riḍā*, 1:218, H#2.

If Thou dost leave them, they will [always try to] lead astray those who worship Thee, and will give birth to nothing but wickedness and stubborn ingratitude."[213]

It is reported from Abul-Hāshim al-Ja'farī: "I asked Imām Riḍā ﷺ concerning the Ghulāt and the Mafūḍa. His Eminence ﷺ said, 'The Ghulāt are heretics (*kāfir*) and the Mafūḍa are idolaters (*mushrik*). Anyone who keeps company with them, or has dealings with them, or shares their table spread with them, or journeys with them, or [inter-]marries [with] them, or considers them to be trustworthy, or acknowledges the truth of what they say, or affirms them [even] with a [single] word, has exited the compass of [submission to] the sovereignty (*welāyat*) of God ﷻ and the guardianship-type regency (*wilāyat*) of the Apostle ﷺ of God ﷻ and of our guardianship-type regency (*wilāyat*), the regency of the Members of the Household of the Prophet ﷺ."

Imām ar-Riḍā ﷺ has explained one of the important reasons for the rise of the Ghulāt phenomenon. Ibrāhīm b. Abī-Mahmūd relates from Imām ar-Riḍā ﷺ that he stated,

"O son of Abī-Mahmūd! Our enemies have forged three types of hadīth reports about us. Some are exaggerations (*ghulū*), some are claims of deficiency and flaws in us, and some are affirmations of accusations that our enemies have made against us. When the people hear exaggerations about us, they anathemize and excommunicate (pronounce *takfīr* on) our adherents (*shī'atuna*), and think of them as believing in our divinity; and when they hear talk of deficiency and flaws in us, they will believe in these claims; and when they hear the accusations of our enemies against us, they will slander and defame us. And [all] this occurs despite the fact that God ﷻ the Exalted has said, [6:108] *Do not revile those who invoke [beings] other than God ﷻ, lest they revile God ﷻ out of spite, and in ignorance.*

[213] Shaykh Saddūq, *al-I'tiqādāt*, p. 99.

"O son of Abī-Mahmūd! If you see the [multitude of] people having deviated to the left and to the right [of the Straight Path], be sure that you attend to the path that we have shown, for, [verily,] we attend to those who attend to us, and we keep our distance from those who distance themselves from us."[214]

In the above passage, we see Imām ar-Riḍā ﷺ explain how the Ghulāt caused the accusation of extremism to be levelled at the Sh'īa. Thus, we see heresiographical writings accusing the Sh'īa of extremism (*ghulūw*), especially the Twelver Sh'īa, and this is because of false hadīth reports which the Ghulāt spread among the populace, and the heresiographers who were adversarial to the Sh'īa believed that all of these hadīth reports were reported by the Sh'īa, as they conveniently lumped the Ghulāt in with the Sh'īa, whereas there was no true basis for this conflation.

Additionally, many heresiographers made the egregious error of ascribing the belief in the imminence and incarnation [of God ﷻ] to the Sh'īa. And this is despite the fact that, as we mentioned in our review of the Sh'īa creed, the Sh'īa's belief in the transcendence and sublimity (*tanzīh*) of God ﷻ surpasses that of other creeds (who usually subscribe to the false belief of anthropomorphism), and rejects immanence and incarnation and anthropomorphism more definitively than other creeds.

In another hadīth report, Imām ar-Reḍā ﷺ explains the reasons for these matters as follows: "Verily, the Ghulāt fabricated some hadīth reports concerning anthropomorphism (*tashbīh*) and predeterminism (*jabr*) which they ascribed to us. These are people who have belittled the grandeur of God ﷻ the Exalted. Anyone who likes them has [thereby] disconcerted us, and anyone who disconcerts them has [thereby] made us happy. Anyone who befriends them has [thereby]

---

[214] Shaykh Saddūq, *Uyūn Akhbār ar-Riḍā*, 2:272, H#63.

shown enmity toward us, and anyone who shows enmity toward them has [thereby] shown friendship toward us. Anyone who establishes a relationship with them has [thereby] severed his ties with us, and anyone who severs their ties with them has [thereby] established a relationship with us. Anyone who causes them anguish has done us a good turn, and anyone who does them a good turn causes us anguish [by so doing]. Anyone who honors them has insulted us, and anyone who insults them honors us. Anyone who accepts them has rejected us, and anyone who accepts us must necessarily reject them; anyone who does right by them has wronged us, and anyone who wrongs them has done right by us; anyone who denies them is affirmed by us, and anyone who affirms them is denied by us; anyone who grants them something has deprived us [of something], and anyone who deprives them of something has granted us [a good]; O son of Khālid, anyone who is a follower or devotee of us (*Sh'īatuna*) will not consider them as their friends or colleagues."[215]

9. The Position of Imām al-Hādī ﷷ and Imām al-Askarī ﷷ

During his tenure, Imām al-Hādī ﷷ also clashed with the Ghulāt who believed in the divinity of the Imāms. Their chieftain was an individual named Muhammad b. Nasīr an-Namīrī, after whom the Nasīrīya cults are named. He had a small number of followers, chief among which were Fāris b. Hātam al-Qazvīnī and Ibn Bābā al-Qomī.

Kashī writes, "They were a cult who believed that Muhammad b. Nasīr an-Namīrī was a prophet. He claimed to be a prophet and that Ali b. Muhammad al-Hādī ﷷ had sent him. He believed in reincarnation and went to extremes concerning Imām al-Hādī ﷷ, claiming divinity for him. He proclaimed incest and homosexuality to be licit and said that both the active and passive partners have carnal desires which God ﷻ has made pure and has not prohibited.

[215] Shaykh Saddūq, *Uyūn Akhbār ar-Riḍā*, 2:130, Hadith #45.

Muhammad b. Mūsā b. Hasan b. Farāt was one of Muhammad b. Nasīr an-Namīrī's lieutenants who aided and abetted him.

It is related that one day, a number of people came upon Muhammad b. Nasīr an-Namīrī who was lying face down with his slave lying on top of him. They scolded him for this deed, but he said, "Being the passive partner [in the act of sodomy] is one of the pleasures [in life] and is a sign of humility before God ﷻ and [a sure sign of] an absence of arrogance"!

Nasr b. Sabāh has stated, "Ali b. Muhammad al-Hādī ﷺ cursed Hasan b. Muhammad, known as Ibn Bābā al-Qomī, Muhammad b. Nasīr an-Namīrī and Fāres b. Hātam al-Qazwīnī. Abū-Muhammad Faḍl b. Shādhān has written in some of his books that Ibn Bābā al-Qomī is a renowned liar.

Sa'd says, "'Abīdī has related to me that Imām Hasan al-Askarī ﷺ sent me a letter in which the following was written: 'I take refuge with God ﷻ from Fahrī and from Hasan b. Muhammad, known as Ibn Bābā al-Qomī. You, too, should be wary of them and keep your distance. I warn you and all of my followers against those two. May God's ﷻ curse be on them both. They deceive the people under our name; they are charlatans and frauds. May God ﷻ torment them, humiliate them and make them abject. Ibn Bābā al-Qomī claims that I commissioned him to prophethood and that he is the Portal to God ﷻ (*bābullāh*)! May God's ﷻ curse be upon him! Satan has seduced and conquered him. May God's ﷻ curse be upon anyone who follows him! Truly, he has tormented me. May God ﷻ torment him in this world and in the world to come!"[216]

[216] Kashshī, Shaykh Muhammad, *ar-Rijāl*, 6:805, Hadīth 999.

Kashī has related from Ibrāhīm b. Shayba that in a letter to Imām al-Hādī he wrote, "Would that I were sacrificed [for your sake], there are some people among us who ascribe virtues to you which are grotesque and which place doubt in one's mind, while they claim that their words are taken from hadīth reports. On one hand, these words are not acceptable to us because they are exorbitant and bombastic; on the other hand, we cannot refute and reject them because they claim to be the words of your forefathers. Thus, we have taken the position of indecision.

"They state concerning the revelation,

> اتْلُ مَا أُوحِيَ إِلَيْكَ مِنَ الْكِتَابِ وَأَقِمِ الصَّلَاةَ ۖ إِنَّ الصَّلَاةَ تَنْهَىٰ عَنِ
> الْفَحْشَاءِ وَالْمُنكَرِ ۗ وَلَذِكْرُ اللَّهِ أَكْبَرُ ۗ وَاللَّهُ يَعْلَمُ مَا تَصْنَعُونَ ﴿٤٥﴾
>
> [29:45] Behold, prayer restrains [man] from loathsome deeds and from all that runs counter to reason; and:
>
> وَأَقِيمُوا الصَّلَاةَ وَآتُوا الزَّكَاةَ وَارْكَعُوا مَعَ الرَّاكِعِينَ ﴿٤٣﴾
>
> [2:43] and be constant in prayer, and spend in charity, that what this refers to is [being with] a man, and not bowing down and prostrating in prayer!

"Similarly, they say that the meaning of *zakāt* is [being with] a man, not the quantity of one's wealth and its purification [by means of paying the poor due (*zakāt*)]!

"These are the kinds of beliefs and immoral practices they have, of which I have reported [only] a portion for you. Now if you believe it to be for the best, be so kind as to oblige your followers and write a letter and save them from the false beliefs which put people on the road to perdition and annihilation. The people who say these things profess to be your friends and call the people to obey them [in their supposed positions as your proxies]. Among these are Ali b. Hasaka and Qāsim al-Yaqtīnī; what do you say concerning the reliability of their hadīth reporting?

"The Imām wrote in response, 'This is not our religion. Stay away from it.'"[217]

It is reported from Sahl b. Zīād al-Ādamī: "One of our people wrote thus to Imām Abul-Hasan al-Askarī ﷺ: "Would that I were sacrificed [for your sake], O my master! Verily, Ali b. Hasaka claims that he is your executor and that you are the alpha and are uncreated (*qadīm*), and that he is your Portal (*bāb*) and prophet, and that you have ordered him to call the people to such beliefs and practices! He claims that the *salāt* (mandatory ritual worship), *khums* (the "fifth" of ones disposable income payable as religious dues to the Imām), *sawm* (ritual fasting), the Hajj pilgrimage and the *zakāt* poor due are all [merely symbolic representations of] your knowledge and of the knowledge of someone such as Ali b. Hasaka, and that anyone who has such knowledge is a Perfect Believer to whom *salāt*, *khums*, sawm, hajj and *zakāt* no longer apply. He has described the rest of the rites, rituals, ordinances and injunctions of Islam and has defined these to be anything that has been proven to you [personally to be valid and true, and that they are no longer religiously incumbent upon them if this is not the case.] And so now a large number of people have inclined toward him. If you deem it to be for the best, be so kind as to oblige your followers and save them from these false beliefs and from their perdition.

"The Imām wrote in response, 'Ibn Hasaka is lying. May God ﷻ curse him! I cannot fathom what it is he wants with my followers? May God ﷻ curse him! I swear [upon my oath] to God ﷻ that the Lord of Providence of the worlds did not commission his Eminence [the

[217] Kashshī, Shaykh Muhammad, *ar-Rijāl*, 6:803.

Prophet] Muhammad ﷺ or the other prophets before him other than [to call people] to the religion of the *Hunafā* and to *salāt*, *khums*, *sawm*, *hajj* and *zakāt* and to *walāyat*. And his Eminence Muhammad ﷺ did not call people to [aught] but the one God ﷻ Who has no partners.

"And we who are the *awsīā* (heirs to, legatees, executors, and successors) of his Eminence are the lesser bondsmen of God ﷻ and do not assign anyone as a partner to Him. If we obey God ﷻ, he will show mercy toward us, and if we disobey Him, He will torment us. [Like other mortals,] we would have no [cause for any] argument against God ﷻ [were he to pass judgment against us]; rather, God's ﷻ argument and proof [against all falsehood] has been completed against us and against all created beings. I take refuge with God ﷻ against people who make such claims, and I divorce myself of such words. Drive these [types of people] away from you. May God's ﷻ curse be upon them!'"[218]

Conclusion

Having reviewed the beliefs and practices of these sects, it is now clear that one of the causes that gave rise to extremist beliefs and to the phenomenon of the Ghulāt was the desire to escape from the burden of having to perform the religiously obligatory duties of *salāt*, *khums*, *sawm*, *hajj*, *zakāt* and allegiance to the *wilāyat* of the Imām, as well as having to take on the yoke of the other injunctions of religion, such as conducting oneself in accordance with the proper mode of ethical conduct (*akhlāq*).

By expressing this motivation, Imām as-Sādiq ﷷ has exposed the Ghulāt and put them to shame. In response to one of his companions' questions, His Eminence ﷷ stated, "Some people claim that Imām Husayn ﷷ was not martyred, but that the people are confused about this matter..." Ultimately, he was asked, "O son of the Apostle ﷺ of God ﷻ! What do you say about a number of your followers

---

[218] Ibid, 6:804.

(Sh'īa) who have such claims?" He said, "These are not my followers (Sh'īa). I hereby renounce them... May God ﷻ curse the Ghulāt and the Mafūḍa! They have belittled the grandeur of God ﷻ the Exalted, and have become heretics and infidels and have gone astray in order to avoid carrying out the incumbent duties imposed on them by their religion (*wājibāt*) and [in order to avoid having to transact life in accordance with a system of social organization in which] the rights [of God ﷻ and others] are respected."

The Imāms ﷺ struggled in earnest with the Ghulāt and with all forms of extremist beliefs and practices, exposing their wicked intentions and their ugly objectives, and cautioning their followers against any sort of association with them. Imām as-Sādiq ﷺ said, "Keep your youth away from the Ghulāt so that they will not be corrupted [by them]. Verily, the Ghulāt are the worst of God's ﷻ creatures. They have belittled the grandeur of God the Exalted, and have deified [God's ﷻ] bondsmen. I swear [upon my oath] to God ﷻ that the Ghulāt are worse than the Jews, the Nazarenes, the Magus, and the idolaters... members of the Ghulāt return to us and repent, but we do not accept their repentance, whereas we do accept [the repentance of] a sinner." When asked what the reason for this was, the Imām replied, "Because the Ghulāt have become habituated against abiding by the requirements of *salāt*, *khums, sowm, hajj, zakāt* [and allegiance to the *welāyat* of the Imām] and is no longer able to put an end to the disruption of these habits and to return to obedience to God ﷻ the Exalted, but the sinner will return to the fold when he becomes aware of his sin."

We thus see that in addition to fighting their severe persecution at the hands of oppressive tyrants, the Immaculate Imāms ﷺ struggled against deviant ideologies and sects and did not sit still for a single moment. And it was thanks to their sincere intentions and efforts and the grace of God ﷻ the Sublime and Exalted that the Sh'īa were able to survive the tempests of time and emerge unscathed and with honor.

6 - False Memes about Sh'īa Islam

As a denomination within Islam, Sh'īa Islam has been subject to the attention of historians and research scholars more than any other sect. There have been various reasons for this disproportional attention, one of which is that, throughout its lifespan Sh'īa Islam has been one of the serious opponents to deviant currents of thought which had been fostered and at times instigated by the illegitimate and oppressive powers who ruled over the realms of Islam. These despotic regimes felt the necessity to apply the full force of their propaganda machinery against the Sh'īa community in order to weaken it. Their disinformation of choice was to project and amplify the meme[219] that the adherents of the Sh'īa are members of a deviant sect that is beyond the pale of the religion of Islam, and to portray the Sh'īa as a sect whose totality can be summed up as a *bid'a^t^* or 'reprehensible innovation'.

On the other hand, the extraordinary attention that the Sh'īa paid to the Members of the Household of the Prophet ﷺ and their benefitting from their teachings, and the love and respect which the Sh'īa showed to the Ahl al-Bayt (as) of The Most Noble Prophet ﷺ

[219] A unit of cultural information, such as a belief, idea or cultural practice, that is transmitted verbally or by repeated action from one person to another, as by imitation.

caused the ruling powers to be concerned about the real possibility that the Sh'īa would eventually be able to spread their teachings and beliefs among the masses of the Muslim populace. Thus, they believed that they had no alternative but to suppress the Sh'īa so as to prevent and preclude the possibility of popular rebellions and insurrections.

We thus can see why the ruling powers took a particular interest in the Sh'īa sect and tried very hard to muffle their activities and the promotion of its ideology and worldview, and why it was critical to their interests and even to their survival that the uninformed masses be warned away from the Members of the Household of the Prophet ﷺ and from their Sh'īa. This they did, more or less successfully, by spreading the false meme that the beliefs of the Sh'īa have no affinity with the principles and creed of Islam! They would introduce the Sh'īa as a sect whose beliefs were foreign and alien to Islam, and as a sect which is worse than the Jewish religion and worse than the religion of the Magus.[220] And they would use different approaches in order to achieve their objectives, the most important of which was the indoctrination and inculcation of minds against the truths of Sh'īa Islam.

The most dangerous and most successful of these memes was the accusation that the principles of Sh'īa Islam are Jewish and that its roots supposedly go back to the teachings of the Jew Abdullāh b. Sabā who, it was claimed, pretended to convert to Islam toward the end of his life with the aim of poisoning Islam with his corrupt beliefs, and travelled from the Yemen through the Hijāz (Western Arabia, the land of revelation), the 'Irāq, *ash-Shām* (the Levant), and Egypt, spreading his poisonous thoughts which, (the myth has it), were the seeds from which Sh'īa Islam sprouted.

---

[220] Zoroastrianism; the dualist religion of ancient Iran.

The Abdullāh b. Sabā Meme[221]

The reason this meme was so successful (millions of Muslims believed and, alas, still believe it) is that whoever instigated the meme was able to get hadīth reports from Sayf b. 'Umar, who is a supposed narrator of hadīth reports who has no external reality and is a figment of the imagination of its inventor, into reputable books of history, the most important being Tabarī's *Tārīkh*. According to the hadīth reports of this imaginary figure, in his travels, the supposed Yemenite crypto-Jew cum newly-converted Muslim Abdullāh b. Sabā (that, in any event, is his "legend") gave glad tidings that the Prophet ﷺ appointed Ali ؑ as his *wasī* (legatee, inheritor, executor and successor), but that 'Uthmān usurped his right. Some of the great Companions of the Prophet ﷺ are supposed to have fallen for the poisonous talk of this Jewish sorcerer, including Abū-Dharr, 'Ammār Yāsir and Mālik Ashtar. The myth also has it that the events which lead to the death of 'Uthmān were instigated by the "Sabāīn."

As pointed out earlier (see footnote #192 on page 182) Allama Askarī has proven the falsity of this story by proving that Sayf b. 'Umar never existed. Allama Askarī's research narrowed the source of this myth to four sources: Tabarī (d. 310 HQ), *at-Tārīkh al-Umam wa'l-Mulūk*; Ibn Asākir (d. 571 HQ), *at-Tārīkh al-Madīna' ad-Damishq*; Ibn Abī-Bakr (d. 741 HQ), *at-Tamhīd wa'l-Bayān fi Maqtal ash-Shahīd 'Uthmān b. Affān*; and Dhahabī (d. 748 HQ), *at-Tārīkh al-Islam*. All four sources report the story from Sayf b. 'Umar, and Tabarī's *Tārīkh* is the source for the other three historians.

In addition to proving that Sayf does not exist by means of various proofs, including a comparative analysis of the content of his

[221] The honorable author was not aware that Allāma Askarī has put paid to this particularly virulent false meme (see footnote #192 on page 182), and therefore, his apologetics concerning it were out of date. As such, I felt the need to replace the entirety of his wording in this section with that of my own.

hadīth reports with those of categorically reliable sources, Allāma Askarī also investigated the worth and reliability of Sayf as a reporter of hadīth from the perspective of the great historians of the Sunni rites from Yahyā b. īMu'īn (d. 233 HQ) to Ibn Hajar (d. 852 HQ) and reports that all of these great historians and specialists in the hadīth science sub-specialty of *ilm ar-rijāl* state that Sayf is *ḍaīf* (unsound), *kadhdhāb* (a liar), *matrūk al-hadīth* (meaning that hadīth scholarship has abandoned any reports related by him), accused of being a *zindīq* (heretic), etc.

So if the question as to whether or not Abdullāh b. Sabā ever actually existed has been put to bed in the negative, then the question becomes: Why did Sayf's fabricated hadīth reports gained such a foothold with Muslim historians? Why did they gain such widespread acceptance despite the damningly weak provenance titles (*asnād*) of Sayf b. 'Umar's reports and despite the existence and indeed prevalence of reliable hadīth reports which contradicted the myth? Why were the provenance titles overlooked and ignored and the reliable reports which contradicted Sayf's reports neglected? Allāma Askarī concludes his study by positing that the dynamic that was at play was that hadīth scientist and historians leaned to what the Muslim community wanted to have taken place rather than to what actually occurred.

And so, the question of whether or not Abdullāh b. Sabā actually existed was turned by some into one with an ideological and even a creedal orientation. It seems that for these people, preserving the sacrality of the odious posture of the execration, anathematization and excommunication of the Sh'īa is dependent on the continued repetition in perpetuity of the false Abdullāh b. Sabā meme, which now definitively discredited, but which never the less continues to be used as a club with which to cudgel the truth about Sh'īa Islam, and prevent its authentic Islamic ideas from seeing the light of day in the mainstream of Sunnite thought and among others who are similarly ignorant of the truth.

The Meme of the Persian Origin of Sh'īa Islam

Obviously, the Omayyad government was an Arab government, and its policy was to dispatch leaders among the *mawālī* (non-Arabs) to the far reaches of the empire in order to curtail their potential for social and political influence. They strove to praise and valorize the Arab and to posit the Arab as superior in every way. In the un-Islamic racist milieu that was created by the Umayyads, the matter of saying that someone was a non-Arab was a weapon in the arsenal used in the propaganda campaign which the Umayyads waged against their opponents. In so far as the Sh'īa were the most vigorous opponents of their regime such that the promotion and propagation of its ideology and creed would weaken the foundations of their dynasty, the Umayyads did not stop their disinformation operations at ascribing the origins of Sh'īa Islam to the likes of Abdullāh b. Sabā. Rather, they endeavored to spread the meme that Sh'īa Islam was an ideological import of Iranian provenance, which accreted to Islam after the conquest of the Iranian plateau.

Certain contemporary so-called historians have insisted on this absurdity and have attempted to conflate and fuse both the Jewish and the Iranian memes together and posit this fusion to be the supposedly true provenance of Sh'īa Islam.

Ahmad Atīatullāh writes, "The teachings of the *'Sab'īya'* [the supposed sect founded by the mythical character Abdollah b. Sabā] comprise the creedal roots of the Sh'īa, which has been derived from Jewish beliefs and influenced by the religion of Mazdak.[222] This sect is

[222] Mazdak (died c. 524 or 528) was a Zoroastrian prophet, Iranian reformer and religious activist who gained influence under the reign of the Sassanid Shahanshah Kavadh I. He claimed to be a prophet of Ahura Mazda, and instituted communal possessions and social welfare programs. He has been

headed by a Jew of Yemenite origin, whereas some of the beliefs of Mazdak the Persian had been transferred to the Arabs and Jews in certain parts of the Arabian Peninsula. Thus, we see that [teachings of] the 'Sab'īya' [sect] is adopted rapidly by some of the people of Iraq, which is adjacent to Iran.

"The thesis of divine right (*al-haqq al-ilāhīa*) is a thesis which was transferred to the Sab'īya and the Sh'īa, who are generally from among the Persians, and posits the view that the caliph after the Prophet ﷺ is Ali ؑ, who has been appointed by God ﷻ to this office, and that this right is transferred by way of heredity to his progeny."[223]

This individual wants to establish a connection between the inheritance of the Imāms ؑ and Iranian ideological accretions on the basis that the Iranians believed in hereditary kingship. This is an opinion which a large number of historians and orientalists have adopted.

The truth is that if we were to look into the matter with just a little more depth, we would have had to say that it was in fact the Umayyads who started this tradition in Islam by transforming the caliphate into an absolute hereditary kingship. dynasty consisted of pure Arab stock, and Qurayshite stock to boot! Which, one would think, makes them immune to imitation from the Persians. And so we can see that talk of Sh'īa Islam being inspired by Iranian belief systems is nothing but an absurd farce. This is all the more so given the fact that Sh'īa Islam is a belief system that is purely and authentically Arab in its provenance and nature.

Certain other so-called historians have claimed that most of the early Sh'īa adherents were Persian. Thus, Shaykh Muhammad Abū-

---

seen as a proto-socialist. Shahbazi, A. Shapur (2005). *"Sasanian dynasty". Encyclopaedia Iranica, Online Edition. Or* Yarshater, Ehsan (1983). *Cambridge history of Iran; The Seleucid, Parthian and Sasanian periods.* **2.** pp. 995–997.

[223] *al-Qāmūs al-Islāmī*, 3:249.

Zahra writes, "The truth is that we believe Sh'īa Islam to have been influenced by Persian thought with respect to the issue of kingship and heredity. The similarity between their beliefs and the order of [hereditary] kingship of the Persians is very clear to see, and this thesis is confirmed by [the fact that] most of the Persians are Sh'īa and that the original Sh'īa were Persians as well."[224]

That most Iranians are Sh'īa is correct, but the point that Abū-Zahra forgets is that the majority of the people of the Iranian plateau adopted the Sh'īa form of Islam during the later periods, and especially after the ascension of the Safavids[225] to power (i.e. between the 16th to 18th centuries, fully 700 years after the Iranians had entered into Islam and adopted one of the four Sunnite rites).[226]

However, as to the assertion that the original adherents of Sh'īa Islam were Persians – that is also incorrect. Historical research demonstrates that the majority of the early Sh'īa were Arab. This fact has been recorded in the ancient historical texts which state that Sh'īa

---

224 Abū-Zahra, *Tārīkh al-Madhāhib al-Islāmīya*, 1:41.

225 Reading Safavid for Abbāsid.

226 There is another curious meme that has come in vogue among Iranian modernists and nationalists and liberals which maintains that the adoption of Sh'īa Islam was Iran's way of combatting Islam, which of course was Sunni. Actually, Islam was not Sunni at the time of 'Umar's invasion of Iran, nor did that term come into usage until a good two or three centuries after that. Of course, the proponents of this meme are blissfully ignorant of the reality that Iran was Sunni for 700 years before adopting Sh'īa Islam under the Safavids, the critical mass of conversions having been reached probably around the year 1600 CE or later. That is why, of the five greatest poets of Iran, Ferdowsī, Mowlavī, Sa'dī, Nezāmī, and Hāfez, all of them are Sunni except Ferdowsī who is the exception who underscores the rule, and who is Sh'īa, bless his heart. This fact also explains the otherwise unanswerable question as to why Asia Minor (present day Turkey) and the Indian subcontinent who "became Islamized through a Persian filter" (as Ustād Algār used to say), are predominantly Sunni and not Sh'īa.

Islam existed only in limited areas within the Iranian territories, the first of which area was the town of Qom, whose residents were Arabs!

Yāqūt al-Hamāwi (the Arab geographer of Byzantine descent; d. 626 HQ) describes Qom as follows: "Qom is a new town in which no trace of non-Arabs can be found. The first person to pay attention to this was Talha[t] b. Ahwas al-Ash'arī... and all of its residents are Imāmī (Twelver) Sh'īa. It was founded during [the governorship] of Hajjāj b. Yūsuf in the year 83 [HQ]... When Ibn Ash'ath was defeated, he returned to Kābol with a group who had made a pact of brotherhood with him. His brothers were Abdullāh, Ahwas, Abdur-Rahmān, Ishāq and Na'īm. They were of the Banī-Sa'd (b. Mālik b. Āmir al-Ash'arī). Among this group, Abdullāh b. Sa'd had a higher rank. He had a son in Kūfa who believed in free will (*qadrī-maslak būd*) and who was an Imāmī (Twelver Sh'īa) and who immigrated from Kūfa to Qom. It was he who was the cause of the spread of Sh'īa Islam among the residents of Qom, and no [Muslim of any of the] Sunnī [rites] can be found in Qom."[227]

As Yāqūt al-Hamāwi has related, Sh'īa Islam did not come to the town of Rey (just south of present-day Tehran and about 100 km north of Qom) until the reign of the Abbāsid al-Mu'tamid: "The residents of Rey were Sunnī (*ahl as-sunna[t] wa'l-jamā'a[t]*) until Ahmad b. al-Hasan al-Mādarātī prevailed over them. He professed to Sh'īa Islam and honored and promoted the Sh'īa in his court. After books had been written about Sh'īa Islam [under his patronage], the people inclined toward it. During this time, Abdur-Rahmān b. Abī-Hātam wrote a book about the excellences and virtues of the Members of the Household of the Prophet ﷺ for him, and this was during the reign of al- Mu'tamid the Abbāsid caliph. The conquest of Rey by Ahmad b. Hasan was in the year 275 HQ."[228]

---

[227] Hamāwi, Yāqūt, *Majma' al-Baldān*, 7:159.
[228] Ibid 3:121.

Maqdasi confirms that the dominant rites (*madhhab*) among the Persians were the Hanafī and Shāfi'ī rites, and does not make any mention of the Sh'īa rite among the Persians during his lifetime: "The populace is made up of four sects: the followers of Abū-Hanīfa are in the east; the followers of Mālik [b. Anas] are in the west; the followers of Shāfi'ī are in Khorāsān and Neyshāpūr (in the north-east); and the People of the Hadīth are in the Levant (*ash-Shām*). In the rest of the territories, the rites are comingled among the populace. In Baghdad, the followers of Ahmad b. Hanbal and the Sh'īa predominate… in Kūfa, the residents are Sh'īa except for the neighborhood of Kanāsa, which is Sunni. And in Mosul, the residents are followers of Ahmad b. Hanbal and there are some Sh'īa there also."[229]

Ibn Faqīh relates a subject that is important for our present purposes from Muhammad b. Ali, the commander of the Abbāsid revolt against the Umayyads. He orders his troops to follow certain instructions categorically. He divides the territory into several regions and orders his forces to go forward to their respective sectors and to attract recruits and gather materiel. He says, "The people of Kūfa and its environs are the Sh'īa of Ali ﷺ. The people of Basra and its environs are 'Uthmānids whose religion can be purchased with silver and gold (*dirham wa dīnār*) [!] The people of Mosul are Harwarīya and are Mariqīn and A'lāj Arabs. The Muslims there have the temperament of the Nazarenes (Christians). The residents of Shām (the Levant) do not recognize any but the people of Abī-Sufyān and the Marwānids. They have a deep hatred [for the Ahl al-Bayt ﷺ] and an intense ignorance [of the true nature of their religion]. The residents of Mecca and Medina are by and large supporters of Abū-Bakr and 'Umar… But Khorāsān is for you. There you will find a large number of suitable forces whose hearts are wholesome and intact and who have not been

---

[229] *Ahsan at-Taqāsīm*, p. 136-142.

divided up into different sects and sub-sects. They have strong bodies and broad shoulders and robust voices... I take the east which is where the sun rises to be a good omen."[230]

A large number of orientalist scholars of Islam and contemporary Muslim historians own to this truth. Dr. Abdullāh Fayyāḍ writes, "Historical evidence proves that Sh'īa Islam arose from among the Arabs and in a milieu in which Arab customs and mores were dominant, including Kūfa; and we cite the following as our reasons:

1. The people who were counted as the companions and devotees of Ali ﷺ and who accompanied him in the wars [which he waged] were predominantly from the Arabs of the Hijāz and the 'Irāq, and we do not see the name of any individual of significance who is of Iranian stock.

2. The people who wrote a letter to Husayn b. Ali ﷺ in the year 60 HQ and asked him to come to Kūfa were all the chieftains of the Arab tribes resident in [the Arab garrison town of] Kūfa and its environs. This we know on the basis of their names, which appears in the Maqtal of Abī-Mikhnaf (d. 157 or 158 HQ).

3. In the revolt of the Tawwābūn, the companions of Sulaymān b. Sard al-Khazā'ī were all from famous Arab tribes."[231]

The great German biblical scholar, historian and scholar of Islam, Julius Wellhausen writes, "Four thousand of the Tawwābūn had gathered in Nakhīla who were of the tribes who lived in the surrounding areas and there were no *mawālī* (non-Arabs) among them... That we should say that the views and opinions of the Sh'īa are in harmony with that of the Iranians and that therefore Sh'īa Islam is influenced by

[230] Hamāwi, Yāqūt, *Majma' al-Baldān*, p. 315.
[231] Kāshāni, Mustafa Sādiqī, *Tārīkh-e Imāmīye*, p. 68.

Iranian thought is mistaken. Rather, historical evidence tells us that Sh'ia Islam first existed in an Arab environment and was only later transferred to the mawālī."[232]

And lastly, Abdullāh Fayyāz quotes the French Catholic Louis Massignon: "Hamdān, which was a large and powerful [Arab] tribe with a glorious past, was very predisposed to Sh'ia Islam."[233]

Other Causes for the Perpetuation of the Meme of the Persian Origin of Sh'ia Islam

Another pretext which some have used to consider Sh'ia Islam to be an essentially Iranian sect is the matter of the marriage of Imām Husayn ﵇ with an Iranian woman. Dr. Mustafā Shak'a writes, "Anyone who says that Sh'ia Islam came into being as a political denomination rather than a religious one reasons as follows: Most Iranians are the followers or the Sh'ia of Ali ﵇ and his progeny. The reason for this is that the Iranians believe their ancestry goes back to Imām Husayn ﵇ because he married Shahrbānū, Yazdgerd's daughter, after she was captured by the Muslims. Shahrbānū [in turn] gave birth to Imām Zayn al-Ābidīn ﵇ thereby making the Iranians his maternal uncles. Thus, their love of Ali ﵇ and his progeny was more political than religious, or at least, the Sh'ia Islam of the Iranians was more political than religious, and they themselves admitted that their love of Ali ﵇ and his progeny was on account of the family ties with the Household of Imām Husayn ﵇."[234]

We respond to Dr. Shak'a by saying that firstly, not all Sh'ia are Iranian, even if the Iranians had become Sh'ia on account of family ties, then what would become of the non-Iranian Sh'ia? Especially the Arabs who were the original Sh'ia and had become so before the Iranians?

---

232 Quoted in Op. Cit. p. 240.
233 Op. Cit., p. 16.
234 Shak'a, Mustafā, *Islām bi lā Madhhab*, p. 173.

It can also be argued that if Shahrbānū's marriage to Imām Husayn ﷺ was the reason for the Iranians to incline toward Sh'īa Islam, why did this not happen in the case of others? We know that Imām Husayn ﷺ was not the only person to marry an Iranian bondmaiden. During the same time, there were others who married Iranian princesses who had been captured in battle, including Abdullāh b. 'Umar, who married Shahrbānū's sister and Yazdgerd's daughter and gave him a son named Sālem. If Imām Husayn ﷺ was the son of the caliph of the Muslims, this was also the case with Abdullā b. 'Umar, whose father attained to the caliphate prior to Ali ﷺ. Why then did all the Iranians not become followers of 'Umar?!

The same goes for Muhammad b. Abū-Bakr, who also married another sister of Shahrbānū's, who gave him Qāsim, the famous magister (*faqīh*) as a son. Muhammad b. Abū-Bakr was also the son of a caliph, and his father anteceded both 'Umar and Ali ﷺ. These three marriages took place during the reign of 'Umar.[235]

Why did all the Iranians not become followers of Abū-Bakr or 'Umar? So this meme can also be discarded as it cannot have been the cause of the Iranians having become Sh'īa Muslims.

Summary of the Discussion

We demonstrated that the seeds of Sh'īa Islam were sown during the time of the Prophet ﷺ and that his Eminence ﷺ watered this seed on different occasions by referring to Imām Ali ﷺ as his legatee and successor to make sure that the seed would sprout into a sapling and grow. He would call people to Ali ﷺ and would tell them that Ali ﷺ was always with the truth (*al-haqq*) and that his followers would be sure to attain to salvation.

The testament of the Prophet ﷺ in favor of Ali ﷺ as his successor and legatee is not something that was claimed by the mythical

[235] Ibn Khallakān, *Wafyāt al-'Ayān*, 1:455.

character of Abdullāh b. Sabā, but is the *nass* (a scriptural source containing an injunction or burden of duty whose meaning is clear and self-evident) from the Prophet ﷺ himself which dates back to the very first call to Islam. The Companions of the Prophet would ask him, among their other questions, concerning the issue of his succession, and he would answer them, to the point where the label *wasī* (inheritor, legatee, executor and successor) became an epithet for Imām Ali ؑ and can still be found in biographical compendiums and lexicons.[236]

The original Shʿīa were among the greatest of the Companions of the Prophet ﷺ and the early adopters of Islam who inclined to and became the devotees or Shʿīa of Imām Ali ؑ and who then promoted and propagated it among the Islamic community. The original Shʿīa were pure Arabs. Jawlad Tashīr writes, "Shʿīa Islam came into being in an environment on the basis of first principles that were authentically Arab."[237]

Those who try to prove that Shʿīa Islam was created by the Persians in order to destroy Islam and to replace it with the restoration of the Zoroastrian religion should be aware that most of the imāms of the Sunnite rite were Iranian. These include Bokhārī, Muslim, Tirmidhī, Ibn Māja, Abū-Hanīfa, as well as a large number of the *fuqahā* and *muhaddithūn*, who are too numerous to name (whereas the Imāms of the Shʿīa were all Arab Sayyids, of course). So then if the purpose of the Iranians in accepting Shīʿa Islam was the destruction of Islam, then surely the objective of the Sunni ʿulamāʾ would have been no different!

---

[236] Ibn Manzūr writes that Ali ؑ was called the *wasī*. See his authoritative *Lisān al-Arab*, 15:394. Zubaydī also writes in his *Tāj al-ʿArūs* (10:392) that *Wasī* is Ali's ؑ epithet. Ibn Abī'l-Hadīd also points to tens of couplets composed by a number of the Companions as his reasons for arriving at the same conclusions. Ibn Abī'l-Hadīd, Abdul-Hamīd, *Sharh-e Nahj al-Balāgha*, 1:143.
[237] *al-Aqīda wa'l-Sharīʿa fī Islām*, p. 205.

But the truth in which there can be no doubt is that Shʿīa Islam is the expression of the path of authentic Islam; a path which has remained immune to deviation after the passing of the Prophet ﷺ of God ﷻ, and has traversed this path with all its difficulties and trials so that the Divine Decree is implemented the way it was meant to be.

Praise be to God, Lord of All Worlds.

Bibliography

Abī-Shayba, *al-Masnaf*

Abī-Ya'lā, *Musnad*

Abu-Dāwud, *Sunan*

Abū-Zahra, *Tārīkh al-Madhāhib al-Islāmīya*

Ahmad b. Hanbal, *Musnad*

Ahmad b. Hanbal, *al-Faḍāil*

Abal-Faraj al-Halabī, *as-Sīra[t] al-Halabīa*

Ash'arī, Abul-Hasan Ali, *al-Maqālāt al-Islāmīīn wa'l-Ikhtilāf al-Musallīn*

Baqdādī, Abdul-Qāhir b. Tāhir, *al-Farq Bayn al-Firāq*

Balādhūrī, *Ansāb al-Ashrāf*

Beyhaqī, *Sunan*

Bokhārī, *Sunan*

Dāramī, *Sunan*

Dhahabī, *Tārīkh al-Islam*

Dhahabī, *Sayr I'lām al-Anbīā*

Ibn Abdul-Barr, *al-Istī'āb*

Ibn Abī-Bakr, *at-Tamhīd wa'l-Bayān fi Maqtal ash-Shahīd 'Uthmān b. Affān*

Ibn Abī'l-Hadīd, Abdul-Hamīd, *Sharh Nahj al-Balāgha*

Ibn Asākir, *at-Tārīkh al-Madīna[t] ad-Damishq*

Ibn Athīr, *Usud al-Ghāba*

Ibn Athīr, *al-Kāmil fi't-Tārīkh*

Ibn Hajar, *as-Sawā'iq al-Mahraqa*

Ibn Hajar, *Tahdhīb at-Tahdhīb*

Ibn Hajr al-Asqalānī, *Fath al-Bārī*

Ibn Hishām, *as-Sīrá an-Nabawīya*
Ibn Jawzī, *Tazkirat al-Khawās*
Ibn Kathīr, *Tārīkh*
Ibn Khallakān, *Wafyāt al-'Ayān*
Ibn Māja, *Sunan*
Ibn Manzūr, *Lisān al-Arab*
Ibn Qutayba, *al-Imāma wa'l-Siyāsa*
Ibn -Sa'd, *Tabaqāt al-Kubrā*
Ibn Taymīya, *Minhāj as-Sunná an-Nabawīya*
Esfahānī, Ahmad b. Abdullāh, Abū-Nu'aym, *Hilīat al-Awliā*
Esfahānī, Abī'l-Faraj, *Maqātil at-Tābiīn*
Ganjī, *Kefāyat at-*Tālib
Golpāyegānī, Sayyid Muhammad Riḍā, *Hidāyat al-'Ibād*
Khārazmī, *Manāqib*
Hākem al-Haskānī an-Neyshāpurī, *al-Mustadrak 'Ālā's-Sahīhayn*
Hamedānī, Hāj Āqā Riḍā, *Mesbāh al-Faqīh*
Hamīdī, *al-Masnaf*
Hamāwi, *Farā'iḍ al-Samtayn*
Hamāwi, Yāqūt, *Majma' al-Baldān*
Hillī, Muhaqqiq al-Awwal, *al-Mu'tabar fi Sharh al-Muqtasar*
Hillī, Allāma, *al-Khulāsa*
Haydar, Asad, *al-Imām as-Sādiq* ﷺ *wa-l-Madhhab al-'Arba'a*
Haythamī, *Majma' az-Zawāid*
Kāshāni, Mustafa Sādiqī, *Tārīkh-e Imāmīye*
Kashshī, Shaykh Muhammad, *ar-Rijāl*
Khārazmī, *al-Manāqib*
Khatīb al-Baghdādī, *Tarīkh al-Baghdād*
Koleynī, Shaykh Muhammad b. Ya'qūb, Thiqat al-Islam, *'Usūl al-Kāfi*
Majlisī, Allama Muhammad Bāqir, *Bihār al-Anwār*
Mufīd, Shaykh, *Tashīh al-I'tiqādāt ash-Sh'ia*
Munāwī, *Kunūz al-Haqāiq*

Munāwī, *Fayḍ al-Ghadīr*
Muttaqī al-Hindī, *Kanz al-Uʻmmāl*
Muslim, *Saḥīḥ*
Muzaffar, Shaykh Muhammad Riḍā, *Aqāid ash-Shʻia*
Muzaffar, Shaykh Muhammad Riḍā, *Tārīkh ash-Shʻia*
Narāqī, Ahmad b. Muhammad al-Fāḍil, *Mustanad ash-Shʻia fī Ahkām ash-Sharʻia*
Najafī, Muhammad Hasan, Sāhib-e Jawāhir, *Jawāhir al-Kalām fī Sharh Sharāyiʻ al-Islām*
Nasāī, *Khasāis Amīr al-Muʼminīn*
Nowbakhtī, *Firāq ash-Shʻia*
Qundūzī, Yanabī, *al-Mawadda*
Rāḍī, Fakruddīn, *at-Tafsīr al-Kabīr*
Rāḍī, Fakruddīn, *Fusul al-Muhimmah*
Saddūq, Shaykh, *al-Iʻtiqādāt fī dīn al-Imāmīa*
Saddūq, Shaykh, *Uyūn Akhbār ar-Riḍā*
Shakʻa, Mustafā, *Islām bi lā Madhhab*
Suyutī, *Durr al-Manthur*
Tabarī, Muhibbiddīn, *Dhakhāir al-Uqbā*
Tabarī, Muhibbiddīn, *ar-Riyāḍ an-Naḍra*
Tabarī, *al-Maʻjam al-Awsat*
Tabarī, *Tafsīr*
Tabarī, *Tārīkh ar-Rusul waʼl-Mulūk*
Tabarānī, *al-Maʻjam al-Kabīr*
Tayālasī, *Musnad*
Tirmidhī, *Jāmiʻ*
Tūsī, Shaykh at-Tāifa, *al-Amālī*
Wāqidī, *al-Maghāzī*
Yaʻqūbī, *Tārīkh*

www.ingramcontent.com/pod-product-compliance
Lightning Source LLC
Chambersburg PA
CBHW021435080526
44588CB00009B/529
* 9 7 8 1 9 2 2 5 8 3 1 5 4 *